WEBSTER'S NEW WRLD™
ENGLISH GRAMMAR
HANDBOOK

by Gordon Loberger, Ph.D., and Kate Shoup Welsh

Webster's New World™ English Grammar Handbook

Copyright © 2002 by Wiley Publishing, Inc., Indianapolis, Indiana

Published by Wiley Publishing, Inc., Indianapolis, Indiana
Published simultaneously in Canada

Library of Congress Control Number: 2001090687

ISBN 0-7645-6488-9

Manufactured in the United States of America
10 9 8 7 6 5

ACKNOWLEDGMENTS

I wish to thank two individuals who have been especially helpful to me in preparing the first edition of this text. Kristen Minks White was a very dedicated and efficient project manager for the preparation of the original manuscript, while Jennifer Moore displayed similar efficiency and dedication in making the necessary revisions prior to publication. Both were very able students enrolled in the professional writing program at Murray State University. Also, a number of my students were helpful in pointing out various trouble spots and elusive errors. I hereby thank them all for their assistance.

This edition was subject to many unforeseen obstacles. Trisha Starr and Terri Puckett, both students in Professor Miles Kimball's technical writing class, worked diligently under pressure to prepare the manuscript. Unfortunately, the semester ended before the project was completed. Ms. Puckett graciously consented to continue working through the semester break/Christmas vacation, dividing her time between this project and her duties as wife, mother, grandmother, homemaker, and employee elsewhere. Her concern for the quality of the text and her dedication to the project were truly "beyond the call of duty." I know that without her assistance, I would have been nearly helpless at times. I offer her my sincerest thanks for all her help, insights, and for her calm, quiet way of overcoming obstacles. Thank you, Terri.

This latest edition is a result of sharp-eyed students in my classes who detected numerous errors in typing and misplaced answers. The errors and suggestions for necessary corrections were passed on to Terri Puckett, who, once again, worked diligently and efficiently to make corrections. I really cannot thank her enough. As I stated in earlier editions, if any errors occur or remain, I must assume responsibility for them.

Gordon Loberger
Murray State University
Murray, Kentucky

It never ceases to amaze me how many people contribute to the writing, editing, designing, printing, and binding of a single book. Thanks must first go to Dr. Loberger, whose fine text, *A Concise Guide to Standard English Usage*, serves as the template for this book. Thanks also go to Sherry Gomoll, for providing me the opportunity to make my own contributions.

Mike Kelly's help through this process has been invaluable, as have the sharp eyes of Mike Shields, who helped greatly with the technical accuracy of this book. Thanks very much to all of them for helping us avoid the embarrassment of publishing a grammar book that contains grammatical errors.

Finally, I'd like to thank my baby daughter, Heidi, for napping at all the right times so her new and hapless mother could work, and my husband, Ian, for taking such good care of us both.

Kate Shoup Welsh
Indianapolis, Indiana

TABLE OF CONTENTS

STANDARD ENGLISH USAGE: A RATIONALE

It should come as little surprise to anyone who has had to struggle through months—even years—of the formal study of grammar in both middle school and high school that certain segments of society place great emphasis on using "correct grammar" and on "speaking correctly." Because the study of grammar was given preeminence in the public-school curriculum (after all, for how many years is one exposed to the basics of English grammar?), nearly every student has been expected to become proficient in such things as diagramming sentences—some of them incorporating uncommon constructions—and in determining the correct use of such forms as *who* and *whom* in complex, convoluted sentence patterns.

Needless to say, although such instruction was generally ineffective, it had a certain degree of merit, for knowledge of the subtleties of one's own language can be a very useful tool. But if any students did learn the proper use of *who* and *whom,* the learning did not often translate into a functionally meaningful experience. In short, it was usually a failure. Students able to recite rules and employ correct forms failed to incorporate proper usage into their everyday speech. Imagine the chagrin of the hapless teacher of English who for hours inveighed against the use of double negatives only to hear students employ that usage time and time again, even while leaving the classroom immediately after instruction. For such a person, the task of teaching grammar probably seems hopeless.

Can, then, proper grammar or standard English usage be taught? Of course it can—and it should be—or this text would not be in existence. But students of grammar must understand the nature of the beast with which they are wrestling, as well as the reasons underlying their efforts.

Students must realize, for instance, that there is a time and place for all things, whether soap, sex, or standard English grammar and usage. Attempts by teachers to instill in students a different standard of usage (in effect, a different dialect) to be used at all times and in all places are surely destined for failure. The person who uses *who* or *whom* properly at all times and is constantly on guard not to split an infinitive, even in the most informal situations, is using the language in a manner that is just as questionable as the person who misuses *who* and *whom* out of ignorance or carelessly splits infinitives in the most formal of situations.

The level of formality one employs in various situations is, then, a matter of *dialect*. Just as people in one area of a country speak in a way slightly different from people in another area of the country, so too do people in one situation speak differently from the way they would speak in another situation—one that would require greater or less formality. In other words, the formality of one's grammar and usage is a matter of dialect and of adapting one's dialect to a given situation. Just as a doctor or mechanic has more than one instrument or tool with which to perform different tasks, so too ought an effective speaker have different modes of speech for different situations.

Custodians of the Language versus Advocates of Usage

The debate over which grammar to use involves two different philosophies. One school would prescribe certain rules of conduct in matters of grammar and usage. People with this view hold that, in one way or another, speakers ought to maintain the highest standards of formal usage at all times and that to do less reflects discredit upon themselves and their general, overall competence in various matters, whether linguistic or otherwise. This position is the one usually held by teachers of English in many public schools—often encouraged and rewarded by principals and parent groups. The standards to which they would have everyone adhere are, of course, their standards, which reflect their own personal value systems.

Another group is of the opinion that the study of grammar ought to be descriptive in nature, observing and noting the nature of language as it is used by people in general. If, they would maintain, they discover that 75 percent of the speakers of a particular dialect employ split infinitives in their speech—whether formal or informal—that fact should be recorded without any judgment being passed on the appropriateness of the usage. They rightly observe that language is a living phenomenon, growing, spreading, changing, and dying in much the same manner that vegetation grows, spreads, changes, and dies. Attempts to restrain change by establishing artificial constraints or rules, they maintain, are hopeless.

Valid arguments in support of both positions are easy to find. Educated people (and more and more people are obtaining college and university degrees) do indeed have a tendency to hold in mild contempt (at the least) people whose language habits do not meet norms that they or others have established. They see a dichotomy such as that suggested by the title of an article by Thomas A. Knott, General Editor of Webster's Dictionaries, in *American Speech* (Vol. IX, April 1934, p. 83). His title is simple and to the point: "Standard English and Incorrect English." The title suggests (though Knott is more tolerant than the title would lead one to believe) that if one does not speak standard English, whatever that happens to be, one is using incorrect English.

In the *Saturday Review of Literature* (14 Nov. 1964, p. 82), Mario Pei, a writer who has given readers a wide range of insights into the phenomena of language through his books and articles, states the following:

> Two voices are raised throughout the land with the same frequency and insistence as that of the Turtle. One is the voice of the Advocates of Usage, the other that of the Custodians of the Language.

The Custodians of the Language, says Pei, "hold that there is a right way and a wrong way of expressing yourself, and that the right way should be prescribed . . . ." The Advocates of Usage, on the other hand, suggest that "language should be subjected to a sort of 'democratic' process similar to the one that prevails in our political life. If enough people say a certain thing in a certain way, that is the way to say it."

This book takes a more moderate approach, neither demanding that all members of society conform to a single set of rules (that is, acknowledging that, in our view, there is a time and a place for formal grammar, and a time and a place for informal grammar, and that different rules sometimes apply to each) nor evangelizing the theory that language must be so elastic that no rules apply. Rather, we seek to gather a useful set of guidelines that writers and speakers can utilize in the boardroom, in the classroom, and in the billiard room.

The Five Clocks

Advocates of both sides of the usage issue have had enough support by writers from various walks of life to fill page after page of numerous magazines for decades. However, in 1961, Martin Joos, a teacher and linguist, published a little book that went far toward creating order out of the chaos of conflicting opinions about language usage. In the book *The Five Clocks* (Harcourt, Brace & World), Joos offers the reader the suggestion that speakers of a language (English) actually modify language usage across five styles or "clocks":

- Frozen
- Formal
- Consultative
- Casual
- Intimate

FROZEN STYLE

The first style, *frozen*, is used "for print and for declamation." It is the style of good literature and, consequently, not usually employed in the various speaking situations—except, perhaps, for humorous effect. Obviously, knowledge of this style is a requirement for those whose duties require a degree of facility with language: teachers, editors, writers, formal speakers, attorneys, and others.

FORMAL STYLE

Formal style, according to Joos, is the style of individuals "who are to remain social strangers." It is the style that is employed when a group has grown too large, and participation among members no longer occurs. The formal style demands advance planning and is characterized by the speaker's detachment from the audience. It is, of course, the form of speech that is used in formal lectures or presentations. In this way, it is closely related to the frozen style.

Because of these prestigious uses, the formal style is sometimes viewed as the dialect to be used on all occasions. Unfortunately, many educators tend to stress the importance of this style to the exclusion of the others. The so-called advocates of usage, however, maintain that the formal style is rightly used in formal situations and tend to discount this style for everyday, general usage.

The importance of the formal style should not be underestimated. Often, the confidence one has in himself as a speaker or writer is directly related to his ability to use the formal style proficiently.

Further, because first impressions often determine the success of a venture, the impression one makes through speech or writing often depends on one's ability to use the formal dialect. Joos, however, makes this observation (and it is well worth remembering): "Formal style is designed to inform . . . . The formal code-labels inform each hearer that he is in a formal frame [and that the hearer] is not to make insertions but must wait until authorized to speak."

In short, the formal style is not the style of general conversation. It is, however, the style of educated speakers and writers; for this reason, those who use the language in any but informal or consultative situations ought to know the proper forms of usage of the formal style.

At the same time, according to Joos, "Good frozen style . . . lures [one] into educating himself, so that he may the more confidently act what role he chooses" (p. 40); and few would argue the point that knowledge of the formal style (which in many ways is essentially the same) gives the speaker or writer the same self-confidence. In addition, Porter G. Perrin, author of the widely respected *Writer's Guide and Index to English* (Scott, Foresman, and Company, 1965), states that "People tend to judge us by superficial traits, in language as in other matters" (p. 29).

Beyond those considerations, however, lie other factors. A dialect such as the frozen and formal styles requires insights into the structure of a language, which has practical applications elsewhere, for example in punctuation. Further, it provides writers and speakers with a wider range of options in expressing themselves than they would have if they were limited to only a single, utilitarian grammatical style. Perhaps with the eye of a prescriptive grammarian, Perrin says that "good Formal English may be the best way (if not the only way) to present certain ideas" (p. 21).

The frozen and formal styles employ restrictions not placed upon speakers of more-informal dialects. As suggested previously, they are most often used in literary and other professional writing and similarly restricted situations, such as addresses (by speakers) on formal occasions. Depending, then, upon what individuals' conceptions of themselves are and what they envision for their futures, they will be more or less concerned with the study of the formal dialect. "Your language," says Perrin, "in the long run represents your personality, and you are responsible for the language you use" (p. 30).

Frozen and formal styles, then, incorporate both similarities *and* differences. The frozen style, as stated earlier, is the style of formal literary works and declamations. It is not the style of everyday speech, as anyone who has tried to "say" a prepared speech or "orate" informal conversation knows. Frozen, written literary language is a dialect of a special kind, incorporating, of course, the principles of formal English.

Formal style, on the other hand, is the careful speech of persons concerned about their language. The speaker who employs this style makes conscious choices of such things as forms of pronouns, adverbs and adjectives, syntax, verb tenses, and subject-verb relationships. *The formal style gains its value from its appropriateness in formal situations other than formal written prose or declamations.* It is the style one uses with confidence for self-expression in those situations obviously more structured than the usual informal situations. Probably for this reason, the formal style has received special emphasis at all levels of education.

CONSULTATIVE STYLE

The other styles of usage are not the focus of this book; therefore, they need be mentioned only briefly here. The *consultative style* is that style of language most frequently used for imparting information among individuals. It is generally relaxed and requires a response by the listener(s). According to Joos, in consultative style, "The diction is kept in accurate balance with the requirements: the pronunciation is clear but does not clatter, the grammar is complete but for an occasional anacoluthon, the semantics is adequate without fussiness" (p. 33). In other words, this is the easy-going style of everyday conversation—of business, instruction, on-the-scene reporting, and discussions involving individuals, whether in pairs or larger groups. This is the style the general speaker adopts for his public participation in events; as such, most individuals feel relaxed and comfortable with it.

CASUAL AND INTIMATE STYLES

The other two styles, *casual* and *intimate*, are personal in nature and are of limited general use. In fact, use of these styles by outsiders—by those who are not a part of the "in group," for example—is sometimes looked upon by its "rightful" users as an intrusion or an affront. Identical twins, lovers, close-knit family members, and members of certain fraternal groups may employ various aspects of one or the other of these styles.

That said, the study of these dialects, or "clocks," while interesting in its own right, is not the purpose of this text, even though it has been the focus of hundreds of studies in recent years. As a basis for further study, one would do well to read Joos' little book.

Why the Study of Formal Usage Is Important

One aspect of grammar that we *are* concerned about, however, is the *why* of the study of formal usage. A few reasons have already been suggested, but beyond those reasons lie other considerations. We live in a rapidly changing society; and, cliché though it may be, we must adapt to those changes. No longer can a young person feel secure in the type of world often portrayed by one's parents. This is the age of technology, of mass communications, of computers. It is, in fact, becoming, with increasing emphasis, a "white collar" society. The gulf between those who adapt to those changes and those who do not is widening at an alarming rate, and that gulf will surely grow wider and wider with each succeeding year. What served one's parents will no longer serve an individual in the electronic age—and that includes the grammar one uses.

The young person, then, who aspires to a successful life among the educated people of the modern workplace has the responsibility of making sure he or she is prepared to function effectively in an environment that subjects one to close scrutiny via videotape and fax machines. Obviously, individuals must assume that their grammar—and their general facility with language—will be easily evaluated, and they must take whatever steps are necessary to insure that their language and grammar reflect positively upon themselves, rather than negatively.

Fortunately, the formal study of language and specific usages or dialects can be an interesting and intellectually challenging endeavor. Sooner or later, most inquisitive people develop a curiosity about how people say things and what certain things "mean." Further, most educated people recognize a need on their part to use a particular dialect at certain times, just as they recognize lapses in usage among others. We all feel a discomfort—no matter how slight—and even a certain degree of embarrassment when educated people, especially our colleagues, make lapses in usage such as saying "between Billy and I," "they was," "Carl and him were," or "the child playing with his friends were." Although we have become more tolerant of various departures from what was once considered standard (the use of *their* rather than *his* with *everyone*, for example), we still expect a certain degree of language proficiency from educated people. We have, in fact, a reasonable expectation that educated people will speak like educated people. Why should we expect less?

Students must assume the task, then, of acquainting themselves with the varieties of English so that they will be able to choose the dialect that will best serve their purposes, whether it be conversing informally with friends and casual acquaintances or preparing material for formal presentation, either written or oral. One must learn to communicate effectively, and sometimes effectiveness is measured by the respect that is accorded not only the substance of presentation, but also the *manner* of presentation.

INTRODUCTION

The best way to describe what this book is, is to tell first what it is not. It is not, you will discover, a grammar book, although it contains detailed descriptions of grammatical constructions and describes many of the ways in which the English language functions. Grammar books have a purpose, either to analyze the workings of a language in an attempt to offer insight into the language or to prescribe rules about how a language ought to be used by speakers of that language.

The first objective of a grammar book—to describe the language—is the objective of descriptive linguists, those language scientists who attempt to remain neutral about what constitutes "correct" grammar and what constitutes "substandard" grammar. Linguists gather detailed information about the workings of a language and piece together an overall picture of that language, much as one would piece together a jigsaw puzzle, until a complete description is available to interested parties. Such a task requires the dedicated efforts of hundreds or thousands of scholars devoting their entire lives to their projects. And then, as students of language know, the task is never completed. Language is too complex and is always changing.

The second objective of many grammar books is to prescribe rules—those lists of *do's* and *don'ts* for writers—as well as to present detailed analyses of writing problems, writing methods, types of discourse, outlining, studies in logic, and so on, all in an effort to make better writers of those students who use the books. Such goals are admirable, and such books have their places. Fortunately, many excellent works of this nature are available to the general public.

This text attempts to do neither of these tasks; yet, at the same time, it attempts, in a limited way, to do both. This book, you will discover, is intended to be a means of reviewing quickly and effectively basic procedures in sentence analysis, reviewing and building upon what you already know so that you will be able to write and speak with the effectiveness of an articulate, educated person.

To accomplish this task, we have presented what some may think are too many detailed descriptions of how the English language functions relative to various things—subjects, verbs, and objects, for instance. At other times, you may think we have been too cursory in our presentations, or have completely omitted vital material and explanations. But this is a book about standard English usage—those practices that often mean the difference between success and failure as a writer or speaker. As a result, this text is meant to be more on the order of a reference book than a standard text.

This book is organized to cover grammar, first at the level of types of words (that is, nouns, verbs, and so on), advancing to cover how those words are used in sentences. Rules for capitalization and spelling are then presented, followed by tips on improving your writing. An appendix contains a handy list of commonly misused words and expressions. Notes, tips, cautions, analysis sections, and sidebars supplement the discussion, alerting you to extra information, providing helpful hints, warning you of pitfalls, and summarizing the key points of each section. To aid you in navigating this information, this book includes a fairly detailed table of contents and an extensive index, enabling you to search for and find quickly specific items about which you need more information. Most of us, when we are writing, do not have the time (nor do we wish to take the time) that is needed to read complete explanations of why something is or ought to be a certain way.

Of course, it should be noted that any author or teacher who attempts to present prescriptive grammar or "standard English" selects those niceties—those rules or ways of saying things—that he or she feels are important. Because of this, a book that presents the study of language from the prescriptive point of view is necessarily selective and presumptuous, presenting those "rules" and usages that the author feels are important enough to be included while omitting all others. At the same time, the author imposes his or her own standards upon the material presented, saying, in effect, "If you want to be an effective speaker or writer, do things my way."

A writer of a text such as this cannot avoid these problems, for decisions on what constitutes the most effective way of saying things are not a matter of historical record, revealed truth, or telephone surveys. Rather, "correct usage" is a matter of using a language in precise ways based on what educated speakers and writers have accepted as appropriate over the years. That, often, is a matter of opinion, both on the part of those writers and speakers and on the part of those of us who, at present, examine their uses of the English language. It is a judgment call at best, but a judgment call based on scrutiny of the language used by a variety of educated people. A text such as this one presents guidelines and standards—however arbitrary they may be—in an attempt to develop good language habits; for good language habits are, after all, one means of achieving success and avoiding personal embarrassment.

Language, of course, is in a state of constant change. Words come and go. The word *parenting*, to which many purists object, has already secured a place in our dictionaries and is now accepted as a "real" word. *Cool* once had a meaning similar to "not warm" and "calm," and when used as slang, "great." It has now taken on, in informal usage, a renewed vitality with the meaning of "fine, acceptable," or as a word expressing general approval, as in the expression, "That's cool." *Inflammable* has, by governmental decree, become *flammable*. What is *not* in one year, decade, or generation *is* in the next, reflecting the needs of the particular group using the language.

If that be the case, you may ask, why not take an "anything goes" approach? The answer is simple and, we suspect, obvious: not anything goes. Readers, listeners, employers, and others have certain expectations; those expectations are higher among educated people and professional groups. What is also obvious is that when a person writes or speaks in formal situations, that person is subjecting himself or herself to public scrutiny that could be beneficial or embarrassing, based on the knowledge of language usage—and that includes vocabulary items. This text has as its main objective the goal of assisting the writer or speaker to use the English language to his or her benefit.

This text does not address all the problems that you may encounter in using the English language effectively. No text can do that. For one thing, this text is highly selective and limited. It presents a brief review of the grammar of the English sentence as a basis for understanding how certain parts of speech (pronouns, adjectives, and adverbs, for example) fit into the overall sentence. This text is also limited in its presentation of words and definitions. Not all troublesome pairs of words are included; for those words and pairs that are, not all definitions are given. Thus, if you believe that a certain word may be used in a way not listed in this text, you should consult a good dictionary to determine the appropriateness of the word or usage in a particular circumstance. A good dictionary is, after all, an important tool for any writer or speaker.

 An especially sensitive matter that this text deals with in only a cursory manner is that of sexism in language. In this matter, an author walks on the prickly cacti of human emotions, for this is an emotional issue. The centuries-old use of *he* as the pronoun of indefinite gender, for instance, is rejected by many writers and groups in today's society. Some of these people advocate eliminating all references to gender, perhaps an admirable goal if the "cleansing" of the language is not carried to extremes (substituting *hystory* for *history,* for example, even though *history* is derived from the Greek word *histor,* meaning "knowing" or "learned," and is gender free—unless you choose to make it gender specific). *He* as a pronoun of indefinite gender, however, is often a preferred pronoun in such constructions as *Everyone is expected to hand in his assignment tomorrow.* Even so, you may avoid such constructions by recasting the sentence in a manner similar to this: *All students are expected to hand in their assignments tomorrow.* At times, though, employing plural nouns can be less effective than using singular nouns. In those cases, you have to decide if you should employ the same nouns, use the awkward *he/she, his/her* combinations, or risk using the *he* pronouns. Because this is a text dealing with standard English usage, and because standard English usage for centuries has employed *he* in such constructions, we have used *he* at times when we thought that other options were less effective. It's a no-win situation at best. Rest assured, however, that we are sensitive to the problem; all the children of both the authors are girls.

Finally, we think we make our position quite clear throughout the text: The level of formality of one's language ought to vary from situation to situation. Not every activity requires correct grammar and formal diction. Standard English—or whatever term is used—is a dialect for formal situations and for less-formal situations in which a speaker may wish to make a positive impression. Grammar—formal or otherwise—is a tool of communication. You should learn to use it wisely and well.

PART I

PARTS OF SPEECH

In a perfect world, people would not forget things; but, as we all know, this is not a perfect world. People tend to forget specific details of the formal training in grammar to which they were exposed in their earlier years of schooling. And because authors of grammar texts treat their subjects in various ways and from their own points of view, a brief refresher course in some of the basics of grammar may be helpful in dealing with materials presented in later sections of this book. After reviewing the material in this part, you should be able to understand the material in the sections dealing with specific usage problems.

Knowledge of which word or construction to use in a certain place in a sentence often depends upon knowing the *function* of each word in a sentence or construction. For that reason, a basic understanding of grammar is essential if you wish to become adept at using the language with confidence. Choosing between *who* and *whom*, for instance, or *well* and *good* depends nearly entirely on the role that these words play in the sentence. Errors in usage are often made by individuals simply because the individuals are unable to analyze their sentences—or unable to analyze them quickly enough to be effective in making desirable choices of such sentence elements as pronouns, adjectives, and adverbs.

Fortunately, the traditional parts of speech that comprise the English sentence are fairly easily learned. Although it is true that sometimes these parts of speech are used in ways that seem complicated, their basic definitions and usages ought to present very few problems. What follows, then, are definitions and explanations of the parts of speech and discussions of some of the problems associated with them.

Parts of speech, also called *word classes,* include the following:

- Nouns
- Pronouns
- Adjectives
- Verbs
- Adverbs
- Function words

Nouns

A standard definition of a *noun* is a word that names a person, place, or thing:

Persons
Jane
Michael
man
girl
clerk
Elton John
typist
brother
Collins
Whitney Houston
Spaniard
airman
wife
daughter
Heidi

Places
Toronto
church
attic
Benton
Kentucky
Laos
the South
Texas
Land Between the Lakes
home
Lake Superior
Antarctica

Things
    car
    dogs
    trip
    honesty
    love
    justice
    honor
    life
    joy
    neatness
    wisdom
    fear
    table
    chair
    Gone With the Wind
    Carnegie Hall
    the Pulitzer Prize

NOUN CLASSES

Nouns are sometimes classified in the following ways:

- Common
- Proper
- Abstract
- Concrete
- Collective

Common Nouns

Nouns that are the names of things in general are called *common nouns*. A common noun does not begin with a capital letter unless it is the first word of a sentence. Some examples of common nouns are the following:

    nail
    car
    teacher
    cat
    fish
    story

Common nouns are often subdivided into two groups:

- Count nouns
- Mass nouns

Count Nouns

Count nouns are those nouns that identify individual items, either singly or as members of groups. In other words, the single entities may be counted. Examples of count nouns are the following:

cat
boxes
tree
fish
herd
Dr. Adams
class
eyeball
bean

Determiners patterning with count nouns may be singular or plural, depending on the number of the noun:

That cow is my uncle's favorite.
Those dogs appear friendly.

A *determiner* is a word that introduces a noun phrase. Determiners specify number and quantity (*all, both, two, many, several*), or that conveys the denotation of a noun phrase (*a/an, the, my, this*). They are discussed in more detail later in this part under the heading "Determiners."

Mass Nouns

Sometimes called *non-count* nouns, mass nouns identify undifferentiated mass—that is, things not usually considered countable by individual items:

sugar
grass
water
darkness
news
money

Mass words are usually singular and are usually modified by words such as *much, more, less,* and *some.*

Although mass nouns are not usually considered countable, countability can be achieved with certain mass nouns through the use of *partitive expressions,* such as *a bit of, some pieces of,* and the like. Following are examples of sentences containing partitive expressions (in italics) with mass nouns (in bold):

Billy offered Jan *a piece of* **advice.**
There wasn't *a shred of* **evidence** to support Joseph's theory about
the robbery.

Some partitive expressions work only with certain mass nouns:

a ball of **wax/yarn**
a lump of **coal/sugar**
a cup of **coffee/milk**
a case of **beer/wine**

Measurements can also be used as partitive expressions with mass nouns:

a spoonful of **sugar**
a ton of **manure**

Proper Nouns

Nouns that name specific things that are identified with an individual
name are *proper nouns*. The first letter of a proper noun is capitalized.
Some examples of proper nouns are the following:

Michael Jordan
Rover
Moby Dick
Wisconsin
History 110
Pepsi Cola
Proverbs
Indianapolis 500

Abstract Nouns

Nouns that name a *quality,* an *attribute,* an *idea,* or anything not having physical properties are *abstract nouns.* Such words as *goodness,
love, truth,* and *mercy* are included in this category. Many abstract
nouns employ the suffixes *ness* (*goodness*), *ty* (*loyalty*), and *th* (*truth*)
to name ideas and intangible qualities.

Concrete Nouns

Nouns that name things that have physical properties—that is, things
that are tangible items—are *concrete nouns.* Some examples of concrete nouns are the following:

wood
rain
smoke
Mr. Peterson
ghost

car
moon
wind
pencil
Jennifer
sunshine
story
lie
Saturday

Borderline cases exist, such as *ghost* and *lie,* because ghosts, supposedly, can be seen and lies can be heard.

 As you've probably noticed, nouns fit into more than one noun category. For example, *Mr. Peterson* is both a proper noun and a concrete noun.

Collective Nouns

A *collective noun* is a singular noun that refers to more than one thing as members of a single unit. Some examples are the following:

herd (the single unit herd is made up of the individual members—cows, for example)
flock
jury
bunch
throng
committee
company
class
team
tribe
school (of fish)
army
platoon
family
Congress

RECOGNIZING THE VARIOUS TYPES OF NOUNS

The following sentences contain examples of various types of nouns:

The little puppy that the family obtained from the animal shelter was fun to play with.

puppy: common (count), concrete
family: common (count), concrete, collective
shelter: common (count), concrete

Politicians often make speeches that include such things as patriotism, love of country, dedication, and self-sacrifice.

> **politicians:** common (count), concrete
> **speeches:** common (count), concrete (you can hear speeches)
> **things:** common (count), concrete
> **patriotism:** common (mass), abstract
> **love:** common (mass), abstract
> **country:** common (count), concrete
> **dedication:** common (mass), abstract
> **self-sacrifice:** common (mass), abstract

All Americans should help to protect the environment by recycling all materials that are reusable.

> **Americans:** proper, concrete
> **environment:** common (mass), concrete
> **materials:** common (count), concrete

Reading these books will fill you with admiration for the talents of the authors.

> **books:** common (count), concrete
> **admiration:** common (mass), abstract
> **talents:** common (count), concrete
> **authors:** common (count), concrete

My parents lived in perfect harmony for years in the same house.

> **parents:** common (count), concrete
> **harmony:** common (mass), abstract
> **house:** common (count), concrete
> **years:** common (count), concrete

The tribe of head-hunters led the explorers through the jungle.

> **tribe:** common (count), concrete, collective
> **head-hunters:** common (count), concrete
> **explorers:** common (count), concrete
> **jungle:** common (count), concrete

The lost travelers felt both joy and relief when they sighted the rescue plane.

> **travelers:** common (count), concrete
> **joy:** common (mass), abstract
> **relief:** common (mass), abstract
> **plane:** common (count), concrete

The class sighed with relief when Professor Jones announced that she had postponed the test for a week.

class: common (count), concrete, collective
relief: common (mass), abstract
Professor Jones: proper, concrete
test: common (count), concrete
week: common (count), concretre

Members of our family have always attempted to tell the truth or to remain silent.

members: common (count), concrete
family: common (mass), concrete, collective
truth: common (count) (truth is often pluralized, as in "We hold these truths to be self-evident . . . ."), abstract

We learned just enough French and German to get by during our stay in Europe last year.

French: proper, concrete
German: proper, concrete
stay: common (count), concrete
Europe: proper, concrete
year: common (count), concrete

MAKING NOUNS PLURAL

Most nouns are made plural by adding an *s*:

cat	cats
dog	dogs
sneeze	sneezes
file	files

Alas, many nouns do not fit this pattern:

- Nouns ending in *s, ss, z, zz, x, ch, sh,* and *tch* are made plural by adding *es* to the singular form:

bus	buses
mass	masses
buzz	buzzes
fox	foxes
lunch	lunches
wish	wishes
watch	watches

- If a noun's singular form ends in a consonant plus *y*, you must change the *y* to *i* and then add *es*:

baby	babies
fly	flies
sky	skies

Proper nouns that end in *y* are exceptions to the rule replacing *y* with *ies*:

Correct: the Kennedys
Incorrect: the Kennedies

- Some nouns that end in *o* are made plural by the addition of *es*:

hero	heroes
tomato	tomatoes

Because this rule is inconsistent, you should check your dictionary for the correct plural form of nouns ending in *o*.

You should be alert for variant spellings of the plural forms of some nouns. For example, *cargo* may take either the *s* or *es* to form the plural. *Bus* may be spelled with one *s* or two in its plural form (*buses* or *busses*).

- For some nouns ending in *f* or *fe*, the ending is changed to *ves* to form the plural:

wife	wives
shelf	shelves
elf	elves

Because this rule is inconsistent, you should check your dictionary for the correct plural form of words ending in *f* and *ef*.

- Some nouns mutate to form the plural:

man	men
woman	women
tooth	teeth
foot	feet
goose	geese
mouse	mice
louse	lice
brother	brethren
ox	oxen
child	children

A few nouns undergo no visible change, but plurals are implied: *fish, deer, sheep,* and so on. With nouns that do not change forms when they are made plural, you can determine plurality or singularity by identifying the verb or determiner that patterns with each noun, as in these examples:

One deer *is* in the field.
Those sheep *are* my uncle's favorite animals.

Some nouns are plural in form but singular in meaning and, therefore, take singular verbs:

Politics *makes* strange bedfellows.
Mathematics *is* an interesting area of study.
The news *is* certainly disturbing.

Some plural nouns refer to instruments or items of clothing that consist of two joined parts (*slacks, scissors, sunglasses, boxers, Daisy Dukes,* and so on). These nouns take a plural verb:

Ethan wore plaid *trousers* to the country club.
Helen's *britches were* a little too big.

Other nouns are plural in form but may be either singular or plural, depending on the meaning intended by the speaker or writer:

Oats is a healthful breakfast.
    (The cereal grain, oats, is construed as a single entity.)
The *oats are* too wet to harvest today.
    (The grains of oats are construed as individual items.)

Ethics is the study of a system of morals.
That man's *ethics are* certainly questionable at best.

The troop's *headquarters are* in the valley.
Headquarters has given the order to retreat.

Other words in this category include the following:

data
strata
phenomena
statistics
measles
shears
pliers
suds

The word *media,* the plural form of *medium,* gives many speakers unnecessary problems. *Media* is plural; therefore, a sentence would read something similar to this:

> The *media are* presenting the story inaccurately.
> The *medium* favored by many artists *is* painting.

Some nouns may be either singular or plural, depending upon whether the context refers to a group or the individuals that comprise the group. These words, such as *family, tribe, choir, committee, team, faculty, band, staff, Congress,* and so on, are sometimes a bit confusing to work with, because a writer's intentions may not be understood, and a writer cannot be certain how a reader will interpret his or her written statements. Notice the following sentences and the brief explanations for each one:

> The tribe *are* beginning to assemble for the ceremony.
> (This sentence suggests that the individual members of the tribe are beginning to assemble. The tribe is not yet complete; the group is not acting in concert. The *individuals,* then, are beginning to assemble. The verb is plural: the individuals *are.*)
> The tribe *is* planning to build a new school building.
> (In this sentence, the tribe, as a group and acting in concert, is united in planning to build a new building. The members are not conceived as individuals. The group *is* making plans.)

> The fraternity *plans* to accept some new members.
> (In this sentence, the fraternity is acting as a single entity. The group *is* making plans.)
> The fraternity *have* not *agreed* on a new house.
> (In this sentence, no unity exists; the individuals have different views. They *have* not *agreed.*)

Sometimes this matter is a bit more complex, especially with the word *jury.* When is a jury acting as a unit, when is it not? The following sentences exemplify the problem:

> The jury *is* debating the verdict.
> (In this sentence, the jury, as a group, is debating an issue; however, if a debate is taking place, obviously a difference of opinion exists and the group would seem not to be united. But in this case, the jury *as a group* is engaged in a common activity—the debate. The members are not viewed as separate individuals acting independently.)
> The jury *have* not been able to reach a verdict.
> (In this sentence, individuals are clearly divided one from the other—or, more accurately—one group from the other. No conception of unanimity of behavior exists. The verb is plural in form.)

Try applying this same rationale to these two sentences:

The class *are* taking different forms of the test.
The class *is* assembled and waiting for the test.

If such a construction as "the class are" seems unnatural or stilted, a speaker or writer may simply insert "the members of" before the nouns, as in this sentence:

The *members* of the class *are* waiting anxiously.

 How can you be certain whether the form of a noun is singular, plural, or both? The answer is simple: Consult a good dictionary.

Many words of Latin origin that once formed their English plurals in the traditional Latin manner may now utilize regular English forms:

antenna	antennas (or antennae)
curriculum	curriculums (or curricula)
syllabus	syllabuses (or syllabi)
memorandum	memorandums (or memoranda)
narcissus	narcissuses (or narcissi)
cactus	cactuses (or cacti)
radius	radiuses (or radii)

 Be careful: *Arbutus* is not usually pluralized with a Latin suffix, while *thesis* still has only the Latin plural form, *theses*. In situations such as these, a good dictionary can be very useful.

MAKING NOUNS POSSESSIVE

Many nouns are inflected to show possession. When a word shows possession, it indicates a relationship between someone who possesses something and the thing that person possesses. This inflection takes the form of an *'s*, although some nouns cannot be inflected in this manner. For example, *cat's* tail, *teacher's* book, *girl's* jacket, and so on, are correct, but not *suit's* fit, *bus's* back, or *house's* roof, and so on. Nouns in this second group show possession by employing the "*of* construction": *fit of the suit, back of the bus, roof of the house*. Usually the possessive form is used with animate nouns (that is, nouns referring to a person, animal, or other creature—for example, *girl, grizzly bear, spider*), while the *of* structure is used with inanimate nouns (nouns that refer to a thing or concept—for example, *train station, algebra*).

Inflection refers to an affix (always a suffix in English) that expresses a grammatical relationship, such as the plural *s* in *mothers* and the *ed* ending in *bathed*.

When a noun becomes possessive, it is called a *determiner*. Determiners are discussed in more detail later in this part (see the section titled "Determiners").

DERIVATIONAL SUFFIXES

Many nouns may be identified by certain kinds of suffixes. These suffixes usually change another part of speech to a noun. Notice the suffixes (called *derivational suffixes* because they cause a noun to be *derived* from another part of speech) on the following words:

> honesty
> Asian
> truth
> disappointment
> happiness
> departure

(Such words as *Asian, Russian,* and *motherhood* are, of course, one type of noun that has been derived from another type of noun.)

GENERAL OBSERVATIONS ABOUT NOUNS

- A noun is a word that names a person, place, or thing.
- A noun must fit into more than one of the five classifications listed. For example, tree is both a common noun and a concrete noun; justice is both a common noun and an abstract noun; English 328 is both a proper and a concrete noun.
- Common nouns are usually not capitalized unless they are the first words of sentences.
- Proper nouns are usually capitalized wherever they appear in sentences.
- Names of school classes (history, geometry, and so on) are not capitalized unless they are the first word of a sentence, the name of a language (French, Spanish, English), or followed by a numeral or letter (History 101, Physics B, Astronomy A).
- Although most nouns are made plural through the addition of an *s* at the end of the word, many nouns do not fit this pattern.
- Some nouns may be either singular or plural, depending upon whether the context refers to a group or the individuals that comprise the group.

- Some nouns borrowed from other languages may be made plural as they were in the contributing language:

    crisis   crises
    alumna   alumnae
    thesis   theses

- Most nouns are made plural through the addition of an *s* at the end of the word.
- Many nouns are inflected to show possession. This inflection takes the form of an *'s*, although some nouns cannot be inflected in this manner.
- Many nouns may be identified by certain kinds of suffixes. These suffixes usually change another part of speech to a noun.

Pronouns

A *pronoun* is a word that can be substituted for a noun, noun phrase, or other pronoun without changing the meaning of the sentence or the basic construction pattern of the sentence. Notice the following pairs of sentences. The first sentence of each pair contains a noun or noun phrase that is replaced by a pronoun in the second sentence.

    I saw *John* yesterday. I saw *him* in the library.
    Main Street is an interesting book. *It* was written by Sinclair Lewis.
    The little boy went fishing. *He* caught two fish.

CLASSIFYING PRONOUNS

Pronouns are classified in one of seven ways, depending on their uses in sentences. Except for certain uses of the personal pronouns, the pronouns in the various categories cause the average speaker of English little trouble if the individual speaks English as his or her first language. Here are the categories of pronouns:

- Personal pronouns
- Reflexive pronouns
- Intensive pronouns
- Relative pronouns
- Indefinite pronouns
- Demonstrative pronouns
- Interrogative pronouns

Personal Pronouns

Personal pronouns are used when a writer or speaker wishes to use a pronoun to substitute for a word that refers to a person, either himself or someone else (or, in the case of *it,* a thing). Examples of personal pronouns are *I, you, he, she, it, we,* and *they.* Here are some examples using personal pronouns:

> *You* are perfect for the part of Iago!
> *I* painted the jalopy British-racing green.
> When *he* proposed, Susan nearly fainted.
> *She* doesn't know the answer to the question.
> When the moped stalled, *I* gave *it* a swift kick to restart *it.*
> *We* were the last couple standing in the dance contest.
> I told Earl and Eunice *they* could go to the movies.

 As a general rule, you should avoid using the pronoun *you* in situations clearly calling for a noun or a different pronoun, especially in formal speaking or writing situations.

> **Incorrect:** When *you* are pregnant, *you* shouldn't do any heavy lifting.
> **Correct:** When *a woman* is pregnant, *she* shouldn't do any heavy lifting.

Reflexive Pronouns

Reflexive pronouns do what their name implies: They "reflect" the person or thing already identified. They are used when the subject of a sentence performs an action on itself or refers to itself in some other way.

 The *subject* of a sentence (or clause) is the noun, pronoun, or noun phrase that normally comes before the verb (for example, *Joann* in "Joann ran the marathon") or, in the case of interrogative sentences, after the verb (for example, *dog* in "Did the *dog* eat the meat loaf?"). Subjects are covered in greater detail in Part II under the heading "Subjects and Predicates."

A reflexive pronoun is made by combining a form of the personal pronoun and the suffix *self* or *selves* (*myself, himself, yourself, themselves,* and so on). Notice the reflexive pronouns in the following sentences:

> You are only fooling *yourself.*
> I often find *myself* asking *myself* questions.
> Roger cut *himself* with a sharp ax.
> My sister saw *herself* in the picture.
> The puppy watched *itself* in the mirror.
> The kittens chased *themselves* around the room.
> I injured *myself* this morning.

Intensive Pronouns

Intensive pronouns are similar in nature to reflexive pronouns; they differ only in their function within the sentence. They are usually found immediately following a noun or pronoun for the purpose of lending emphasis to the noun or pronoun that they follow. Here are some examples of intensive pronouns:

I *myself* painted that picture.
The captain *himself* guided the plane.
You *yourself* must do the work required of each person.
I shall do it *myself.*
John *himself* is the culprit.
The players *themselves* voted for the captain.

Relative Pronouns

Relative pronouns connect adjective or noun clauses to other elements of the sentence. That is, a relative pronoun substitutes for the noun being modified by an adjective clause and relates that clause to the noun:

The boy **who** *was here* is my nephew.
The person to **whom** *I talked* was the new president.

In the first sentence, *who* substitutes for *the boy*. Without the relative pronoun, the sentence would be constructed as the following:

The boy (the boy was here) is my nephew.

 You'll learn more about noun and adjective clauses in Part II, "Sentence Elements," in the section titled "Clauses."

The four most frequently used relative pronouns are *who/whom, which, that,* and *what*. In general, *who/whom* refers to persons, and *which* refers to animals, things, or to collective nouns referring to persons. *That* refers to persons, animals, or things. Consider these examples of relative pronouns (in bold) used to introduce adjective clauses (in italics):

The boy **who** *was here* is my brother.
The table **that** *he sold* was new.
The dog **that** *bit me* was a family pet.
The cow for **which** *you are looking* is in the barn.
The person to **whom** *you were speaking* is the captain.
The worker **that** *injured himself* has gone home.
The committee **that** *made that decision* has been highly praised.

Sometimes the relative pronoun is omitted from the grammatical construction in which it would normally be found:

> Leslie is the person ( ) I wish to see. (*whom*)
> Here is the coin ( ) we found. (that)

Indefinite Relative Pronouns

Indefinite relative pronouns introduce noun clauses. The indefinite relative pronouns are the following:

> who
> whom
> what
> whoever
> whomever
> whatever
> whichever

The indefinite relative pronouns have indefinite antecedents, thus their name. Notice the use of the relative pronouns in these two sentences:

> The person **who** *gave you that book* is our new librarian.
> **Whoever** *gave you that book* did not give you the right one.

In the second sentence, the relative pronoun *whoever* is an indefinite pronoun, because *whoever* has no antecedent. In the first sentence, however, the relative pronoun *who* is not an indefinite pronoun because it has the antecedent *person* and introduces an adjective clause.

 An expression's *antecedent* is the expression to which the expression refers. As stated in the preceding paragraph, "person" is the antecedent of "who gave you that book."

Using Relative Pronouns to Introduce Nominal Relative Clauses

The relative pronouns *who, whoever, whom, whomever, that, which, whichever, what,* and *whatever* may introduce nominal relative clauses—that is, clauses that are used as noun substitutes:

> Everyone knew *what I wanted for my birthday.*
> *Whoever wins the race* will receive the prize.
> Give the keys to *whomever lost them.*
> That is exactly *what we need for the job.*

Notice the relative pronouns are inflected for case according to their uses in the various grammatical entities in which they occur. The cases of pronouns are discussed later in this section under the heading "The Cases of Pronouns."

Indefinite Pronouns

Indefinite pronouns are words that are substituted for nouns without referring to a definite person, place, or thing. The most frequently used indefinite pronouns are the following:

anyone
everyone
someone
no one
one
all
some
somebody
anybody
everybody
every
everything
either
neither
any
many
other
both
some
none
nobody

 Indefinite pronouns should not be confused with the indefinite relative pronouns discussed in the section titled "Relative Pronouns."

These pronouns are called *indefinite* because they do not indicate the exact person or thing to which they refer:

Both are acceptable to me.
Everything is fine between Sue and Sam.
Someone has taken my new chemistry book.
Have you told *anyone* our secret?
Somebody took my sandwich.
Everybody is busy doing the lesson.
We knew that *no one* had taken the car.
I don't have *any,* but John has *some.*
You may have *either* of the books.

Notice that these indefinite pronouns do not introduce clauses, as do the indefinite relative pronouns. Note, too, the difference in usage of the indefinite pronouns in these two sentences:

The runner **who** *wins* will have earned the prize.
　(*Who* relates to the noun phrase, *the runner,* in this sentence.)

Someone should explain the rules to Bill.
　(*Someone* has no antecedent and is unrelated to anyone or anything in the sentence. Because it is not related to an antecedent, it is not a relative pronoun.)

Most indefinite pronouns require singular verbs. *Each, either, neither, someone, somebody, anyone, anybody, everyone, everybody, no one, nobody,* and *one* (and a person) are singular. Prepositional phrases following indefinite pronouns usually do not influence verb number (prepositional phrases are discussed in more detail in the section titled "Prepositional Phrases" in Part II, "Sentence Elements"):

Each (of the puppies) **was** healthy.
Every one (of the workers) **is** ready to eat lunch.
Neither (of the books) **was** interesting to me.

The exceptions to this rule are in the cases of a fraction or a percent and such words as *all, most, more, part, some, such, rest, any,* and *none,* which will be singular if bulk or a total number or amount is intended, and plural if numbers are considered. That is, if the object of the preposition in a phrase modifying the subject of the verb (even if the prepositional phrase is unstated or understood) is a count noun, the verb is plural; if the object of the preposition is a mass noun, the verb is singular:

Thirty percent *of the water* **is** contaminated.
Thirty percent *of the professors* **are** members of the organization.

Some *of the apples* **are** spoiled.
Some *of the soup* **is** cold.

The words *both, few, many, others,* and *several,* on the other hand, are plural and take the plural form of the verb:

Many **believe** in UFOs.
Both **have** brown hair.

In formal writing and speaking, indefinite pronouns and noun phrases preceded by indefinite determiners (*each, every, any, either,* and so on) require the singular masculine pronoun form (*he, his, him*):

> *Any* dog worth his salt barks when a stranger knocks at the door.
> *Each* student must do *his* own work.

 Because of the sensitivity of many people—both writers and nonwriters—and the mistaken notion that gender-based pronouns refer exclusively to males, some writers and speakers make a conscious effort to avoid them. One method of doing this is to make all nouns plural, requiring the use of *they, them,* and *their:*

> All *students* must do *their* own work.

Because this type of construction is not always the most effective means of expressing oneself, some individuals are attempting to legitimize the use of *they, their,* and *them* as substitutes for the masculine pronoun forms:

> Every student must do *their* own work.

Although this usage may someday be acceptable in formal English, it is not yet recognized as an alternative to the *indefinite masculine* pronoun. At present, it tends to call attention to itself and may reflect questionably upon the user. It is probably best avoided.

Demonstrative Pronouns

Demonstrative pronouns serve to point out particular persons, places, or things, even though they may not be named directly. These types of pronouns may sometimes refer to a complete idea expressed elsewhere. The demonstrative pronouns are the following:

> this
> that
> these
> those

Following are some example sentences using demonstrative pronouns:

> *This* is the way to kick a football.
> *That* is a new coat.
> She told me that *these* are good apples.
> *Those* were the ones she wanted to buy.
> *This* is a good apple.

Everyone should taste one of *these*.
I played the entire game, and *that* is something I seldom do.

Demonstrative pronouns are of two types: The *substitutional pronouns* demonstrated in the preceding sentences, in which the pronoun substitutes for the entire noun phrase, and the *prenominal demonstratives,* in which the pronoun precedes a noun, as in the following sentences:

This apple is a really good apple.
That woman is a really fine speaker.

Interrogative Pronouns

Interrogative pronouns are the pronouns that are used in asking questions. The interrogative pronouns are the following:

who
whom
whose
which
what

Here are a few example sentences using interrogative pronouns:

What did you say?
Who did you find in the garden?
Which car is yours?
Who are you?
Who was that masked man?
Which topic did you select for your report?

Interrogative pronouns also signal indirect questions in noun clauses:

I asked him *whom* he intended to contact.
We all wondered *what* he intended to do.

RECOGNIZING THE VARIOUS TYPES OF PRONOUNS

 The following sentences contain examples of various types of pronouns (personal, reflexive, intensive, relative, indefinite, demonstrative, interrogative):

The little boy injured himself by falling off his wagon.
        himself: reflexive
        his: personal

Who was that person I saw you talking to yesterday?
> **who:** personal
> **I:** personal
> **you:** personal

> *That* in *that person* functions as a determiner, much as *a* or *the* would.

The car that I drive I call my "golden chariot."
> **that:** relative
> **I:** personal
> **I:** personal
> **my:** personal

The little girl hurt herself, but she didn't cry at all.
> **herself:** reflexive
> **she:** personal

Everybody was surprised when his car started without delay.
> **everybody:** indefinite
> **his:** personal

What do you think about the situation in Antarctica?
> **what:** interrogative
> **you:** personal

I suppose I'll have to clean up this mess myself.
> **I:** personal
> **I:** personal
> **myself:** intensive

> *This* in *this mess* functions as a determiner (see the preceding note).

That book belongs to my roommate.
> **my:** personal

> *That* in *that book* functions as a determiner (see the preceding note).

The money is gone, but I certainly didn't spend any.
> **I:** personal
> **any:** indefinite

This is a pretty shirt, but no one seems to want it.
> **this:** demonstrative
> **no one:** indefinite
> **it:** personal

Each of you must do your work yourself.
> **each:** indefinite
> **you:** personal
> **your:** personal
> **yourself:** intensive

Somebody is spreading gossip about my friend.
> **somebody:** indefinite
> **my:** personal

The person who took your car is now in jail.
> **who:** relative
> **your:** personal

We considered ourselves untalented performers.
> **we:** personal
> **ourselves:** reflexive

I guess I'll have to do it myself.
> **I:** personal
> **I:** personal
> **it:** personal
> **myself:** intensive

THE CASES OF PRONOUNS

Unlike nouns, which do not change form when they are used in various ways in a sentence (except to indicate possession), certain pronouns—chiefly personal pronouns—do change form depending on their placement in a sentence:

- Pronouns being used as a subject of a sentence or clause are said to be in the *nominative case.*
- Pronouns being used as an object are in the *objective case.*
- Pronouns being used to show ownership or similar relationships are in the *possessive case.*

The following table contains the various cases of personal pronouns. Note that *first person* refers to the speaker talking about himself. *Second person* refers to the person being addressed (the *you* of a sentence). The *third person* is the *he, she,* or *it* that the speaker is talking about.

Personal Pronoun	Nominative Case	Objective Case	Possessive Case
First-person singular	I	me	my, mine
First-person plural	we	us	our, ours
Second-person singular	you	you	your, yours
Second-person plural	you	you	your, yours
Third-person singular	he, she, it	him, her, it	his, her, hers, its
Third-person plural	they	them	their, theirs

Certain relative pronouns can also be inflected for case; the following table shows the various cases of relative pronouns.

Nominative Case	Objective Case	Possessive Case
who	whom	whose
whoever	whomso	whosoever
whoso	whomsoever	
whosoever	whomever	

When a pronoun is made possessive, it is considered a *determiner*. Determiners are covered in more detail later in this part in the section titled "Determiners."

Nominative Case

Examples of nominative-case pronouns include the following:

I
he
she
we
they
who
whoever
whoso
whosoever

Pronouns in the nominative case can function as the following:

- The subject of a sentence

    They bullied their way into the club.
    I love Parcheesi.

- A subject complement

    The queen is *I.*
    The winners were *they.*

A *subject complement* is the complement of a linking verb such as *be* or *seem*. You'll learn more about subject complements in Part II.

- An appositive with another nominative

    Gymnasts, *he* for example, are incredibly nimble.

An *appositive* indicates a relationship between (typically) two noun phrases that refer to the same entity or overlap in their reference. ("Pirmin Zurbriggen, the greatest ski racer of his generation, is also an accomplished dirt-biker.") Appositives are discussed in more detail in Part II under the heading "Appositives."

- A complement of the infinitive *to be* when *to be* has no subject

    To be *she* would be a hardship.

Objective Case

Examples of objective-case pronouns include the following:

    me
    him
    her
    us
    them
    whom
    whomever
    whomso
    whomsoever

Pronouns in the objective case can function as the following:

- Objects of all kinds

    Beth's father gave *her* away at her wedding.

- Subjects of infinitives (infinitives are discussed in the section titled "Infinitive Phrases" in Part II)

    I wasn't sure whether *to kiss him* or *to clobber him.*

- An appositive with another object

    Dora gave James, *her brother,* a tie for Christmas.

- A complement of the infinitive *to be* when *to be* has a subject

    What I wouldn't give *to be her.*

Possessive Case

Examples of possessive-case pronouns include the following:

my
your
his
her
its (*never* it's)
our
their
whose
whosoever

Pronouns in the possessive case can function as the following:

- Adjectives

    My sweater looks better on Julie than it does on me.

- The subject of a gerund

    Seeing *him* is painful for Gladys.

A *gerund* is a word that ends in *ing* that shares characteristics of nouns and verbs. For example, in the sentence "Sculpting hedges is Robyn's favorite activity," the gerund *sculpting* requires a direct object (*hedges*) in order to be unambiguous, in the same way many verbs require direct objects (direct objects are covered in more detail in Part II in the section titled "Direct Objects"). At the same time, the phrase "sculpting hedges" acts as the subject of the sentence, much as nouns do. For more information on gerunds, turn to the section titled "Gerund Phrases" in Part II.

PRONOUNS AS NOMINALS

Pronouns, as substitutes for nouns (or *nominals*), may serve the same functions in sentences as nouns. Where nouns serve as subjects, objects, and the like, pronouns may also serve in those functions. Unlike nouns, which do not change forms when used as subjects or objects, pronouns do; therefore, you should understand the specific uses of pronouns in each sentence or sentence part. Here, briefly, is a summary of the rules governing pronoun use:

- Pronouns used as subjects, subject complements, and complements of the infinitive *to be* without a subject must be in the nominative case:

> *She who* sings well will be accepted.
> (*She* is the subject of *will be accepted. Who* is the subject of *sings.*)

> The thief was *he who* had the wallet.
> (*He* is the subject complement. *Who* is the subject of *had.*)

> The winner was thought to be *I.*
> (*I* is the complement of the infinitive *to be.* A pronoun used in this situation is in the nominative case, because *to be* has no subject.)

> Give the book to *whoever* asks for it.
> (*Whoever* is the subject of *asks;* and the entire clause, *whoever asks for it,* is used as the object of the preposition *to.*)

You'll learn more about subjects, subject complements, and complements of the infinitive *to be* in Part II.

- Pronouns used as objects of all kinds must be in the objective case:

> Give the money to *me.*
> (*Me* is the object of the preposition *to.*)

> We found *her* in the library.
> (*Her* is the direct object of *found.*)

> They gave *us* the information yesterday.
> (*Us* is the indirect object.)

An *indirect object* is typically placed between the verb and the direct object, and typically has the role of recipient or beneficiary of the action. For example, *Maria* in "I told Maria the truth" is the sentence's indirect object. Indirect objects are discussed in more detail in Part II under the heading "Indirect Objects."

> Chasing *us* through the field, the puppy became tired.
> (*Us* is the object of the participle *chasing.*)

A participle is a non-finite form of a verb—that is, a verb that does not indicate tense. A participle combines characteristics of a verb with those of an adjective. The present participle of any verb ends in *ing;* the past participle of a regular verb is identified with the past tense, ending in *ed.* Participles are

discussed in more detail in Part II under the heading
"Participial Phrases."

> Finding *me* can sometimes be difficult.
>> (*Me* is the object of the gerund *finding*.)

> To find *her*, search near the fishing hole.
>> (*Her* is the object of the infinitive *to find*.)

> Everyone thought *her* to be *me*.
>> (*Her* is the subject of the infinitive *to be*. *Me* is the complement
>> of the infinitive *to be*. Because *to be* has both subject and com-
>> plement, both pronouns used as subject and complement are in
>> the objective case. See the section titled "Infinitive Phrases" in
>> Part II.)

 You'll learn more about objects in Part II.

Bear in mind that sometimes sentences may be convoluted and
confusing; and when you attempt to analyze them, you may be destined to stumble through jungles of dense grammatical growth. If,
however, the sentence is separated into its constituent parts, the relationship of both the sentence parts and the use of the pronouns can
be understood. Consider, for example, this sentence:

> Present the award to (*we, us*) students (*who, whom*) you consider to be the
> most talented of all (*who, whom*) entered the competition.

To analyze this sentence and to determine the correct pronouns to
use in each instance, you need only to consider the sentence constituents. First, examine the first part of the sentence:

> [You] present the award to (*we, us*) students . . .

What sounds right is right in this case: Someone will present the
award to us. *Us* and *students* both function as the object of the preposition. Objects are in the objective case.

Second, rearrange the second part of the sentence to put the elements into the normal order for an English sentence—that is, subject,
verb, object:

> . . . you consider (*who, whom*) to be the most talented of all (*who, whom*)
> entered the competition.

This part of the sentence may be analyzed in two ways:

- One method is to substitute *he* or *him* for the *who* or *whom* to
  see if the sentence sounds "natural." In this way, you can
  determine that *You consider he* . . . certainly does not sound
  right—and it isn't.

- The other—and most reliable—method is to analyze the role of the pronoun in the construction. In this case, the infinitive *to be* has both a subject (*whom*) and a complement (*the most talented*). In such cases, both the subject and complement are in the *objective* case.

Therefore, the sentence should read as follows:

Present the award to us students whom you consider to be the most talented of all who entered the competition.

Who versus whom

Many speakers and writers of English have difficulty determining whether *who* or *whom* is correct in any given situation. One easy litmus test is to try substituting *he* or *him* for *who* or *whom* to test the pronoun usage. (*He* and *him* are the closest pronouns in spelling to *who* and *whom*. Just omit the *w* and change the vowels.) Consider the following sentence:

Give the bat to him *(who, whom)* cares for the equipment.

In such a case, you first determine whether *who* or *whom* patterns with *him* or functions in some other way. Examine the sentence, determine that *cares* is a verb, and examine *who* or *whom* in terms of that verb—that is, which of these sentences makes better "sentence sense":

Give the bat to him. *Him* cares for the equipment.
Give the bat to him. *He* cares for the equipment.

Here's a convoluted sentence along with a detailed analysis to explain the *who-whom, he-him* system:

(He, him) (who, whom) makes the highest scores we shall certainly recognize.

First, find the natural beginning of the sentence. In this case, it is *We shall certainly recognize . . . .* Now the next word seems obvious: *him.* A native speaker of English surely would not "recognize *he*." What's left? *(Who, whom) makes the highest score.* Substitute *he* or *him* and the answer is readily apparent:

He makes the highest score.

Now we can put the sentence back together in its original form with the proper pronoun selections:

Him who makes the highest scores we shall certainly recognize.

Granted, these sentences may be a bit unusual, and few writers—if any—would use such sentences; but this same process may be used in other, less "rearranged" sentences. The writer who can analyze these sentences should be able to avoid making mistakes in other situations.

PRONOUNS AFTER *AS, THAN,* AND *BUT*

The use of pronouns after *as, than,* and *but* poses some problems. When used in comparisons in formal writing, *as* and *than* function as conjunctions. Therefore, the form of the pronoun after these words depends upon the function of the pronoun in the comparative clause.

A *clause* is a sentence or sentence-like construction within another sentence; a comparative clause, then, is a clause containing a comparison. Clauses are covered in more detail in the section titled "Clauses" in Part II.

A *conjunction* is a sentence element that links parts of a sentence together. See the section titled "Conjunctions" later in this part for more information.

Following are several pairs of sentences. In the first sentence of each pair, the verb in the comparative clause is absent (understood). The second sentence in each pair contains the verb in the comparative clause:

> Her brother talks the same way as she.
> Her brother talks the same way as she talks.
>
> She talks on the radio much better than I.
> She talks on the radio much better than I talk.
>
> They gave him more credit than me.
> They gave him more credit than they gave me.
>
> We admire Charles more than her.
> We admire Charles more than we admire her.

But is a preposition when it means "except," thus the pronoun following *but* is in the objective case. Notice these two sentences:

> We paid everyone but him. (everyone except him)
> No one but him can bake a cake like that. (no one except him)

As, meaning "in the capacity or position of," functions as a preposition, but its use is distinct from that of *like.* For instance, these two sentences have quite different meanings:

> He spoke *like* a professor who is an authority on bats.
> He spoke *as* a professor who is an authority on bats.

The first sentence states the *manner* of the person speaking, not his actual position or role in life. The second sentence establishes the *authority* of a person who is a professor and an expert on the subject of bats. In both cases, a pronoun in the objective case would be required if a pronoun were substituted for *a professor*:

> He spoke *like **him*** who is an authority on bats.
> He spoke *as **one*** who is an authority on bats.

 You would be unlikely to say *as him who . . . ;* but such a construction would be appropriate in some situations, since *as* means "in the capacity of."

SELECTING THE CORRECT PRONOUN

Following are numerous sample sentences that demonstrate the selection of the correct form of pronoun:

> Harold, John, and (*I, me*) are going to Memphis next month.
> **I**

> I thought that you, (*he, him*), and (*she, her*) would study together.
> **he**
> **she**

> The man in the front row was thought to be (*I, me*).
> **I**

> (*She, Her*) who wins the race will receive the trophy.
> **She**

> Donna said that it was not (*she, her*) who found the money.
> **she**

> The guilty ones, (*he, him*) and (*she, her*), confessed readily.
> **he**
> **she**

> Did you enjoy (*him, his*) playing the violin?
> **his**

> Give the book to (*whoever, whomever*) comes to the door.
> **whoever**

> Ask (*whoso, whomso*) you will, the answer will still be no.
> **whomso**

> Why did you believe (*I, me*) to be (*he, him*)?
> **me**
> **him**

I saw the winners, (*he, him*) and (*she, her*).
   him
   her

It most surely was not (*he, him*) or (*I, me*) (*who, whom*) you saw.
   he
   I
   whom

Award the prize to (*whoever, whomever*) you believe to be deserving.
   whomever

Was the trouble the fact that (*he, him*) was believed to be (*I, me*)?
   he
   I

He is 98; can you imagine (*him, his*) jumping rope?
   him

Let's you and (*I, me*) look for the lost golf ball.
   me

She thought the man in the front row to be (*I, me*).
   me

Yes, it was (*she, her*) (*who, whom*) you should have seen.
   she
   whom

Don't you remember (*him, his*) asking us to do this work?
   his

No one knows (*who, whom*) he said should get into line first.
   who

The coach always calls upon (*whosoever, whomsoever*) he sees first.
   whomsoever

(*Who, Whom*) did she say called upon her last evening?
   who

We have no objections to (*you, your*) going with us.
   your

Several people believed you to be (*I, me*).
   me

Was it (*they, them*) (*who, whom*) you asked to finish painting?
> **they**
> **whom**

Could it have been (*they, them*) (*who, whom*) you thought would fight?
> **they**
> **who**

No, it was not (*they, them*) about (*who, whom*) I was speaking.
> **they**
> **whom**

Then it must have been (*he, him*) and (*I, me*) (*who, whom*) should have taken the initiative.
> **he**
> **I**
> **who**

It was (*we, us*) graduate students (*who, whom*) you saw.
> **we**
> **whom**

Give it to (*we, us*) contestants (*who, whom*) you deem to be the most diligent among all (*who, whom*) entered the program.
> **us**
> **whom**
> **who**

(*Whoever, Whomever*) we see winning the race will be the ones (*who, whom*) will be rewarded first.
> **whomever**
> **who**

Both Jack and (*she, her*) enjoyed the professor's laughing at the anecdote.
> **she**

(*Those, Them*) individuals (*who, whom*) make the highest scores (*we, us*) shall most certainly recognize.
> **those**
> **who**
> **we**

Isn't it strange that (*they, them*) were thought to be (*we, us*)?
> **they**
> **we**

Give it to (*whoever, whomever*) asks for it.
whoever

Give it to (*whoever, whomever*) he says should have it.
whoever

He is making (*we, us*) members a set of instructions.
us

Mr. Smith thinks that you, (*he, him*), and (*she, her*) will win.
he
she

Is it (*we, us*) of (*who, whom*) he thinks this?
we
whom

(*We, Us*) early arrivals will have first choice of seats.
we

Can you envision (*me, my*) doing such a foolish thing?
my

(*He, Him*), as well as (*she, her*) and (*they, them*), are no better than (*we, us*) are.
he
she
they
we

Neither (*he, him*) nor his brothers are so tall as (*I, me*).
he
I

The men were asked to meet (*he, him*) and (*she, her*) at the bus.
him
her

Here come Lewis, Sam, and (*she, her*) with John and (*he, him*).
she
him

Who but (*he, him*) could have done such a thing to (*we, us*) people?
him
us

(*She, Her*) (*who, whom*) they nominate we shall support.
> **her**
> **whom**

Was it both (*he, him*) and (*she, her*)?
> **he**
> **she**

No one enjoyed (*his, him*) lecturing on that particular topic.
> **his**

The lady in the front seat was believed to be (*she, her*).
> **she**

Very few people thought (*I, me*) to be (*he, him*), however.
> **me**
> **him**

It is up to (*whoever, whomever*) we select to do the work.
> **whomever**

It is up to (*whoever, whomever*) you think can do the work.
> **whoever**

Neither (*he, him*) nor (*she, her*) studies more than (*they, them*) or (*I, me*).
> **he**
> **she**
> **they**
> **I**

It was (*she, her*), not (*he, him*), who believed (*we, us*) to be (*they, them*).
> **she**
> **he**
> **us**
> **them**

Two of the students, (*he, him*) and (*she, her*), were chosen.
> **him**
> **her**

Yes, (*he, him*), not (*I, me*), is one of those who are somewhat older than (*she, her*).
> **he**
> **I**
> **she**

The leaders seemed both Beth and (*her, she*).
    she

Why don't you sit between (*she, her*) and (*I, me*)?
    her
    me

It is not (*I, me*) who am wanted; it is (*he, him*).
    I
    he

Each of you is much wiser than (*he, him*), (*she, her*), or (*I, me*).
    he
    she
    I

Each of (*we, us*) members is asked to invite (*whoever, whomever*) he wishes.
    us
    whomever

Neither of (*we, us*) officers can go with you, (*she, her*), and (*he, him*).
    us
    her
    him

Many people think that (*I, me*) am (*he, him*).
    I
    he

Neither of you believes (*I, me*) to be (*he, him*), however.
    me
    him

None of those people have taken you to be (*I, me*).
    me

A girl (*who, whom*) Jack and (*I, me*) thought was (*she, her*) spoke to (*we, us*) today.
    who
    I
    she
    us

It could not have been (*he, him*), (*she, her*), and (*I, me*) (*who, whom*) you saw.
> **he**
> **she**
> **I**
> **whom**

It was her best friend (*who, whom*) she was expecting.
> **whom**

She has never found a person (*who, whom*) pleases her entirely.
> **who**

The people with (*who, whom*) he works praise him highly.
> **whom**

Everyone (*who, whom*) the dean called to his office approved the plan.
> **whom**

(*Who, Whom*) was the man to (*who, whom*) you spoke?
> **who**
> **whom**

Give the clothing to (*whoever, whomever*) you believe to need it.
> **whomever**

The small man with the nervous gestures is (*he, him*).
> **he**

Allan and (*he, him*) were a hilarious comedy team.
> **he**

Everyone except (*she, her*) and (*I, me*) was invited.
> **her**
> **me**

No dictator will govern (*we, us*) Americans.
> **us**

He invited everyone but (*she, her*) and (*I, me*).
> **her**
> **me**

With John and (*he, him*) as forwards, we'll make a good score.
> **him**

We left without either (*he, him*) or (*she, her*).
>**him**
>**her**

The next victim will probably be Tina or (*I, me*).
>**I**

Everyone in camp but (*she, her*) can swim.
>**her**

Is that piece of cake for Louis or (*I, me*)?
>**me**

The delegates were Sarah and (*he, him*).
>**he**

A tap at the door brought Mrs. Jones and (*he, him*) to the window.
>**him**

Aunt Phyllis invited (*she, her*) and Leslie to New York.
>**her**

The coach showed George and (*I, me*) a new tennis serve.
>**me**

(*He, Him*) and (*I, me*) were away for two weeks.
>**he**
>**I**

Vote for (*whoever, whomever*) you wish; I shall vote for the one (*who, whom*) I believe can best accomplish our goals.
>**whomever**
>**who**

PRONOUN REFERENCE

Writers and speakers must be certain that the pronouns they employ refer specifically to the nouns for which the pronouns are substituting. If the noun-pronoun relationship is not clear, the result is a problem in *faulty reference*. To avoid faulty reference, a writer or speaker should either place the pronoun close to the noun for which it substitutes, or use a noun rather than a pronoun. Notice the easily detected problem in this sentence:

The professor told Lynne that she had lost her book.

The reference problem in this sentence is obvious: Does *she* refer to *Lynne* or to *The professor*? To which one does *her* refer? One way to clarify the sentence is to re-cast the sentence:

The professor lost Lynne's book and told her so.

Also, avoid using *they* to refer to unknown or unidentified individuals or groups:

I read in the paper that they plan to raise our taxes again. (vague)
I read in the paper that the city council plans to raise our taxes again. (clear)

Finally, readers always appreciate having the antecedent of a pronoun on the same page as the pronoun. A noun on one page and a *he* or *she* on the next page may require a reader to return to the previous page to understand the sentence. Many readers find this mildly annoying and confusing.

 ## GENERAL OBSERVATIONS ABOUT PRONOUNS

- A *pronoun* is a word that can be substituted for a noun or noun phrase without changing the meaning of the sentence or the basic construction pattern of the sentence.
- Pronouns are classified in one of seven ways, depending on their uses in sentences.
- Unlike nouns, which do not change form when they are used in various places in the sentence, pronouns do change form to show they are being used as a subject of a sentence or clause, as an object, or to show ownership or similar relationships.
- Sometimes the relative pronoun is omitted from the grammatical construction in which it would normally be found.
- Most indefinite pronouns require singular verbs, even when a phrase following the pronoun contains a plural noun.
- The case of a pronoun (or noun) is determined in each instance by the function of the pronoun or noun in the sentence or phrase of which it is a part.
- Pronouns in the nominative case can function as the subject of a verb, a subject complement, an appositive with another nominative, and a complement of the infinitive *to be* when *to be* has no subject.

- Pronouns in the objective case can function as objects of all kinds, subjects of infinitives, an appositive with another object, and a complement of the infinitive *to be* when *to be* has a subject.
- Pronouns in the possessive case can function as adjectives and as the subject of a gerund.
- Pronouns, as substitutes for nouns, may serve the same functions in sentences as nouns.
- Writers and speakers must be certain that the pronouns they employ refer specifically to the nouns for which the pronouns are substituting. If the noun-pronoun relationship is not clear, the result is a problem in faulty reference.

Adjectives

An *adjective* is a word that describes or limits a noun or pronoun, meaning that an adjective identifies by placing restrictions on any noun with which it is associated. For example, the adjective *small* in the phrase "the small boy" not only describes the boy, but it also limits the focus to a certain boy, not just any boy—specifically, to the *small* boy.

Usually, an adjective answers one or more of the following questions:

- Which?
- What kind of?
- How many?

For example, examine the following sentences:

The small boy is my brother.
(*Small* both describes and tells which boy.)
A new car is a valuable possession.)
(The adjective *new* describes the noun *car* and tells what kind of car.
The girl had four apples.
(The adjective *four* limits the plural noun *apples* to a certain number by telling how many—in this case, four.)

 Although numerals and word numbers (*six, 44,* and so on) are sometimes considered to be adjectives, some teachers of grammar consider them to be members of a special class of prenominal modifiers—*post-determiners*—which pattern between determiners and adjectives in noun phrases. For our purposes, it seems more practical to consider numerals to be adjectives.

 See the section titled "The Hyphen" in Part II for the correct way to punctuate two or more words used as single adjectives before nouns, as in this example:

> Roger had a down-in-the-mouth look about him this morning.

TYPES OF ADJECTIVES

Three major types of adjectives are generally recognized:

- Attributive
- Appositive
- Predicate

Attributive Adjectives

Attributive adjectives are those that are found immediately before the word(s) that they modify. Each of the adjectives in italics in the following sentences is an attributive adjective.

> He was reading a *good* book.
> The *old* man stood by himself in the rain.
> We saw an *old, dark, wooden* house in the woods.

Appositive Adjectives

Appositive adjectives follow the words that they modify. These adjectives are usually used in pairs and employ the conjunction *and* or *but* between them.

> The tree, *tall* and *straight,* stood in the yard.
> The doctor, *young* but *experienced,* remained calm.
> We all knew the child, *tired* and *wet,* would come home.
> The players, *cold* but *happy,* smiled at the photographer.

Predicate Adjectives

Predicate adjectives are adjectives that occur after linking verbs or after a form of the verb *to be* and that modify the subjects of those verbs. As the name implies, these adjectives occur in the predicate of a sentence or clause, but they must modify the subject of the sentence or clause to be considered predicate adjectives. The adjectives in italics in the following sentences are predicate adjectives.

> That girl is *beautiful.*
> My new car looked *dirty.*
> The baby's forehead felt *hot.*
> The sky was *dark* and *gloomy.*

The adjectives in the following sentence are not predicate adjectives, because they do not modify the subject of the verb in the grammatical unit of which they are a part:

The explorer's only company was a huge, white polar bear. (*Polar* is considered part of the compound noun.)

The linking verbs after which most predicate adjectives are located include the following:

seem
appear
look
taste
feel
smell
become

A few verbs not usually considered linking verbs until they are closely examined are verbs such as *work, run, stand,* and a few others:

The boards covering the old well *worked* loose.
Be sure the keg does not *run* dry before the party begins.
The defendant *stood* mute before his accusers.

 Linking verbs are covered in more detail later in this part in the section titled "Linking Verbs."

Proper Adjectives

A fourth classification, proper adjective, should be recognized, although it is semantically different from the other classifications, and members of this group are also members of the other three groups. *Proper adjectives* are adjectives derived from proper nouns or are proper nouns used as adjectives. A proper adjective is generally initial-capped (that is, the first letter of the word is capitalized). The proper adjectives in the following sentences are in italics:

The *American* flag is red, white, and blue.
Although he is an *Asian* tourist, he enjoys the *Colorado* climate.
We enjoyed seeing *Kentucky* bluegrass again.

DEGREES OF COMPARISON

Adjectives have three degrees of comparison. These three degrees of comparison show relationships between or among the words they modify:

- Positive
- Comparative
- Superlative

Positive Degree

The *positive degree* expresses a quality without a comparison; a statement is made concerning only one entity:

The tree is *big.*
The grass is *green.*
The water is *cold.*
The twins are *tall.*

Although *twins* in the last sentence is plural, the entity (*twins*) is not being compared to anything or anyone else.

Comparative Degree

The *comparative degree* expresses a higher or lower degree than the positive. It is used to compare two things, and the inflectional suffix is usually *er.*

Roger is *shorter* than Bill.
Mary seems *taller* than Betty.
She is the *younger* of the two sisters.
Of the two wrestlers, John is the *stronger.*
She looks *better* than anyone else in the choir.

Else in comparative situations

Else is required in comparisons of the same class; otherwise, they are omitted:

Calvin is taller than *anyone* in this class. (Calvin is not in the class. If he were, he would, apparently, be taller than himself.)
Calvin is taller than *anyone else* in this class. (The word *else* indicates that Calvin is in the class.)
Jane is more intelligent than *anyone* in the group. (Jane is not in the group.)
Jane is more intelligent than *anyone else* in the group. (Jane is a member of the group.)

Superlative Degree

The *superlative degree* is the highest or lowest degree when comparing more than two persons or things. The inflectional suffix for the superlative degree is usually *est*. Adjectives of three or more syllables usually take *most* instead of *est*.

> Susan is the *brightest* of all the students in class.
> Carl is the *tallest* player on the team.
> That was the *most beautiful* sunset I have ever seen.

 Use the *comparative degree* of an adjective or an adverb when speaking of two things and the *superlative degree* when speaking of three or more:

> This is the *smaller* of the *two* puppies.
> The black one is the *smallest* of the *three* puppies.

More and most with all, any, and any other

More and *most* are used in special ways with *all, any,* and *any other* to indicate comparisons, especially class (group) and unit (individual) comparisons:

Jeremy is *more* energetic than *any* worker in the group. (Jeremy is obviously not in the group, because he cannot be more energetic than himself.)

Jeremy is *more* energetic than *any other* worker in the group. (Jeremy is a member of the group and is being compared to the other workers in the same group.)

Jeremy is the *most* energetic of *all* workers in the group. (Jeremy is one of the workers; and of all workers in the group, Jeremy is the most energetic.)

Jeremy is *more* energetic than *all* the workers in the group. (The combined energy of all the workers in the group is less than Jeremy's energy. Jeremy is not in the group.)

Jeremy is *more* energetic than *all other* workers in the group. (Jeremy is a member of the group and has more energy than the combined energy of the other workers.)

Adjectives Expressing Absolute Qualities

Adjectives that express within themselves the highest degree of comparison will not submit to further comparison. They express *absolute qualities*. Examples of such words are the following:

unique
perfect
round
square

honest
vertical
horizontal
perpendicular
exact
endless
frozen
dead
full
empty
straight

You compare such words as these by using *more nearly* and *most nearly*. Here are some examples:

My picture is *more nearly perfect* than your picture.
That figure seems *more nearly square* than this one.
Roger's glass is the *most nearly empty* of the three.

The logic reflected by the preceding observation is readily apparent: If something is empty or square or perfect, something else cannot be any emptier or "squarer" or perfect to an even greater extent. A number of writers and authors of textbooks, however, recognize a legitimacy in comparing some of the absolutes. For instance, "more perfect" means something similar to "nearer to a state of perfection," a meaning clearly intended by the writers of the Constitution of the United States of America when they wrote this famous preamble:

"We the people of the United States, in Order to form a more perfect Union, establish Justice, insure domestic Tranquility, provide for the common defense, promote the general Welfare, and secure the Blessings of Liberty to ourselves and our Posterity, do ordain and establish this Constitution for the United States of America."

 You may often find examples of fine writing that employ such constructions as "more perfect," "sincerest form [of flattery]," and "more honest." In general, you ought to avoid calling attention to your writing style by employing such constructions.

This same meaning of "nearer to" may be applied to such words as *complete* and *unique*. Consider a sentence such as the following:

The addition of the various stage directions makes this the most complete edition of Shakespeare's works I have ever read.

"Most nearly complete" does not, logically, fit into the context of the sentence. How can anyone really know when an edition of Shakespeare's works will ever be complete? Although you could argue for a better sentence (perhaps by replacing *complete* with *inclusive*), writers feel less hesitant now than in some previous years to use the comparative form with *perfect* and *unique*. However, you should employ such constructions judiciously. In a formal situation—writing or speaking—you should probably consider alternate constructions; and you surely would want to avoid using the comparative suffix (*er*) or the comparative *more* with such words as *dead, empty, full, infinite,* and *equal*.

NOUNS THAT ACT LIKE ADJECTIVES

Possessive nouns pattern in sentences in nearly the same manner as adjectives:

> I found *John's* book in the garage.
> The *cat's* claws were really sharp.

Although the possessive form of nouns and adjectives pattern and function in similar ways (and you should use care not to confuse the two), adjectives may usually be distinguished from nouns by determining whether a restrictor can be placed before the word in question:

> The sun was *really* bright yesterday.
> The crew planned to demolish the *very* tall building.

Nouns do not admit of this construction. You would be unlikely to say the following:

> We rode to town in the *really* school bus.
> We had a picnic in a *very* city park.

Some nouns pattern before other nouns and function as adjectives. These nouns cannot be inflected with *er* or *est* and may themselves take modifiers:

> The company developed small *puppy* chow.

In this sentence, *puppy* modifies *chow* and has its own modifier, *small*. How we treat *puppy* is somewhat a matter of choice, depending mostly on how technical our discussion becomes. What is important at this point is that we recognize that some words have the qualities of nouns but function as adjectives.

Some linguistically oriented texts treat words by establishing a three-part classification for words: *form, function,* and *position*. In this way, a word may be a noun in form, an adjective by position, and a modifier by function. A word could likewise be an adjective in form, a nominal by position, and a subject of a verb by function, as in this sentence:

The *destitute* were determined to persevere.

Adjectives may be located in sentence constructions that you may easily overlook, for example, in object-complement constructions, as in this sentence:

All of us considered the singer *talented.*

 For more information about object complements, see the section titled "Object Complements" in Part II.

RECOGNIZING THE VARIOUS TYPES OF ADJECTIVES

The following sentences contain examples of various types of adjectives:

The furry animal was identified as a Chinese panda.
> **furry:** attributive, positive
> **Chinese:** positive, proper

The audience found the speaker witty and humorous.
> **witty:** predicate, positive
> **humorous:** predicate, positive

The building, old and abandoned, was scheduled for demolition.
> **old:** appositive, positive
> **abandoned:** appositive, positive

The work was very difficult, but the eager students enjoyed it.
> **difficult:** predicate, positive
> **eager:** attributive, positive

The frightened child tore his coat on a rusty nail.
> **frightened:** attributive, positive
> **rusty:** attributive, positive

My brother won the second prize in the composition competition.
> **second:** attributive, positive
> **composition:** attributive, positive

The shy, timid child would not participate in the various activities.
> **shy:** attributive, positive
> **timid:** attributive, positive
> **various:** attributive, positive

Your dog is certainly very frisky.
    frisky: predicate, positive

The cowardly lion delighted the laughing children.
    cowardly: attributive, positive
    laughing: attributive, positive (*laughing* is a verb form known as a *participle,* not really an adjective; however, participles function as adjectives in sentences)

The poor often have educational weaknesses.
    educational: attributive, positive

The biggest berries are those on the very edge of the patch.
    biggest: attributive, superlative
    very: attributive, positive

My neighbor's house is much larger than mine.
    neighbor's: attributive, positive (this is an example of a possessive noun patterning in the same way as an adjective)
    larger: predicate, comparative

Driving a large truck through city traffic is not easy.
    large: attributive, positive
    city: attributive, positive
    easy: predicate, positive

When the snow is deep, we know winter is here.
    deep: predicate, positive

All the climbers felt tired from the long hike.
    tired: predicate, positive
    long: attributive, positive

The city police drove the homeless wanderer to a shelter.
    city: attributive, positive
    homeless: attributive, positive

My laptop computer is very efficient.
    laptop: attributive, positive
    efficient: predicate, positive

The young of most species need parental protection.
    most: attributive, positive
    parental: attributive, positive

I made my wife happy by giving her a diamond ring.
> **happy:** attributive, positive (*happy* is an adjective modifying the direct object in this sentence, thus it is called an "object complement")
> **diamond:** attributive, positive

He laced his boots tight to keep out the swamp water.
> **tight:** attributive, positive
> **swamp:** attributive, positive

I made a complete fool of myself at the party last night.
> **complete:** attributive, positive
> **last:** attributive, positive

The National Scout Museum has many regular visitors each year.
> **regular:** attributive, positive
> **each:** attributive, positive

Even a very short speech can be very boring.
> **short:** attributive, positive
> **boring:** predicate, positive

The milk tasted sour to the fussy child.
> **sour:** predicate, positive
> **fussy:** attributive, positive

The polar bear rested on a snow-white glacier.
> **polar:** attributive, positive (in such constructions as this, words like *polar* would often be considered a part of the noun phrase *polar bears,* not a separate adjective)
> **snow-white:** attributive, positive

GENERAL OBSERVATIONS ABOUT ADJECTIVES

- An *adjective* is a word that describes or "limits" a noun or pronoun, meaning that an adjective identifies by placing restrictions on any noun with which it is associated.
- Usually, an adjective answers one or more of the following questions:
  - Which?
  - What kind of?
  - How many?

- Three major types of adjectives are generally recognized:
  - **Attributive:** *Attributive adjectives* are those that are found immediately before the word(s) that they modify.
  - **Appositive:** *Appositive adjectives* follow the words that they modify. These adjectives are usually used in pairs and employ the conjunction *and* or *but* between them.
  - **Predicate:** *Predicate adjectives* are adjectives that occur after linking verbs or after a form of the *verb to be* and that modify the subjects of those verbs.

- *Proper adjectives* are adjectives derived from proper nouns or are proper nouns used as adjectives.
- Adjectives have three degrees of comparison. These three degrees of comparison show relationships between or among the words they modify:
  - **Positive:** The *positive degree* expresses a quality without a comparison; a statement is made concerning only one entity.
  - **Comparative:** The *comparative degree* expresses a higher or lower degree than the positive. It is used to compare two things, and the inflectional suffix is usually *er*.
  - **Superlative:** The *superlative degree* is the highest or lowest degree when comparing more than two persons or things. The inflectional suffix for the superlative degree is usually *est*. Adjectives of three or more syllables usually take *most* instead of *est*.

- Certain adjectives usually do not admit of comparison. They express *absolute qualities*. Examples of such words are *unique, perfect, round, square, perpendicular, endless, dead, full, empty,* and *straight*.
- Although possessive nouns pattern in sentences in nearly the same manner as adjectives (and you should use care not to confuse the two), adjectives may usually be distinguished from nouns by determining whether a restrictor can be placed before the word in question.
- Some nouns pattern before other nouns and function as adjectives. These nouns cannot be inflected with *er* or *est* and may themselves take modifiers.

Verbs

A *verb* expresses an act, occurrence, or a state of being.

Because a discussion of verbs must also include a discussion of verb phrases, supplemental discussions of the various forms of verbs are found in other sections of this text—specifically, in Part II in the section titled "Verbals." The limited presentation that follows should be sufficient to enable you to grasp the essentials necessary to make informed choices concerning standard English usage.

KINDS OF VERBS

Verbs may be classified in a number of ways; but for the purposes of this text, they will be classified as follows:

- Transitive
- Intransitive
- Copulative
- Auxiliary

Transitive Verbs

Transitive verbs are those verbs that pattern with direct objects—that is, they express an action that directly affects a grammatical unit (usually a noun or pronoun) elsewhere in a clause or sentence. Stated another way, a transitive verb shows an action that is "passed on" to the direct object. In effect, these verbs serve as a *transition* between the subject (the *actor*) and the direct object (the thing acted upon, sometimes called the *patient*). Each of the following sentences contains a transitive verb and a direct object. The transitive verbs are in italics, and the direct objects are in bold:

The farmer *painted* his old **barn.**
My cat *caught* a **mouse** yesterday.
Carl's brother *told* us an interesting **story**.

Active voice versus passive voice

Verbs such as those in the three preceding sentences are transitive verbs in the *active voice.* In sentences with verbs in the active voice, the subject of the verb is the *doer* of the action, or the *actor.* A sentence in the active voice usually patterns in one of the following two orders:

Actor ⇨ Action ⇨ Patient

Subject ⇨ Verb ⇨ Direct Object

Sentences with verbs in the passive voice usually pattern with the actor-action-patient elements in a reverse order. In such sentences, the actor remains passive and often patterns as the object of a preposition at the end of the sentence. The element that is the direct object in a sentence in the active voice becomes the subject of the sentence in the passive voice. Each of the following sentences is cast in the passive voice:

The **barn** *was painted* by the farmer.

A **mouse** *was caught* by my cat yesterday.

We *were told* an interesting story by Carl's brother.

Note that in sentences in the passive voice, some form of the verb *to be* (*am, is, are, was, were, been, be*) is used with the main verb, which employs the past-participle form. The following sentences demonstrate the changes that take place when a sentence is converted from the active voice to the passive voice.

Active voice: The sexton rang the bell yesterday.

Passive voice: The bell was_1 $rung_2$ (by the sexton)$_3$ yesterday.

Note the following about the two preceding sample sentences:

* Auxiliary has been added to the verb phrase.
* Main verb assumes past-participle form.
* Actor is the object of a preposition after the verb. The prepositional phrase is in parentheses to indicate that it is often omitted when a sentence is cast in the passive voice. Such sentences as the one following are quite common:

The bell was rung yesterday.

Intransitive Verbs

If a sentence has a verb that shows action of some sort but does not have a direct object, it has a verb known as an *intransitive verb.* Although intransitive verbs do not pattern with direct objects, such verbs may express the same actions or types of action as transitive verbs. Each of the verbs in the following sentences is intransitive, because the sentences do not have direct objects:

The farmer *painted* until dark.
All the children *laughed* at the funny clown.
The children *played* in the yard.
The ship *disappeared* into the fog.
The mail *arrived* before noon.
The farmer *worked* in the heat of the afternoon.
We *wandered* aimlessly through the forest until dawn.

In the first sentence, for example, the verb *painted* is an action verb; but because the sentence does not state what the farmer painted, the verb is intransitive rather than transitive.

Most verbs may be used as either transitive or intransitive verbs, as in the following pairs:

We *worked* the puzzle as a group. (transitive)
We *worked* inside the hot building. (intransitive)

The children *played* the piano for their parents. (transitive)
The children *played* in the muddy water. (intransitive)

A relatively few verbs in English may be either transitive or intransitive, but usually not both. The following table shows words that are typically transitive only and intransitive only.

Transitive Only	Intransitive Only
enjoy	disappear
find	belong
like (meaning "enjoy")	go
excuse	laugh
reward	wonder
feed	giggle
sell	feast

Of course, these words could be used in some rather unusual sentence constructions, such as, perhaps, in the following question-and-answer sequence:

Question: What do you do for a living?
Answer: I sell.

Such constructions are not common, but the point here is that verbs are usually transitive or intransitive and that few verbs are exclusively one or the other.

Copulative Verbs

A *copulative verb* (also called a *copular verb*) is a verb that usually patterns with a modifier or noun (or noun substitute) that is necessary to complete the meaning of the sentence.

There are two main kinds of copulative verbs:

- The verb *to be*
- Linking verbs

The Verb *To Be*

The forms of the verb *to be,* in addition to *be,* are the following:

am
is
are
was
were
been

Notice how these forms pattern in the following sentences. In the first group, the sentences have adjectives following the form of the verb *to be:*

The grass *is* green.
The book *was* really heavy.
The children *were* dirty and very tired.
The skies have *been* overcast for several days.

In the second group, *be* is followed by a nominal (noun or noun substitute):

Sally *is* the president of the senior class.
I *am* the person responsible for the accident.
You may *be* the driver today if you wish.
Sue and Allison *are* the missing students.

In the final group, *be* is followed by an adverb of time or place or by a phrase that expresses time or place:

The papers *are* not here.
The car *was* in the garage.
The boys *were* here yesterday morning.

 Adverbs are discussed later in this part in the section titled "Adverbs."

Few problems arise in constructing sentences using these different sentence forms—as long as sentences contain nouns after the verb *to be* and not pronouns. When pronouns are in the third position, the pronoun must be in the *nominative* case, as in the following sentences:

> The winner was *he* with the red shirt.
> The president is *she* who was elected by the members.
> It is *I* whom you wish to see.
> The driver must have been *he*.

In informal situations (and even in formal situations upon occasion), you often hear the objective form of the pronoun employed after a form of the verb *to be*:

> That's *me*.
> It might have been *her*.
> It's *him*.

Because the level of usage that is employed in various situations should be governed by the nature of the situations, any pronouncements concerning the acceptability or unacceptability of such expressions as "It's me" would be presumptuous. However, in formal speaking and writing situations, where you are often judged by the appropriateness of your speech habits, you should strive to take a formal approach to usage. And in formal situations, if you err (rhymes with "her"), you should err on the side of formality.

Linking Verbs

Linking verbs are also copulative verbs, because they require a subject complement to complete the meaning of the sentence. Linking verbs are verbs such as *looked* in the following sentence:

> The children *looked* tired after playing in the water.

Any verb that can be substituted in the place of *looked* is probably a linking verb. Some common linking verbs include the following:

appear
become
grow
remain
seem
get
look
sound
smell
feel
taste
continue

Notice how these words function as "links" between the subjects and the subject complements in the following sentences:

This meat *smells* rotten.
The apple at the top of the tree *appeared* ripe.
The custodian *seems* satisfied with his work.
That music *sounds* loud and noisy to our parents.
The soldiers *grew* weary of the training exercise.

LINKING VERBS VERSUS THE VERB *To Be*

There are some obvious and some subtle differences between linking verbs and the verb *to be*:

- Linking verbs often suggest a possibility rather than offer an absolute observation, as does *be*. Notice:

  The milk *tasted* sour.
      (Although the milk tasted sour, it may not have *been* sour. This is a linking verb.)
  The milk *was* sour.
      (The statement is unqualified. The milk was indeed sour.)

- Linking verbs often imply certain kinds of action or activity such as smelling, tasting, becoming, and so on. The verb *to be* does not do so directly.
- Linking verbs are not used as auxiliaries in verb phrases, while the various forms of *be* are; and linking verbs do not "stack up" as *be* may (as in the phrase "may have been dancing").

UNUSUAL LINKING VERBS

Some words that are not generally thought of as linking verbs perform the same function as linking verbs and therefore should be considered linking verbs:

to go
to stand
to work
to run
to turn
to fall
to lay

(There are a few other linking verbs with limited use.) A few of these words are used in the following sentences:

The prisoner *stands* mute before the court.
The water *lay* calm and peaceful in the moonlight.
The tire *worked* loose from the rim.
Every time the President enters, the crowd *falls* silent.

LINKING VERBS AND AUXILIARIES

Linking verbs may be preceded by auxiliaries, as in the following sentence:

The mirror *may have* **appeared** broken to you.

 Auxiliaries are discussed in the next section, "Auxiliaries."

MODIFIERS AND LINKING VERBS

With verbs pertaining to the senses (*feel, taste, become, smell, sound, grow, look, appear,* and the like), an adjective form is required if the modifier relates to the subject; an adverb form is required if the modifier relates to the verb.

Linking verbs are followed by a subject complement. When the same words are followed by *adverbials,* the words are not linking verbs; rather, they are action verbs. For example, the verb in the second sentence of each pair below is not a linking verb:

The negotiators *looked sleepy* from meeting all night long.
> (*Looked* is a linking verb, not an action verb; thus, the modifier is an adjective, not an adverb.)

The negotiators *looked sleepily* at one another.
> (In this sentence, *looked* is an action verb and *sleepily* indicates the manner in which they looked, not how they looked (as in the first sentence); thus, the modifier is an adverb.)

The hikers *grew* weak from lack of water.
The trees *grew* quickly from all the sun and rain.

Leslie *appears* wise and competent.
Peter *appears* nightly with the day's news.

 See the sections "Adjectives" and "Adverbs" in this part for more information about these types of modifiers.

Following are several sample sentences, with the correct modifier indicated:

Neither John nor he seems (*angry, angrily*). Each has shaken the other's hand.
> **angry**

Sarah looked (*angry, angrily*) at Ruth and me when Joe and he smiled at us.
> **angrily**

Ben looks (*bad, badly*) because of his illness.
    bad

Each of the girls looks (*beautiful, beautifully*) wearing her new clothes.
    beautiful

His milk tastes (*sour, sourly*) to both him and me.
    sour

From where we were sitting, the thunder sounded (*loud, loudly*).
    loud

The roses in the vase smell (*sweet, sweetly*) to her and me.
    sweet

You must cook the meat (*tender, tenderly*) so that it will taste good.
    tender

The instructor in masonry taught us students to build a wall (*strong, strongly*).
    strong

His moving to another state makes us friends feel (*sad, sadly*).
    sad

Boil the eggs (*soft, softly*) while he and she set the table.
    soft

She looked (*angry, angrily*) because I believed her to be him.
    angry

The engine runs (*smooth, smoothly*) because Joe and I overhauled it.
    smoothly

While Ed and I were on the mountain, the whistle of the train sounded (*faint, faintly*) in the distance.
    faint

The mother looked (*proud, proudly*) as the committee honored both him and her.
    proud

Each of the fellows feels (*unhappy, unhappily*) about failing his examinations.
    unhappy

Harry, as well as they, seems (*happy, happily*) to be home again.
>**happy**

He looked (*sad, sadly*) at his family as he announced his resignation.
>**sadly**

The mother looked on (*proud, proudly*) as her son received the award.
>**proudly**

That which we call a rose by any other name would smell as (*sweet, sweetly*).
>**sweet**

This new dish tastes (*delicious, deliciously*).
>**delicious**

Puppies appear so (*playfully, playful*) in pictures of homes.
>**playful**

Both men felt (*strange, strangely*) after the accident.
>**strange**

The incense smelled (*fragrant, fragrantly*).
>**fragrant**

The doctor looked (*hopefully, hopeful*) at the patient.
>**hopefully**

AUXILIARY VERBS

An *auxiliary* is one of a small set of verbs that combine with a main verb to express various shades of meaning, usually of time or voice (refer to the discussion of active and passive voice, earlier in this section). The three primary auxiliaries are *be, have,* and *do.* Others include the following:

- **Modal auxiliaries:**

    may
    might
    can
    could
    shall
    should
    will
    would
    must

- **Marginal auxiliaries:**

> dare
> need
> ought to
> used to

- **Semi-auxiliaries (auxiliary-like verbs):**

> be going to
> have to
> had better

You must be careful when examining sentence patterns not to confuse sentence patterns with *be* as the main verb with sentence patterns with *be* as an *auxiliary* or *helping* verb, because forms of the verb *to be* are often used as auxiliaries. The first of each pair of the following sentences employs *be* as the main verb, while the second employs *be* as an auxiliary. The main verbs in the sentences are italicized.

> Carl *is* a basketball player.
> Carl is *playing* basketball.

> The men *were* here by noon.
> The men were *planning* to be here by noon.

> These *are* the plans I have submitted.
> We are *submitting* these plans.

RECOGNIZING THE VARIOUS TYPES OF VERBS

The following sentences contain examples of various types of verbs:

> All the children were standing in line and waiting for ice cream.
> > **were:** auxiliary
> > **standing:** intransitive
> > **waiting:** intransitive

> If you see my roommate, tell her not to take my notes to class.
> > **see:** transitive (active)
> > **tell:** transitive (active)

> The children were overjoyed at seeing the eclipse.
> > **were:** to be

> We were washing the car when the storm arrived.
> > **were:** auxiliary
> > **washing:** transitive (active)
> > **arrived:** intransitive

The floor had been scrubbed to a high gloss by the new recruits.
> **had been:** auxiliary
> **scrubbed:** intransitive

Try catching a fly with your hands; it is really difficult.
> **try:** transitive (active)
> **is:** to be

We waited until four o'clock; then we left without James.
> **waited:** intransitive
> **left:** intransitive

The group left James sleeping in a car in the parking lot.
> **left:** transitive (active)

We considered the alternatives and then made our decision.
> **considered:** transitive (active)
> **made:** transitive (active)

Before we leave, we want to congratulate you on a job well done.
> **leave:** intransitive
> **want:** transitive (active)

The children watched the duck on the pond.
> **watched:** transitive

We all thought about the lost hunting party.
> **thought:** intransitive (*about the lost hunting party* is a prepositional phrase)

My brother gave Mother a pretty lame excuse.
> **gave:** transitive

Some people dream about frightening things.
> **dream:** intransitive

Some people have no dreams at all.
> **have:** transitive

VERB TENSES AND ASPECTS

Tense refers to the time of a situation. English makes use of two tense categories, which are indicated by the form of the verb:

> **Present:** walks, is walking, has been walking
> **Past:** walked, was walking, had been walking

Tense is indicated by the inflection of the first or only verb in the verb phrase:

- Present tense for all verbs (except modal auxiliaries—that is, *may, might, can, could, shall, should, will, would, must*) is indicated by the *s* form for third-person singular and by the base (uninflected) form for others:

  > Edward *saves* cereal box tops to collect prizes. (third-person singular)
  > I *save* fabric scraps in order to make quilts. (all other forms)

- Regular verbs (and many irregular verbs) employ the *ed* inflection to indicate past tense:

  > We *saved* the man's life by administering CPR.

 Auxiliaries are also used to make clear distinctions in time. For example, auxiliaries such as *will* and *be going* indicate that the action expressed by the main verb will occur sometime in the future.

 Unlike tense, which indicates a verb's location in time in absolute terms (past or present), a verb's *aspect* refers to the way the time of the situation is regarded. Aspects are expressed by a combination of an auxiliary and a main verb. In English, two types of aspects apply:

- **Perfect aspect:** This aspect is used to the time of one situation in relative terms to the time of another situation.

  > I *have climbed* this mountain many times before now.

- **Progressive aspect:** This aspect indicates the duration of a situation.

  > I *am strolling* the Boardwalk.

Aspects always appear in sentences in conjunction with tenses to form the following:

- **Present perfect:** has walked, have walked
- **Past perfect:** had walked
- **Present progressive:** am walking, is walking, are walking
- **Past progressive:** was walking, were walking

The perfect and progressive aspects can be combined, as in the case of *has been walking.*

IRREGULAR ENGLISH VERBS

Although the vast majority of verbs in the English language have a predictable pattern when it comes to indicating tense, there are, alas, numerous verbs that differ in this regard. Except in the case of the highly irregular verb *be*, which has eight forms, irregular verbs may have as many as five different forms:

- Base
- *s* form
- *ing* form
- Past
- *ed* participle

 The *ed* participle is used in conjunction with *had, has,* or *have* to indicate past-perfect or present-perfect tense.

Except in the case of *be*, the *s* and *ing* forms are predictable for all irregular verbs. For your reference, the following table indicates the base, past forms, and *ed* participles of several irregular verbs.

Base	Past	*ed* Participle
begin	began	begun
bend	bent	bent
bite	bit	bitten
bleed	bled	bled
blow	blew	blown
break	broke	broken
build	built	built
burn	burned or burnt	burned or burnt
burst	burst	burst
buy	bought	bought
cast	cast	cast
come	came	come
cost	cost	cost
cut	cut	cut
dig	dug	dug
dive	dived or dove	dived or dove
dream	dreamed or dreamt	dreamed or dreamt
drink	drank	drunk
drive	drove	driven
feed	fed	fed
feel	felt	felt
fight	fought	fought
find	found	found
fit	fitted or fit	fitted or fit
get	got	got or gotten
hang	hung	hung

(continued)

(continued)

Base	Past	*ed* Participle
have	had	had
hear	heard	heard
hide	hid	hidden
hit	hit	hit
hold	held	held
hurt	hurt	hurt
keep	kept	kept
kneel	kneeled or knelt	kneeled or knelt
lean	leaned or leant	leaned or leant
leap	leaped or leapt	leaped or leapt
learn	learned or learnt	learned or learnt
let	let	let
lie	lay	lain
light	lighted or lit	lighted or lit
lose	lost	lost
make	made	made
mow	mowed	mowed or mown
put	put	put
quit	quitted or quit	quitted or quit
read	read	read
rid	ridded or rid	ridded or rid
ring	rang	rung
run	ran	run
saw	sawed	sawed or sawn
say	said	said
see	saw	seen
set	set	set
sew	sewed	sewed or sewn
shear	sheared	sheared or shorn
show	showed	showed or shown
shrink	shrank	shrunk
sing	sang	sung
smell	smelled or smelt	smelled or smelt
speak	spoke	spoken
speed	speeded or sped	speeded or sped
spell	spell or spelt	spell or spelt
spoil	spoiled or spoilt	spoiled or spoilt
stand	stood	stood
sting	stung	stung
strike	struck	struck
sweat	sweated or sweat	sweated or sweat
swell	swelled	swelled or swollen
swim	swam	swum
take	took	taken
tear	tore	torn
wed	wedded or wed	wedded or wed
wet	wetted or wet	wetted or wet

Base	Past	*ed* Participle
win	won	won
wind	wound	wound
write	wrote	written

Irregularities within irregularities: cost/costed and hang/hanged

Cost in the sense of "estimate the value or cost of" is a regular verb; *cost* in the sense of "to require expenditure or payment" or "to require effort, suffering or loss" is an irregular verb. When the word *cost* is used to mean "estimate the value or cost of," its past tense and past participle forms are *costed*.

Incorrect: Rescuing the drowning child nearly *costed* Edgar his life.
Correct: That house *cost* me an arm and leg.
Incorrect: Evelyn *cost* the antiques on our behalf.
Correct: Joseph *costed* the car at $4,100.

The verb *to hang* has multiple meanings; the regularity or irregularity of the various verb forms depends on the intended meaning. *Hang* denoting suspension by the neck (as in an execution or suicide) is a regular verb (*hang, hanged, hanged*); all other forms are irregular, and use the forms listed above.

MOODS OF VERBS

In English, writers employ three *moods* or *modes* to indicate various relationships or conditions:

* The *indicative* mood
* The *imperative* mood
* The *subjunctive* mood

The Indicative Mood

The *indicative mood* is employed to state a fact or to ask a question and is the form common to most sentences, whether declarative or question:

We *visited* some friends last night.
Did Roger *ask* his father for advice?
Everyone *was waiting* for the rain to stop.

The Imperative Mood

The *imperative mood* is employed when a sentence states a request, command, or suggestion:

> *Call* me in the morning.
> *Stop playing* with your food!
> Please *remain* in your seats until the bell rings.

The Subjunctive Mood

The *subjunctive mood* is employed to express a condition contrary to fact, a wish, a supposition, a prayer, or a doubt, as well as in "that clauses." The subjunctive mood is most commonly employed, however, in contrary-to-fact statements such as the following:

> I wish I *were* young again.
> If we *were* rich, we could buy new motorcycles.

Notice that in the subjunctive mood, *were* is used for both singular and plural subjects. The same holds true for sentences containing "if clauses" reflecting past events:

> If the President *were* there, he wasn't recognized.

When expressing a doubt, the verb *to be* is employed:

> If that *be* the situation, I'm going home.
> If there *be* any doubt, check the directory.

The *present subjunctive* occurs with verbs such as *insist:*

> I insist that you *prepare* your assignment as instructed.
> He recommended that I *be* inoculated against typhoid.

Certain idiomatic expressions also require the subjunctive mood:

> *Come* spring, I'll be in the mountains.
> He appeared, as it *were,* ready to fight for nothing.
> Torpedoes *be damned!* Full speed ahead!

 An *idiomatic expression,* or *idiom,* is an expression that is peculiar to itself grammatically or that has a meaning that cannot be derived from the conjoined meaning of its elements.

"As if" clauses are contrary to fact and take the subjunctive:

> He acts *as if he were* the only one who can solve the problem.

MAKING VERBS NEGATIVE

Sentences are typically negated through the verb via the insertion of *not,* or, in informal speech or writing, by attaching not's contraction, *n't,* to the end of the first or only verb. In sentences containing auxiliary verbs, *not* follows the auxiliary, or *n't* is attached to the auxiliary:

> Shelley should not think twice about asking for a raise.
> Roger must not concern himself with trivial details.

If the sentence contains no auxiliary verb, then the appropriate form (based on tense and person) of the auxiliary *do* is inserted to indicate a negative expression:

> Do not dream of leaving us here!
> Evelyn did not panic, despite Jake's extreme lateness.

Exceptions to the Rules

A few verbs do not adhere to these rules:

- The verb *to be* requires no auxiliary when being converted to express a negative thought:

  > Cats are not as personable as dogs.
  > Calvin was not the best candidate for mayor.

- The verb *to have* allows for both alternatives. All the following sentences are considered acceptable negations of the sentence "Heidi has her own crib":

  > Heidi has not her own crib. (formal)
  > Heidi hasn't her own crib. (informal)
  > Heidi does not have her own crib. (formal)
  > Heidi doesn't have her own crib. (informal)

Expressing Negation Other Than through the Verb

Words such as *no, not,* and the like may be used to negate a sentence without making the verb negative. Compare the pairs of sentences below. The first sentence in each pair employs the traditional negation (through the verb); the second sentence in each pair uses an alternative means to convey the same negative idea:

> Brittany hasn't a clue about the Civil War.
> Brittany has no clue about the Civil War.

> Mother did not speak a word of my being grounded.
> Mother spoke not a word of my being grounded.

Avoiding Double Negatives

A double negative occurs when a sentence contains two negative ideas, thus effectively canceling them out:

> I *don't* talk to *nobody* in my neighborhood.
> I *don't have nothing* to do today.

Although sentences such as the above are quite common in informal speech, the meaning they express is in fact a positive idea—the opposite of what most speakers intend:

> I *talk* to *somebody* in my neighborhood.
> I *do have something* to do today.

You must be on the lookout, then, to avoid such constructions. That said, certain double-negative constructions have gained acceptance in contemporary speech:

> Josie's new glasses *did not go unnoticed.*
> Ian *wasn't unhappy* with his choice of suits.
> Jane is *not unlike* her sisters in that respect.

To the trained ear, however, such constructions sound somewhat stilted or affectatious. Perhaps a more effective way of stating the same ideas in formal situations would be the following.

> Josie's new glasses *were noticed.*
> Ian was *relatively happy* with his choice of suits.
> Jane is *somewhat like* her sisters in that respect.

 Do not use *but* after negative ideas. Complete such expressions as *cannot help* or *could not help* with a gerund, not with but and an infinitive.

> **Correct:** We *cannot help admiring* the beautiful painting.
> **Incorrect:** We *can't help but admire* the beautiful painting.

SUBJECT-VERB AGREEMENT

One fundamental requirement for every sentence you write or speak is that the subject and verb of the sentence agree. That is, if the subject of your sentence is plural, that should be reflected in the verb form—regardless of tense, aspect, or mood. Because of the inherent complexity of the English, however, it is sometimes not clear how such agreement is achieved. For this reason, several rules concerning subject-verb agreement follow:

- A verb must at all times agree with its subject in both person and number.
- Most indefinite pronouns require singular verbs. *Each, either, neither, someone, somebody, anyone, anybody, everyone, everybody, no one, nobody,* and *one* (and a person) are singular. The words *both, few, many, others, several, we, you,* and *they* are plural and take the plural form of the verb.
- Prepositional phrases following indefinite pronouns usually do not influence verb number:

> *Each* of the puppies **was** healthy.
> *Neither* of the books **was** interesting to me.

The exceptions to this rule are in the cases of a fraction or a percent and such words as *all, most, more, part, some, such, rest, any,* and *none* will be singular if bulk or a total number or amount is intended, and plural if numbers are considered. That is, if the object of the preposition in a phrase modifying the subject of the verb (even if the prepositional phrase is unstated or understood) is a count noun, the verb is plural; if the object of the preposition is a mass noun, the verb is singular:

> Thirty percent *of the water* **is** contaminated.
> Thirty percent *of the professors* **are** members of the organization.
> Some of the apples **are** spoiled.
> Some of the soup **is** cold.

- The word *number,* if preceded by *a* and followed by *of,* takes a plural verb. When *number* is preceded by *the,* it takes a singular verb:

> *A number* of students **are** in the lobby.
> *The number* of defects in the material **is** disappointing.

When preceded by the word *any, number* is singular when it refers to a single item and plural when it refers to more than one item:

> *Any new number* (dress) **is** likely to be expensive.
> *Any number* of guests **are** expected at the party.

- Two or more subjects connected by *and* require a plural verb, except in the case of singular subjects connected by *and,* which require a *singular* verb if the subjects denote the same person or thing:

> The *winner **and*** still *champion* is Mike Slugger.

Additionally, singular subjects joined by *and* require a singular verb if the subjects denote foods commonly served together as one dish:

> Biscuits and gravy **is** my favorite breakfast dish.

This is an especially perplexing concept to deal with, because much of what is visualized as consisting of a single entity is in the language user's mind. Items being served (as on a food line, for instance) are not a meal, thus:

> Ham and eggs **are** being served this morning.
> Ham and eggs **is** Carl's favorite morning treat.

In situations where such usage may sound awkward or stilted, you have the option of simply reversing the sentence order:

> Carl's favorite morning *treat* **is** ham and eggs.

- Expressions indicating quantity or amount to be considered as a unit require a singular verb. These expressions often refer to amounts of money, units of time, or measurements:

> Five dollars **is** the price of that shirt.
> Two hundred yards **is** a long way to crawl.

- Nouns plural in form but singular in meaning require a singular verb.

> Politics **makes** strange bedfellows.

- *There, here,* and *where* are not usually subjects. If these words begin a sentence, the number of the verb is determined by the number of the nominal (noun) following them:

> There **are** four *cats* in my bedroom.
> There **is** one *cat* too many for me to tolerate.

- When the correlative conjunctions *both-and* join the parts of a compound subject, the verb is plural:

> Both the lion **and** the tiger **are** friendly animals.

- Two or more singular subjects joined by *or* or *nor* require a singular verb:

> Either John **or** his sister **is** the president.
> Neither the storm **nor** the hail **frightens** us.

- When the words *or, either-or, nor, neither-nor,* or *not only-but also* join the parts of a compound subject, the verb must agree with the nearer subject:

  Either the cat *or* its **kittens are** eating the food.
  Not only his neighbors *but also* **John has** a new pool.

- Intervening phrases and clauses not introduced by coordinating conjunctions do not affect the number of the verb. These phrases and clauses often begin with words such as *including, as well as, no less than, together with, with,* and *accompanied by:*

  My **mother,** *together with* my sisters, **is** at the store.
  The **chief,** *accompanied by* six officers, **has** talked to the protesters.

- If two or more subjects are joined by *and,* and are preceded by *each* or *every,* the verb is singular:

  Each person **and** his partner **is** expected to arrive promptly.
  Every worker **and** her tools **is** needed for this new task.

- A collective noun requires a singular verb if the noun is considered as a unit. Such a noun requires a plural verb if individuality is considered:

  The *family* **is** enjoying the reunion.
    (The family group is viewed as a single entity or unit.)
  The *jury* **are** unable to reach a unanimous verdict.
    (The members of the jury are seen as separate individuals, not as part of a unified whole acting in concert.)

  This is another potentially confusing principle. A group may be in disagreement and still be acting in unison:

  The *sorority* **is** debating the issue of instituting a smoke-free policy for the house.
    (In this sentence, the sorority is acting as a single entity. The group *is* debating.)

- If one subject is used affirmatively and the other negatively, the verb agrees with the one that is used affirmatively:

  John, not the workers, **is** responsible for the error.
  Not the team but the *coaches* **are** late for the game.

- A verb is *never* affected by a subject complement.

  The *gift* he gave his friend **was** books.
    (*Books* is the subject complement.)

- If a verb has a relative pronoun (*who, that, which*) as its subject, the verb must agree with the antecedent of the relative pronoun:

> The group of children *that were* here is going to the new school.
> (The antecedent of *that* is *children*, not *group*. Thus, "children *were*," and "group *is* going." If *group* is intended as the antecedent, then *was* is the correct form of the verb.)
> The man parked his old cars in the barn *that was* abandoned.
> (The antecedent of *that* is *barn*, not *cars*.)

You must be very certain that you understand the relationship of the sentence parts and the role the relative pronoun plays in some sentences—especially those sentences with the word *only* in them. Notice the difference in meaning of the following two sentences:

> She is one of the **seniors** *who were* absent from class.
> (In this sentence, the relative *who* refers to *seniors*, thus you would rightly employ a plural verb form, *were*.)
> **She** is the only one of the seniors *who was* late.
> (Only one senior was late. Who? *She was*. The *who* refers to *she*, not to *seniors*.)

These sentences can be confusing; however, one way to determine the antecedent of the relative pronoun is by trying to locate the word *only* or similar words. Such words are often a giveaway for the use of the relative. Also, try restructuring the sentence by placing the prepositional phrase first:

> **Logical:** Of the seniors who were absent from class, she is one.
> **Illogical:** *Of the seniors* who were *absent from class, she is the only one.* (How could seniors [plural] be absent from class if she was the only one?)

You'll learn more about how sentence parts relate to one another in Part II.

- When the subject is a title of a book, newspaper, work of art, a clause, a direct quotation, or a name of a firm or an organization, a singular verb is required:

> "The Chrysanthemums" **is** a story by Steinbeck.
> *Weekly Ramblings* **is** a high school newspaper.
> Gittlejax and Harber **is** representing our interests.
> "Who would count eternity in days" **is** from a poem by Theodore Roethke.

- The expression *many a* requires a singular verb:

  Many a day **is** required to do some tasks.

- A relative pronoun used as a substitute for the first-person pronoun (*I*) requires a verb form that is consistent with the form of the verb that would be used with the personal pronoun:

  Give the prize to *me* who **am** the winner.
      (*Who* equals *me* equals *I*, which takes *am*. ["I am the winner."])
  It is *I* who **feel** guilty about the confusion.
      (*Who* equals *I*, which takes *feel*. ["I feel guilty."])

- Elements of modifying clauses that come between a verb and its subject do not influence subject-verb agreement:

  The *air controller* **whom you saw guiding the planes** *was* rewarded for her excellent work.

- Appositives and parenthetical expressions do not affect subject-verb agreement:

  The work *crew*—John, Rolinda, and their brothers—**was** already at work when we arrived.
  My *daughter*, the person who wrote the stories, **is** an English major.

- The pronoun *none* is often used in place of *no one* or *not one*. *None* may be either singular or plural but is now more commonly plural:

  None of the students **have** finished their work.
  None of the oranges **are** ripe yet.

Logic would seem to dictate the use of a singular verb because none means less (or fewer) than one, but idioms often defy logic. In this case, however, a simple substitution test can be helpful: *None* can be construed as singular if *not one* or *no one* may be substituted for it. *None* may be considered plural when no persons or any of a group of things or people may replace it—that is, oddly, when *none* applies to more than one:

  He received no reward, and *none* **was** expected.
  None (*no persons*) **are** more insecure than victims in hostage situations. (*None* refers to *victims*, which is plural, thus the plural verb is used.)

When *none* precedes a singular noun, use a singular verb:

  None of the *cake is* left on the table.

From A.D. 1450 to 1650, *none is* was the preferred usage by a margin of 3 to 1; from 1650 to 1917, *none are* was preferred 7 to 4; from 1917 to the present, *none are* is preferred, but usage is varied, as noted previously.

- When in doubt about the use of verbs with *idioms* (words and expressions peculiar to a language), consult a good dictionary:

   The jar of jam is inedible: *It* (*the jam*) **is** moldy.
   The jar of preserves is inedible: *They* (*the preserves*) **are** moldy.
   (Logically, *preserves* should be a mass noun, as is *jam*.)
   His *pants* **are** at the cleaners.
   The *pair* of scissors **is** on the table.

SELECTING THE CORRECT VERB FORM

Following are numerous sample sentences that demonstrate the selection of the correct verb forms:

   Robert, as well as John and we, (*was, were*) late today.
   was

   Neither David nor she (*was, were*) able to go to Alaska.
   was

   (*Has, Have*) either Frank or she studied Greek?
   has

   Here (*come, comes*) Tina and they.
   come

   James and I thought it to be LuAnn and her; however, neither (*was, were*) there.
   was

   (*Was, Were*) you and she at home when Tom and he called?
   were

   Every one of the girls (*was, were*) at the station to meet Joe and me.
   was

   There (*is, are*) Leslie and Anita, as well as she, walking with Frank and him.
   are

   (*Has, Have*) her brother and she decided to go with you, him, and them?
   have

The dean, as well as the professors, (*is, are*) kind to John and me.
> **is**

John, Tom, and I (*is, are*) the committee.
> **are**

A number of the members (*has, have*) visited Lynne and me.
> **have**

Neither the dean nor the professors (*advise, advises*) you and me to study French this semester.
> **advise**

You, not he, (*is, are*) the one whom we chose.
> **are**

Neither Mr. Black nor his son (*was, were*) able to assist us students.
> **was**

John, together with the rest of us seniors, (*was, were*) in Dayton last week.
> **was**

Every man and woman (*is, are*) responsible for what has happened.
> **is**

The team (*has, have*) agreed upon a practice time.
> **has**

Measles (*is, are*) very contagious.
> **is**

Spaghetti and meat balls (*was, were*) on the menu.
> **was**

Ten percent of the students (*is, are*) absent.
> **are**

The number of people absent (*is, are*) smaller than expected.
> **is**

Ten miles (*is, are*) a rather long distance to walk with someone who you know is unable to walk far.
> **is**

The jury (*is, are*) unable to come to a verdict.
> **are**

She is one of those people who (*is, are*) always late.
> **are**

Many a person (*has, have*) been disappointed by someone in whom he placed his confidence.
> **has**

Eleanor is the only one of those workers who (*is, are*) resting.
> **is**

The Merry Wives of Windsor (*is, are*) usually enjoyed by all who have the opportunity to see the play.
> **is**

Books (*is, are*) always an appropriate gift for us readers.
> **are**

Two thirds of the material (*has, have*) been wasted.
> **has**

Both you and he (*is, are*) accountable to someone whom you consider to be most capable of handling authority.
> **are**

Betty is one of those readers who (*skips, skip*) every other page.
> **skip**

Do you believe that $100 (*is, are*) too much to pay for this item?
> **is**

Here (*come, comes*) those who you believe are troublemakers.
> **come**

The team (*is, are*) on its way to Louisville.
> **is**

Corned beef and cabbage (*is, are*) one of his favorite dishes.
> **is**

This is one of those books that (*is, are*) usually popular with those people who you think are avid readers.
> **are**

That he drives no better than we (*is, are*) an accepted fact.
> **is**

Each junior and senior (*is, are*) insistent upon seeing someone who you believe can answer important questions.
>   **is**

The fact that you were believed to be she and that I was believed to be he (*is, are*) difficult to comprehend.
>   **is**

Where (*is, are*) those candidates whom you have declared to be eligible?
>   **are**

Do you think the preserves (*is, are*) good on toast?
>   **are**

Not only he but also she (*think, thinks*) that you are the guilty one.
>   **thinks**

The team (*has, have*) gone to their homes.
>   **have**

Bread and butter (*is, are*) his favorite snack.
>   **is**

Neither Sue nor her many friends (*has, have*) studied Latin.
>   **have**

She, not her sisters, (*is, are*) attending the conference.
>   **is**

Each of the 20 cousins (*was, were*) at the reunion.
>   **was**

He was the only one of the swimmers who (*was, were*) rescued.
>   **was**

Each of you (*is, are*) to be congratulated.
>   **is**

The girl whom you saw talking to my brothers (*was, were*) she whom you have long admired.
>   **was**

Three freshmen—you, he, and she—(*was, were*) selected.
>   **were**

The committee (*is, are*) John, Joe, Sue, and they.
is

You, as well as I, (*is, are*) older than she.
are

Mine is one of the papers that (*is, are*) late.
are

Give the book to me who (*is, am, are*) the author of it.
am

No, it is not I who (*is, am, are*) the guilty one.
am

Each of you (*knows, know*) that it was I who called.
knows

Neither of them (*believes, believe*) it was he who wrote the book.
believes

Neither she nor they (*is, are*) so young as I.
are

He spoke to me who (*is, am, are*) responsible.
am

We teachers, as well as they, (*has, have*) promised to help.
have

AIDS (*is, are*) running rampant among some segments of society.
is

Ice cream and cake (*is, are*) his favorite dessert.
is

A man's best friend and companion (*is, are*) his dog.
is

The father and husband (*was, were*) thoughtful of the family.
was

One hundred and eighty feet (*is, are*) the length of the lot.
is

Some of the food (*has, have*) already been thrown away.
has

Most of the students (*has, have*) already left the campus.
have

Such as this (*is, are*) not permitted.
is

Such as they (*is, are*) not accepted here.
are

Here (*go, goes*) he, she, and I to take the test.
go

The family (*is, are*) planning to meet in Toledo.
is

Isaac is the only one of those students who (*was, were*) willing to help.
was

Dennis is one of those players who (*takes, take*) the game seriously.
take

TROUBLESOME VERBS

Three sets of verbs are somewhat troublesome, even to native speakers of English:

- Sit-set
- Lay-lie
- Raise-rise

The easiest and most practical way to learn the correct usage of these troublesome verbs is to learn the exact definition of each, and, when you are in doubt about which word to use, substitute the definition for the word. If this method is used, making errors is nearly impossible.

Lay-Lie, Sit-Set, Raise-Rise

To *lay* means to "put" or "to place." To *lie* means "to rest" or "to recline."

To *set* means "to put" or "to place." To *sit* means "to rest."

To *raise* means "to lift." To *rise* means "to come up" or "to ascend."

Also, in their usual meanings, *lie, sit,* and *rise* are always intransitive (have no direct objects), and *lay, set,* and *raise* are usually transitive and therefore have direct objects to complete the meaning. Note these examples:

Let us *lie* here and rest.
I *laid* the book on the shelf.

She *sits* by the window to read.
I *set* the book on the table.

The flames did not *rise* very high.
Did you *raise* the flag?

In addition, the verbs *lay* and *set* may be used as intransitives in certain of their secondary meanings:

The hen *lays* well.
The sun *set* at six o'clock.
The cement did not *set* well.
The boys eagerly *set* out on their camping trip.

You should be certain that the principal parts of these verbs are firmly fixed in your mind as a means of avoiding usage problems:

Present Tense	Past Tense	Past Participle
I lay	I laid	I have laid
I lie	I lay	I have lain
I set	I set	I have set
I sit	I sat	I have sat
I raise	I raised	I have raised
I rise	I rose	I have risen

May-Can, Shall-Will

The verbs *may-can* and *shall-will* also give people trouble. *Can* implies ability, while *may* denotes permission or possibility:

I *can* lift that bundle.
Mother says I *may* go to the game tonight.
I *may* go swimming; I'm not certain.

Shall is used with the first-person pronoun:

I *shall* sing to you.

Will is used with second- and third-person pronouns:

You *will* be the first speaker tomorrow evening.
He *will* lend you the money.
The robin *will* build a nest in the tree.

Although usage is changing, traditional use of *shall* and *will* incorporates a few more subtleties, some of which could be confusing at times:

- If you wish to express determination, desire, or promise, reverse the normal order given previously and use *will* in the first person and *shall* in the second and third persons:

  I *will* go to Atlanta. No one can stop me!
  You *shall* do as you are told.
  They *shall* be punished as I promised.

- In asking questions, *shall* is used in first-person constructions. In second- and third-person constructions, the choice depends on the correct form that would be used in the *response* or answer to the question:

  Shall (not *can*) I do this task for you?
  Shall you finish this test on time?
      (The response or answer is "I shall.")
  Will that dog bite?
      (The response or answer is "He will.")

- *Shall* is used in all persons in noun clauses that serve as objects after verbs such as *deciding, demanding, insisting, willing,* and *wishing* if the subjunctive mood is not employed:

  He demands that the insurgents *shall* surrender immediately.
  He demands that the insurgents *surrender* immediately.
      (The subjunctive mood of the verb is employed in this sentence.)

- In indirect quotations (where the speaker's thoughts are presented but not his exact words), the tense form that is employed is the one that would be correct for the speaker.

  The president said that he *shall* retire soon.
  (His actual words were, "*I shall* retire soon.")

As stated previously, usage of *shall* and *will* is changing, which means that many writers and speakers use the various forms of *shall* and *will* interchangeably. In fact, the preceding statements are probably only vaguely known—if known at all—to many writers. Nevertheless, those students, writers, and speakers who are concerned about the quality of their speech, especially in formal situations, should be familiar with the forms of standard English outlined previously.

Should-Would, May-Might

The uses of *should* and *would* correspond to those of *shall* and *will*. For example, for expressing simple future, you use *should* with the first person and *would* with second and third persons:

> I *should* like to tell you the story of my life.
> The workers *would* need more water in the noonday sun.

The past tense form of *may* is *might*. The past tense form of *shall* is *should:*

> I *may* go to the game; I'm not certain.
>   (*May* expresses present or future intentions or possibility.)

> I *might* have done it; I don't remember clearly.
>   (*Might* expresses past situations.)

> I *shall* finish my work tomorrow.
>   (*Shall* expresses a present or future situation.)

> I *should* have left while I still had the chance.
>   (*Should* expresses a past situation.)

Might is used in other special situations. For instance, *might* is used to state hypothetical situations:

> If the moon were nearer, we *might* be able to drive without lights.

Might is also used to express "weaker possibility or probability" than *may*:

> Martha *may* become an attorney some day.
>   (A reasonable possibility exists.)

> Of course I can jump 30 feet. I *might* be able to pole vault to the moon, too.
>   (The possibility is weak or nonexistent.)

Bring-Take

The verbs *bring* and *take* are sometimes misused, although the formal rule governing the use of these two verbs is quite simple: Use *take* to indicate direction *away* from the speaker; use *bring* to indicate direction *toward* the speaker:

> I shall *take* these books to the library when I go.
> *Bring* your work to class when you come next Friday.
> When you go to Washington, *take* light clothing.
> I shall *bring* my dog when we come hunting here tomorrow.

Selecting the Correct Troublesome Verb

Following are numerous sample sentences that demonstrate the selection of the correct troublesome verbs:

He spent the summer just (*laying, lying*) about the house.
lying

Someone (*lay, laid*) the dictionary on my glasses.
laid

Jackie (*lay, laid*) down on the back seat of the car.
lay

I saw your hat (*laying, lying*) on the hall table.
lying

Did you (*bring, take*) your sister to the party last night?
take

Mother said I (*can, may*) go to the river to swim.
may

I (*should, would*) like to propose a toast to the new bride.
should

She had just (*laid, lain*) down when the telephone rang.
lain

Have the workers (*laid, lain*) the cornerstone yet?
laid

The children were (*laying, lying*) on an old army blanket.
lying

(*Set, Sit*) the box in a place where we'll find it again.
set

Don't leave any money (*laying, lying*) in plain sight.
lying

The wreck (*lay, laid*) in 20 feet of water.
lay

I am determined that I (*shall, will*) spank you for misbehaving.
will

The chairman insists that all members (*shall, will*) vote this time.
   shall

My cat loves to (*lay, lie*) on the window sill.
   lie

The old shirt was (*laying, lying*) in a corner of the closet.
   lying

(*Shall, Will*) you be ready to go to the game on time?
   shall

The cat (*shall, will*) catch the mouse sooner or later.
   will

Do you remember where you (*laid, lay*) my pen?
   laid

Did you (*bring, take*) your report to class when you came today?
   bring

(*Can, May*) you go with us to the movies tonight?
   may

You shouldn't have (*laid, lain*) in the sun so long.
   lain

I could see Jack (*laying, lying*) on the deck.
   lying

The general said he (*shall, will*) attack at dawn.
   shall

I can assure you of this: I (*shall, will*) win the trophy.
   will

(*Can, May*) I help you build this table, please?
   may

If you are quiet, we (*shall, will*) sing to you.
   shall

I'm so tired I can't (*raise, rise*) myself from this bed.
   raise

Did you (*bring, take*) some apples to your sister when you went to visit her?
take

Maria has been (*setting, sitting*) by the telephone all evening.
sitting

Bill just (*sat, set*) still and didn't say a word.
sat

Extra chairs were (*sat, set*) in the aisles by the ushers.
set

Had you (*sat, set*) there awhile, you would have caught a fish.
sat

He plans to (*set, sit*) the new cabin on the beach.
set

Some careless person had (*sat, set*) in the fresh paint.
sat

The river has been (*raising, rising*) all night.
rising

When you come to work on your car, (*bring, take*) your new tools.
bring

I'm stuck; (*can, will*) you help me?
will

The new tax would (*raise, rise*) prices again.
raise

The (*raise, rise*) in prices would affect us all.
rise

Our hopes (*raised, rose*) and fell at the same instant.
rose

(*Can, May*) I do this task with only one uninjured hand?
can

Do you think you (*shall, will*) finish this quiz before noon?
shall

(*Bring, Take*) me to your leader!
take

I (*may, might*) do that task if I have enough time.
may

The witness (*may, might*) have seen the defendant in her home.
might

The old hen (*sat, set*) on the nest for two weeks.
sat

We saw smoke (*raising, rising*) behind the barn.
rising

The moon (*raises, rises*) about 7 p.m. and (*sets, sits*) about 8 a.m.
rises
sets

Because of its heavy load, the plane could not (*raise, rise*).
rise

The glue we used on the shelf would not (*set, sit*) right.
set

The ball has (*laid, lain*) in the water for two days.
lain

You people (*shall, will*) follow instructions or be punished!
shall

All of us (*may, might*) go to the beach next week.
may

I (*shall, will*) not be able to attend class tomorrow.
shall

We all hope that the New Kids (*shall, will*) appear on stage.
will

I knew we (*should, would*) be disappointed with the results.
should

Rents are (*raising, rising*) too rapidly.
rising

The weather (*may, might*) be too hot for us to go camping.
> **may**

A thick film of oil (*laid, lay*) on the water.
> **lay**

Can't you (*set, sit*) still a while longer?
> **sit**

If his temperature (*raises, rises*), call a doctor.
> **rises**

The dog has been (*laying, lying*) on my bed.
> **lying**

Shall I (*bring, take*) my things to your room right now?
> **take**

You should have tried harder; you (*may, might*) have won.
> **might**

Were the logs (*setting, sitting*) near the fireplace?
> **sitting**

Leslie forgot where she had (*laid, lain*) her gloves.
> **laid**

Last night Carl (*laid, lay*) awake worrying about the storm.
> **lay**

Melva (*laid, lay*) the sleeping child in her crib.
> **laid**

The old dog (*laid, lay*) himself down in the cool sand.
> **laid**

We (*shall, will*) answer when we are requested to do so.
> **shall**

If you plan to be there, I'll (*bring, take*) the money to your room tonight.
> **take**

(*Can, May*) I help you correct these tests?
> **may**

Regardless of his instructions, I (*shall, will*) do as I wish!
will

Henry asked his father if he (*could, might*) go to the races.
might

If you wish, you (*can, may*) take my car for a short ride.
may

Books were (*laying, lying*) on tables and chairs.
lying

Elizabeth said she (*shall, will*) ask her boss for a (*raise, rise*).
shall
raise

The stragglers (*may, might*) experience an unpleasant surprise.
may

Carl (*can't, couldn't*) have done that; he was with me today.
couldn't

Can you (*raise, rise*) yourself to a sitting position?
raise

My favorite hen (*lays, lies*) three eggs a day.
lays

The food did not (*set, sit*) very well with the hungry players.
sit

The twins have (*laid, lain*) in bed since dawn.
lain

Try to (*set, sit*) a good example for children to follow.
set

One hymn begins, "I (*should, would*) like to tell you what I think of Jesus."
should

Are the scouts (*setting, sitting*) out those young trees?
setting

We should try to (*lay, lie*) aside our prejudices.
lay

The farm hands (*sat, set*) the posts in concrete.
> **set**

If the weather is nice tomorrow, I (*shall, will*) go sailing.
> **shall**

I insist: you (*shall, will*) defend yourself.
> **shall**

I could see the old dog (*laying, lying*) in the sun.
> **lying**

I (*shall, will*) sing that song this evening.
> **shall**

(*Bring, Take*) these tools to the barn when you go.
> **take**

We (*may, might*) go swimming if the water is warm enough.
> **may**

Peter found a young hen (*setting, sitting*) on some old eggs.
> **sitting**

Latecomers (*may, might*) not find seats that they like.
> **may**

Mabel said that she (*shall, will*) be willing to help.
> **shall**

(*Shall, Will*) you take me to the picnic tomorrow?
> **shall**

 ## GENERAL OBSERVATIONS ABOUT VERBS

- A *verb* expresses an act, occurrence, or a state of being.
- Verbs may be classified in a number of ways; but for the purposes of this text, they are classified as follows:
  - **Transitive verbs:** *Transitive verbs* are those verbs that pattern with direct objects—that is, they express an action that directly affects a grammatical unit (usually a noun or pronoun) elsewhere in a clause or sentence.
  - **Intransitive verbs:** If a sentence has a verb that shows action of some sort but does not have a direct object, it has a verb known as an *intransitive verb*.

- **To be:** The verb *to be* is a copulative verb, which means that it usually patterns with a modifier or noun (or noun substitute) that is necessary to complete the meaning of the sentence.
- **Linking verbs:** *Linking verbs* are also copulative verbs, because they require a subject complement to complete the meaning of the sentence.
- **Auxiliaries:** An *auxiliary* is one of a small set of verbs that combine with a main verb to express various shades of meaning, usually of time or voice (refer to the discussion of active and passive voice). The three primary auxiliaries are *be, have,* and *do.*

- In sentences with verbs in the *active voice,* the subject of the verb is the *doer* of the action, or the *actor.* Sentences with verbs in the *passive voice* usually pattern with the actor-action-patient elements in a reverse order.
- *Tense* refers to the time of a situation.
- Unlike tense, which indicates a verb's location in time in absolute terms (past or present), a verb's *aspect* refers to the way the time of the situation is regarded. Aspects are expressed by a combination of an auxiliary and a main verb.
- Although the vast majority of verbs in the English language have a predictable pattern when it comes to indicating tense, a number of verbs differ in this regard.
- In English, writers employ three *moods* or *modes* to indicate various relationships or conditions:
  - **The indicative mood:** The *indicative mood* is employed to state a fact or to ask a question and is the form common to most sentences, whether declarative or question.
  - **The imperative mood:** The *imperative mood* is employed when a sentence states a request, command, or suggestion.
  - **The subjunctive mood:** The *subjunctive mood* is employed to express a condition contrary to fact, a wish, a supposition, a prayer, or a doubt, as well as in "that clauses." The subjunctive mood is most commonly employed, however, in contrary-to-fact statements.

- One fundamental requirement for every sentence you write or speak is that the subject and verb of the sentence agree. Following various rules ensures that subjects and verbs agree.
- Three sets of verbs are somewhat troublesome, even to native speakers of English: *sit-set, lay-lie,* and *raise-rise. May-can, shall-will, should-would, may-might,* and *bring-take* are other verb sets that cause difficulties.

Adverbs

An *adverb* is a word that modifies a verb, an adjective, or another adverb. In certain constructions, an adverb may also modify a preposition, a conjunction, a verbal, a noun, or a pronoun. As a general rule, adverbs tell *how, when, where, why, under what conditions,* and *to what extent.*

In their grammar text *Descriptive English Grammar* (published by Prentice Hall Inc.), House and Harmon recognize two categories of adverbs:

- **Primary adverbs:** Primary adverbs are those that have existed in the English language since the Old English period (A.D. 450–1100) or became adverbs prior to the end of the Middle English period (A.D. 1101–1500). These adverbs, according to House and Harmon, are usually not inflected for comparison and are usually monosyllabic. These are such words as the following:

  here
  how
  never
  then
  there
  twice
  too
  where

- **Derivative adverbs:** Derivative adverbs are those that may be identified by their suffixes (*ly, wards, ways, wise, s,* and *like*). A few of these words are the following:

  slowly
  boldly
  backwards
  westward
  forwards
  towards
  sideways
  easylike
  always
  dog-like
  casual-like

CLASSES OF ADVERBS

According to their functions in sentences, adverbs are divided into three classes:

- Simple
- Interrogative
- Conjunctive

Simple Adverbs

Simple adverbs are usually one-word adverbs modifying the word or phrase appearing next to them. In the following sentences, the entity modified is in bold print; the type of entity is in parentheses. The adverbs are in italics.

> The horse **runs** *swiftly.* (verb)
> The *softly* **falling** snow made no noise. (*falling,* a participle, functions as an adjective.)
> He found the *bright* **red** shirt in a store. (adjective)
> He was lying *just* **around the corner.** (prepositional phrase)
> Many people like **to ski** *rapidly* down the mountains. (the verbal *to ski* is an infinitive.)
> By **saving** *faithfully,* he had accumulated a small fortune. (the verbal, *saving,* is a gerund.)
> Sally arrived *almost* **before you did.** (adverb clause)
> The *newly* **rich** are not considered socially elite. (adjective serving as subject of verb)

Sometimes an adverb appears to modify an entire sentence and is therefore called a *sentence adverb* or *sentence modifier,* as in this example:

> *Unfortunately,* he doesn't care what people think about him.

Sentence modifiers are discussed in more detail in Part II in the section titled "Sentence Modifiers."

Simple adverbs are divided into five classes. The five classes are these:

- **Manner:** Adverbs of manner indicate *how* the action takes place.

  > The little girl read *silently.*

- **Time:** Adverbs of time indicate *when* the action takes place.

  > We worked in the field *yesterday.*

- **Place:** Adverbs of place indicate *where* the action takes place.

  The package was *there* when we returned.

- **Degree:** Adverbs of degree indicate *how much.*

  We were *really* surprised.

Very and *too* with past participles require intervening words such as *much, greatly, highly, little,* and the like. To omit such an intervening word causes the intended past participle to function as part of a passive verb phrase:

  The class was *very **much** satisfied* with the examination.
  We were *too **highly** motivated* to stop as we should have.

- **Number:** Adverbs of number indicate *order* or *how many times.*

  Bill arrived *first.*
  He spoke *twice.*

Interrogative Adverbs

Interrogative adverbs are used in asking questions, as in the following examples:

  Where have you been?
  When were you in Texas?
  Why did you burn that picture?

Conjunctive Adverbs

Conjunctive adverbs are used to connect dependent clauses to the remainder of the sentence. The most widely used conjunctive adverbs are the following:

where
when
whenever
while
as
why
before
after
until
since

These words are commonly referred to as *subordinating conjunctions,* because they join dependent clauses to main clauses.

A *dependent clause* (also called a *subordinate clause*) is a clause that cannot stand alone. You'll learn more about this and other types of clauses in Part II in the section titled "Clauses."

Note the following examples:

He left the party *before* I did.
Since I was not there, he left without me.
I visit my sister *whenever* I'm in Louisville.

ADVERBIAL FORMS

An adverb may be a *word,* a *phrase,* or a *clause.* In the following two sentences, the adverb is a word:

The little boy walked *slowly.*
We all did our work *rapidly.*

Notice that the adverbs in the following two sentences are phrases:

The children ran *into the street.*
My brother found the ball *under the porch.*

In the following two sentences, the adverb is a clause:

When I arrived at school, I talked with my professor.
The girls played ball *until the rain began to fall.*

COMPARISON AND USAGE

Adverbs, like adjectives, have three degrees of comparison:

- Positive
- Comparative
- Superlative

Positive Degree

The *positive degree* expresses a quality without a comparison; a statement is made concerning only one entity:

Ian drove the car *quickly.*
Heidi speaks *beautifully.*

Comparative and Superlative Degree

These different forms of comparison show a relationship between or among two or more actions or things. The *comparative degree* expresses a higher or lower degree than the positive. It is used to compare two things. The *superlative degree* is the highest or lowest degree when comparing more than two persons or things. These degrees of comparison are formed by adding *er* (comparative) and *est* (superlative) to the positive degree or by using the words *more* and *most,* as in the following examples:

Mickey runs *fast.* (positive)
Sally runs *faster.* (comparative)
Shirley runs *fastest.* (superlative)

My neighbor plays piano *skillfully.* (positive)
I play piano *more skillfully.* (comparative)
My friend plays the piano *most skillfully.* (superlative)

Adverbs that end in *ly* and adverbs of more than two syllables usually form the comparative and superlative by using *more* and *most*:

Betty finished the test *more rapidly* than Bill.

 You must choose the comparative form carefully and not confuse the comparative of an adverb with the comparative of an adjective:

Incorrect: He learns things *easier* than Frances.
Correct: He learns things *more easily* than Frances.

Adjectives are often erroneously employed in place of adverbs:

Incorrect: That person runs good.
Correct: That person runs well.

Some adverbs are compared irregularly, as in these examples:

well ⇨ better ⇨ best
much ⇨ more ⇨ most

 Use the *comparative degree* of an adjective or an adverb when speaking of two things and the *superlative degree* when speaking of three or more:

This is the *smaller* of the *two* puppies.
The black one is the *smallest* of the *three* puppies.

RECOGNIZING THE VARIOUS TYPES OF ADVERBS

The following sentences contain examples of various types of adverbs. Listed below each sentence are the adverbs themselves (adverbial phrases and clauses notwithstanding), the word or construction modified, and the type of word or construction modified.

Move quietly if you wish to observe wildlife.
quietly: move (verb)

I shall study really hard to pass my examinations.
really: hard (adverb)
hard: study (verb)

We thought the team played unusually well yesterday.
unusually: well (adverb)
well: played (verb)
yesterday: played (verb) (*yesterday,* a noun by form, functions as an adverb in this instance by telling *when*)

The scouts found some extremely valuable Civil War mementos.
extremely: valuable (adjective)

The spectators clapped enthusiastically for the clowns.
enthusiastically: clapped (verb)

To play well, you must practice continually.
well: to play (infinitive)
continually: practice (verb)

A teacher is always happy to see her students succeed.
always: is (verb)

He had too many bricks to carry at one time.
too: many (adjective) (*too,* in this case, is an intensifier meaning "more than enough")
An intensifier *is an adverb that adds emphasis to or amplifies an adjective. The word intensifier is also used to describe an adjective that creates an emphasizing or amplifying effect.*

The books were found in the very back of the room yesterday.
very: back (noun) (*very* functions much as *too* earlier in this list)
yesterday: found (verb)

The truck stopped briefly before proceeding farther.
briefly: stopped (verb)
farther: proceeding (verb)

I certainly believe that my neighbor is completely honest.
> **certainly:** believe (verb)
> **completely:** honest (adjective)

You will surely be penalized if you don't do your work correctly.
> **surely:** penalized (verb)
> **correctly:** do (verb)

The gunfighter walked slowly and cautiously down the street.
> **slowly:** walked (verb)
> **cautiously:** walked (verb)

Students are now required to spend more money for education.
> **now:** required (verb)

I did well on my tests, but I received very low grades.
> **well:** did (verb)
> **very:** low (adjective)

We went northward toward the clearing.
> **northward:** went (verb)

I have serious reservations about your totally unbelievable tale.
> **totally:** unbelievable (adjective)

The hikers wandered aimlessly through the deep woods.
> **aimlessly:** wandered (verb)

The clergyman spoke sincerely about the joys of giving.
> **sincerely:** spoke (verb)

We argued enthusiastically for the new gymnasium.
> **enthusiastically:** argued (verb)

We were more confident than we had reason to be.
> **more:** confident (adjective) (*more,* too, is an intensifier)

It finally happened: that really old tree was blown down.
> **finally:** happened (verb)
> **really:** old (adjective)
> **down:** blown (verb)

He called twice, but we hardly heard him.
> **twice:** called (verb)
> **hardly:** heard (verb)

We all worked long and hard, but we had hardly begun the task.
>   **long:** worked (verb)
>   **hard:** worked (verb)
>   **hardly:** begun (verb)

We left early, but we truly intended to return later.
>   **early:** left (verb)
>   **truly:** intended (verb)
>   **later:** return (verb)

COMMON PITFALLS WITH ADVERBS AND ADJECTIVES

Many writers and speakers of the English language commonly encounter certain pitfalls when employing adverbs and adjectives:

- Misplaced modifiers
- Squinting modifiers
- Hedge words

Misplaced Modifiers

Misplaced modifiers are those located in places other than near the words they modify and that seem to modify words other than those they are intended to modify. For example, note the placement of *nearly* in this sentence:

>   I *nearly* won a million dollars in the lottery.

Does this sentence mean what it says—that someone nearly won that money but actually did not win any money, or does it mean this:

>   I won *nearly* a million dollars in the lottery.

This type of error causes confusion on the reader's part. The clause in italic type in the following sentence presents the same problem: What, exactly, does the sentence mean?

>   Carl purchased a new fishing pole from the store *that he liked.*

Did Carl like the new fishing pole, or did he like the store? One of the following revised sentences would be more appropriate, depending on the intended meaning:

>   Carl purchased a new fishing pole that he liked from the store.
>   Carl purchased from the store that he liked a new fishing pole.

Squinting Modifiers

Squinting modifiers are, in a way, misplaced modifiers, except that they are placed in a sentence in such a manner that they may modify either of two nouns in the sentence. In the following sentence, the word *quickly* could modify either *eating* or *caused:*

Seeing the children eating *quickly* caused Mother to lose her temper.

One of the following revised sentences would be more appropriate, depending on the intended meaning:

Mother quickly lost her temper upon seeing the children eating.
Mother lost her temper upon seeing the children eating quickly.

Serious writers try to avoid these kinds of errors. Although the errors may seem harmless enough, they cause a reader to focus upon the manner of composition rather than upon the thought the writer is attempting to convey to the reader.

Hedge Words

Writers and reporters for the various media are increasingly sensitive to possible legal repercussions regarding the things they report. As a result, many of them, seemingly to protect themselves and their organizations, tend to overuse "hedge words"—that is, words that allow the speaker or writer to hedge on the meaning of his statement. Readers and listeners are subjected to such statements as the following:

The *alleged* burglary occurred last night.
Smith died of an *apparent* heart attack.

Such hedge words are unnecessary if the police report indeed shows that a burglary occurred and if the medical report lists a heart attack as the cause of Smith's death. In any case, the second sentence above would certainly make more sense if it were written another way. (Besides, what *is* an "apparent heart attack"?)

Apparently, Smith died of a heart attack.
Smith died apparently of a heart attack.

 ## GENERAL OBSERVATIONS ABOUT ADVERBS

- An *adverb* is a word that modifies a verb, an adjective, or another adverb. In certain constructions, an adverb may also modify a preposition, a conjunction, a verbal, a noun, or a pronoun.
- As a general rule, adverbs tell *how, when, where, why, under what conditions,* and *to what extent.*

- According to their functions in sentences, adverbs are divided into three classes:
  - **Simple adverbs:** Simple adverbs are usually one-word adverbs modifying the word or phrase appearing next to them.
  - **Interrogative adverbs:** Interrogative adverbs are used in asking questions.
  - **Conjunctive adverbs:** Conjunctive adverbs are used to connect dependent clauses to the remainder of the sentence. The most widely used conjunctive adverbs are *where, when, whenever, while, as, why, before, after, until,* and *since.*
- An adverb may be a *word,* a *phrase,* or a *clause.*
- Adverbs, like adjectives, have three degrees of comparison:
  - Positive
  - Comparative
  - Superlative
- Readers and writers of English commonly encounter certain pitfalls when employing adverbs and adjectives:
  - **Misplaced modifiers:** *Misplaced modifiers* are those located in places other than near the words they modify and that seem to modify words other than those they are intended to modify.
  - **Squinting modifiers:** *Squinting modifiers* are, in a way, misplaced modifiers, except that they are placed in a sentence in such a manner that they may modify either of two nouns in the sentence.
  - **Hedge words:** *Hedge words* are those words used to help the speaker or writer avoid making an absolute statement, such as *alleged* in "The alleged burglary occurred last night."

Function Words

Unlike content words, such as nouns, verbs, adjectives, and adverbs, *function words,* also called *structure words,* are words that have a grammatical (or syntactic) role in a sentence or clause as opposed to a lexical (or semantic) meaning. Function words include the following:

- Determiners
- Prepositions
- Conjunctions
- Interjections
- Auxiliary verbs

Auxiliary verbs are discussed in this book in the context of verbs rather than function words; refer to the section titled "Auxiliary Verbs" earlier in this part.

DETERMINERS

A determiner is a word that limits the potential referent of a noun phrase. There are various types of determiners:

- Definite and indefinite articles
- Demonstratives
- Quantifiers
- Possessives

Possessives are discussed earlier in this part in the section titled "Making Nouns Possessive" and thus are not covered here.

Definite and Indefinite Articles

The presence of a *definite article* (there is only one: *the*) typically denotes a definite noun phrase, as in *the woman*. That is, the speaker or writer refers to a specific woman (*the woman*), not just any woman (*a woman*). *A woman* illustrates the use of an *indefinite article*—that is, no specific woman is being discussed. There are two indefinite articles: *a* and *an*.

Many grammarians consider the words *a, an,* and *the* to be adjectives rather than determiners.

The decision to use either *a* or *an* is based upon the initial sound of the word following the article and not on the spelling. For instance, a word beginning with a silent *h* actually begins with a vowel sound. Examine these examples:

> We discovered *an* old house in the woods.
> I had never seen *a* wooden ship before.
> Please remain in this room for *an* hour.
> Should we adopt *an* honor system?
> Jane wore *a* uniform of blue. (*Uniform,* of course, begins with a *y* sound, as in the word *you.*)

Using *a, an,* and *the* before separate items

Repeat the article *a, an,* or *the* before separate items if it is otherwise not clear that the items are indeed separate. For example, the following sentence does not easily reveal the number of cows that the farmer had:

The farmer had *a* black and white cow.

If the farmer had only one cow, the sentence is acceptable; but a better sentence, perhaps, would be one of the following:

The farmer had a cow that was black and white.
The farmer had *a* black and *a* white cow. (In this sentence, of course, the farmer had two cows.)

Demonstratives

A *demonstrative* is a word whose role is to locate a referent in relation to a speaker, an addressee, or some other person. Examples of demonstratives are the following:

this
these
that
those

This should be used when the referent is physically closer to the speaker; *that* should be used when the referent is physically more remote from the speaker.

 This, that, these, and *those* must agree in number with the words that they modify:

These **books** are mine.
This **chair** is broken.

Quantifiers

A *quantifier* indicates a relative or indefinite quantity, such as the following words:

all
many
several
few

Quantifiers are distinguished from numerals, which provide an absolute indication of quantity (*nine* ladies dancing).

All the king's men wore breeches and tunics.
Many of the dogs were abused as puppies.
I find I can read for *several* hours at a time.
Few children enjoy lima beans.

PREPOSITIONS

A *preposition* is a word or, in some instances, a word group that relates one sentence element (the *object of the preposition*) to another sentence element. Because a preposition must have an object, the preposition and the object of the preposition and any modifiers that pattern with them constitute a *prepositional phrase*.

 Prepositional phrases are discussed in more detail in Part II in the section titled "Prepositional Phrases."

Prepositions show certain relationships. One popular way of remembering these relationships is by remembering this statement: Anywhere a mouse can go, a preposition can go.

in
into
out
around
behind
under
beneath
beside
to
from
on
round
over
by
between
among
off
through
throughout
against

Of course, other relationships exist, such as the following prepositions:

with
except
since
than
during
about

Of, in, and *to,* in that order, are the most frequently used prepositions in English.

In each of the following sentences, the preposition is in boldfaced italics, and the object of the preposition is in bold print. The word to which each prepositional phrase relates is in italics.

The *canoe* **with** its **passengers** negotiated the rapids.
The *book* **with** the torn **pages** is Mitzi's.
Not a cloud could be *seen* **in** the **sky.**
The yellow duckling *jumped* quickly **into** the **water.**

Prepositions often have the same form as adverbs; however, adverbs can be distinguished from prepositions by the fact that adverbs do not pattern with objects. In the first sentence below, *up* is an adverb; in the second sentence below, *up* is a preposition, while *up the tree* is a prepositional phrase:

The little girl looked *up.*
The squirrel ran *up* the tree.

Here's another example: In the first sentence following, the word *down* obviously modifies the verb and is not a part of a separate grammatical unit, whereas in the second sentence, the word *down* is a part of the prepositional phrase, *down the street.*

The prisoner looked *down* as he entered the courtroom.
We looked *down* the street before entering the building.

Types of Prepositions

For the purposes of this book, only three types of propositions need be identified:

- Simple
- Participial
- Phrasal

Simple Prepositions

A *simple preposition* is made up of either a simple or a compound word, as in the following:

up
down
in
into
from
to
with
inside
around
before

upon
along
without

Sometimes two-word prepositions such as *inside* and *before* are called *complex prepositions,* because they have the form of complex words.

Participial Prepositions

A *participial preposition* takes the *ing* form of certain verbs, such as the following:

assuming
beginning
barring
considering
following
including
involving
regarding

Note in the following sentences how these *ing* words function as prepositions:

The speaker presented his plans *involving the students.*
She talked with her instructor *regarding her flying lessons.*
The witness *recalling the details* was quite specific.
The quotation *including the error* was stricken from the record.
All of the animals *seeking shelter* walked to the barn.
The project *involving nuclear energy* was terminated.

Phrasal Prepositions

A *phrasal preposition* is, as its name suggests, a unit of two or more words serving as a single preposition (these types of prepositions are also called *compound prepositions*). Often the phrasal preposition is itself a prepositional phrase. These prepositional phrases usually pattern together and are seldom modified in any way—that is, very seldom do speakers or writers change their constructions or add modifiers within the word groups. A few of these word groups include the following:

by way of
in place of
in spite of
in case of
on behalf of
in addition to
in lieu of

in front of
by means of
in contrast to
in comparison with
with regard to

The following examples use phrasal prepositions:

Use the rear stairs *in case of* fire.
We drove to Nashville *by way of* Paducah, Kentucky.

Verb-Adverbial Composites

Words that are used as prepositions or as single-word adverbs are sometimes linked to verbs to form *verb-adverbial composites* (VACs). The words in italics in the following sentence comprise a VAC:

Mother *called up* the plumber as soon as she could.

In sentences containing phrases such as *called up, fell out, give in,* and *run into,* the VAC is recognizable by the fact that it substitutes for a single word. In the preceding sentence, for example, the VAC may be replaced by the single word *telephoned.* When such a replacement is made, the possibility of a prepositional phrase employing the adverbial is eliminated:

Mother *telephoned* the plumber as soon as she could.

The other examples of VACs in the preceding paragraph may be replaced with the single words *quarreled, surrender,* and *meet.*

 Only one preposition in the English language—*near*—can be inflected: *near, nearer, nearest.*

Two- or Three-Part Prepositions

Another type of preposition found in English is the *two-* or *three-part preposition.* These types of prepositions consist of words such as *together, due, as,* and other words followed by a word that is easily recognized as a preposition. Such prepositions include the following:

ahead of
out of
apart from
owing to
as for
instead of
because of

aside from
contrary to
due to
up to
together with

Analyzing a sentence with these constructions in it as adverb plus prepositional phrase would require stretching logic to its extreme. For example, examine the following sentence:

Fritz is up to his neck in trouble again.

In this sentence, the phrase *up to his neck* clearly indicates the amount of trouble that Fritz is in: Fritz is in trouble again. How badly? Up to his neck.

Now try analyzing the sentence this way:

Fritz is up in trouble again.

How far? To his neck. The basic sentence parts, *Fritz is up*, surely do not reflect sound "sentence sense," even though it has the basic sentence pattern of N_1 $V_{to be}$ ADV. However, *Fritz is in trouble*, which has the same basic sentence pattern, makes sentence sense. The missing words, *up to his neck*, clearly pattern as a single unit—that is, as a prepositional phrase. Thus, calling *up to* a two-part preposition seems to reflect a certain amount of sound judgment.

 Sentence patterns are discussed in detail in Part II under the heading "Types of Sentences."

Prepositions and Guide Words

The English language employs many expressions that require certain prepositions to show proper relationships. These expressions are, in a sense, peculiar to themselves because of the sometimes seemingly elusive meaning of the preposition. Nevertheless, standard English requires the showing of the proper relationships in all instances. If you have doubt about the correct preposition, you should consult a standard dictionary, looking up the *guide word* (the key word that controls the preposition).

Following is a list of guide words and prepositions. Although it is fairly up to date, language is always in a state of change; therefore, the following list will one day become obsolete. For now, however, it reflects general desired standards of usage. You should note that not all uses of any guide word or preposition are listed. If you recall a particular usage of a preposition and that usage is not listed, check a dictionary to determine the appropriateness of that usage.

ABHORRENT OF (repulsion): We are all *abhorrent of* greed.

ABHORRENT TO (opposed): His ideas are *abhorrent to* reason.

ABSOLVE OF (to free from penalty or obligation): His excuses do not *absolve* him *of* his responsibility.

ABSTAIN FROM (to refrain): Please *abstain from* interrupting the speaker.

ACCEDE TO (to consent or agree): I *accede to* your demands for an inspection.

ACCOMPANIED BY (with a person): Jane was *accompanied by* her brother.

ACCOMPANIED WITH (to have things): The professor, *accompanied with* all his books, entered the room.

ACCORD WITH (to agree with): His views are in *accord with* ours.

ACCORDANCE WITH (agreement): His plans were in *accordance with* our plans; they took the train to El Paso.

ACCORDING TO (in accordance with): He did the work *according to* our instructions.

ACCUSED BY (a person): He was *accused by* his brothers of disrupting the family reunion.

ACCUSED OF (a deed): We all were *accused of* misbehaving in class.

ACQUIESCE IN (to consent, assent): We *acquiesced in* all of the chairman's plans.

ACQUIT OF (to free, exonerate): He was *acquitted of* the charge of murder.

ADAPT FROM (take from): The movie was *adapted from* Hemingway's first novel.

ADAPT TO (make to fit): I *adapted* a Honda engine *to* my Yamaha.

ADDICTED TO (given over to habit): Many people are *addicted to* coffee.

ADEPT IN (skilled): Native Americans were quite *adept in* hunting.

ADHERE TO (follow, adhere, devoted): He *adhered* closely *to* the instructions to abandon the building.

ADMIT OF (to afford possibility or opportunity): This plan *admits of* numerous errors.

ADMIT TO (confess): He should *admit to* his part in the robbery.

ADVERSE TO (opposed, antagonistic): No one should be *adverse to* cleaning up the environment.

AGREE IN (an opinion): They *agreed in* their selection of candidates for president.

AGREE ON (a matter): We all *agreed on* the next course of action.

AGREE TO (a proposal): The boys seemed to *agree to* my suggestion.

AGREE WITH (a person): They *agreed with* the committee that they should make a report.

AGREEABLE TO (in accordance, conformity): We are certainly *agreeable to* reasonable proposals.

AIM TO (try): I *aim to* consider every facet of the plan.

AMBITION FOR (desire for): It was Lady Macbeth's *ambition for* her husband's success that lead to their downfall.

AMBITIOUS OF (extensive, elaborate): The most *ambitious* biography *of* MacArthur has just been published.

ANGRY AT, ABOUT (a situation): I'm certainly *angry at* the way the test turned out. Edgar is *angry about* the theft of his wallet.

ANGRY AT (a thing): I was *angry at* my car because it wouldn't start.

ANGRY WITH (a person): I was very *angry with* Jane for not doing her part of the project.

APPREHENSIVE OF, FOR (fearful): We were all *apprehensive of* danger. We were *apprehensive for* our lives.

ARGUE ABOUT (a situation): We *argued about* dividing the lost treasure.

ARGUE FOR (a cause or position): Carl *argued for* an end to tests.

ARGUE WITH (a person): I *argued with* my father over use of the car.

ARRIVE IN (a large city): They *arrived in* Denver at midnight.

ARRIVE AT (a small place): The group *arrived at* the park at the scheduled time.

AUTHORITY OF, FOR (actions or acting): We understood the *authority of* parents over children and for acting as we did.

AUTHORITY ON (a subject): My lawyer is an *authority on* taxes.

BESIDE (by the side): The spider sat *beside* Miss Muffet.

BESIDES (in addition to): We have two tests *besides* a paper due on Wednesday.

CAPABLE OF (able): I'm sure he is not *capable of* such a thing.

CAREFUL OF (painstaking, cautious): He was *careful of* not spilling the gasoline.

CARELESS OF (neglectful): You should not be *careless of* your appearance.

CENTER IN (focus upon): Our studies *centered in* Asian culture.

Avoid the usually illogical "center around."

CHARACTERISTIC OF (attribute): Feathers are a *characteristic of* birds.

COLLIDE WITH (crash): The car *collided with* a huge oak tree.

COMPARE TO (to liken): Shall I *compare* thee *to* a summer's day?

COMPARE WITH (to examine for similarities): If you'll *compare* my prize *with* yours, you'll find mine is smaller.

COMPLY WITH (consent, obey): We must *comply with* all requirements before graduation.

CONCENTRATE ON, UPON (to focus): Please *concentrate* your attention *on* the chalkboard.

CONCERN FOR (troubled): He is really *concerned for* his old dog.

CONCERN IN (interest): He showed no *concern in* that matter.

CONCERN WITH (involved): We are not *concerned with* that project.

CONCUR IN (an opinion): We all *concurred in* the decision to go to the theater.

CONCUR WITH (a person): If you all *concur with* me, we'll begin the task.

CONFIDE IN (a person): No one is able to *confide in* Mitzi.

CONFIDE TO (a person about something): John *confided to* Bill that he had cheated on the examination.

CONFORM TO (to be in accordance): Our plans *conform to* the latest specifications.

CONFORMITY WITH (agreement, harmony): Our spending is in *conformity with* our earnings.

CONNECT BY (join): The two rooms are *connected by* a short hall.

CONNECT WITH (associate): We could *connect* his success *with* his hard work and diligent study.

CONTEND AGAINST (an obstacle): We had to *contend against* a strong tide to land our small boat.

CONTEND FOR (a prize or principle): We felt obligated to *contend for* equality and justice for all.

CONTEND WITH (a person): He had to *contend with* an irate store manager.

CONTRAST (*n*) BETWEEN: The *contrast* in temperatures *between* noon and midnight is nearly unbelievable.

CONTRAST (*v*) TO (to examine for differences): His methods *contrast* sharply *to* mine.

CORRESPOND TO (things): The claws of a bird *correspond to* a human being's fingers.

CORRESPOND WITH (a person): We did not *correspond with* each other until I left for California.

DESIRE FOR (wish, craving): I have a sincere *desire for* fried fish.

DESIRE OF (longing): I am aware of the *desire of* students to avoid tests.

DESIROUS OF (adjective form): I am *desirous of* that award.

DESIST FROM (refrain, stop): *Desist from* your abhorrent behavior.

DEVOID OF (without): Most planets are *devoid of* life forms.

DIE BY (violence): He *died by* suffocation in quicksand.

DIE FROM (exposure): He *died from* the iciness of the water.

DIE OF (disease, injury): He *died of* smallpox last year.

DIFFER ABOUT (a situation): George and I *differed about* the answer we would give.

DIFFER, DIFFERENT FROM (something else): My report is quite *different from* yours. My ideas *differ from* yours.

DIFFER WITH (disagree): You may *differ with* me if you wish.

DISAGREE WITH: We all *disagree with* your view of the matter.

DISAPPOINTED BY (what happened): The farmer was *disappointed by* the failure of his crops.

DISAPPOINTED IN (a thing obtained): My brother was *disappointed in* the new bicycle he received for Christmas.

DISAPPOINTED WITH (a thing not obtained): We were *disappointed with* your not being elected chairman.

DISDAIN FOR (contempt): He has *disdain for* all administrators.

DISSENT FROM (withhold consent or approval): He always *dissents from* the group's thinking.

DISTASTE FOR (aversion): I have a *distaste for* offensive people.

EMPTY OF (without): My mind is *empty of* any original thoughts.

ENAMORED OF (charmed or fascinated by): He is *enamored of* the star of a movie.

Avoid use of enamored by in place of enamored of.

ENGAGE IN: Do not *engage in* idle chatter.

ENTER INTO (plan or program): We *entered into* a plan to save money for next Christmas.

ENVIOUS OF: You should not be *envious of* your friends.

EXPERT IN: George is an *expert in* repairing diesel engines.

FOREIGN TO: His way of thinking is *foreign to* my background.

FREE FROM (independent): She tries to be *free from* all responsibility.

FREE OF (void): The moon is *free of* any life forms.

FRIGHTENED AT (a thought): He was *frightened at* the prospect of having heart surgery.

FRIGHTENED BY (a thing): As he tramped through the woods, he *was frightened* by a big, black bear.

You are, of course, afraid *of* something.

GLAD OF (pleased): All his friends were *glad of* his company.

GRADUATE (*v*) FROM: We were happy that he would *graduate from* Yale.

Would be graduated from is less widely used today.

GRADUATE (*n*) OF: The new chairman is a *graduate of* Yale.

GUARD AGAINST: We must all *guard against* hazardous waste.

HATRED FOR: My daughter seems to have a *hatred for* vegetables.

HINT AT: Will you *hint at* the solution to the puzzle?

IDENTICAL WITH: The kissing fever virus is *identical with* that of hoof-and-mouth disease.

ILL FROM (an action): The children became *ill from* eating the sour apples.

ILL OF (a disease): All the children were *ill of* chicken pox.

ILL WITH (ailing): My brother is *ill with* a high fever.

IMPATIENT AT (someone's conduct): The new teacher was *impatient at* the class's behavior.

IMPATIENT FOR (thing desired): We were all *impatient for* the opening of the new ice cream parlor.

IMPATIENT OF (restraint): The driver was *impatient of* tardiness or delay.

IMPATIENT WITH (a person): Sally was often *impatient with* her friends.

IMPLICIT IN: His expectations were *implicit in* his discussions with the group.

IN ACCORDANCE WITH: You ought to act *in accordance with* the law.

INDEPENDENT OF: Children often wish to be *independent of* their parents.

INFER FROM (conclude): I *infer from* your statement that you have resigned.

INFERIOR TO: My report is obviously *inferior to* your project.

INITIATE INTO (to originate): The police *initiated* an investigation *into* the apparent murder.

IN SEARCH OF: The expedition left *in search of* the abominable snowman.

INSEPARABLE FROM: The twins were *inseparable from* each other.

JEALOUS OF: You should refrain from being *jealous of* your friends.

KIND OF (not *kind of a*): He had a *kind of* makeshift airplane.

JOIN IN (participate): Everyone wanted to *join in* the singing.

JOIN TO (connect): *Join* the wire *to* the terminal for results.

JOIN WITH (associate): You may *join with* us if you wish to protest this statement.

LISTEN TO: For greater insight, *listen to* your elders.

LIVE AT (an address): I wonder who *lives at* 1703 Parklane Drive.

LIVE IN (house, geographic location): The former president now *lives in* Georgia.

LIVE ON (a street or road): My sister *lives on* Cherrylog Road.

MARTYR FOR (a cause): He was one of the *martyrs for* freedom in South Africa.

MARTYR TO (a disease): My father was a *martyr to* rheumatism.

MASTERY OF: Alexander gained *mastery of* the entire known world.

MEDDLE INTO: Try not to *meddle into* someone else's business.

MONOPOLY OF: The company gained *monopoly of* the entire cereal business.

NECESSITY FOR (followed by an infinitive): We all felt the *necessity for* all of us *to fight* for our rights.

NECESSITY OF (followed by a gerund): He knew the *necessity of getting* good grades in his classes.

NEED FOR (followed by an infinitive): There is a *need for* Bill *to improve*.

NEED OF (followed by a gerund): The *need of finding* more money is obvious.

OBEDIENT TO: Mankind is forced to be *obedient to* the laws of nature.

OBJECT TO: How can anyone *object to* that proposal?

OBLIVIOUS OF: The children were *oblivious of* the danger nearby.

Oblivious to is also acceptable, but a bit less so.

OVERCOME BY (an element): The firemen were nearly *overcome by* smoke.

OVERCOME WITH (an emotion): The audience was *overcome with* love for the heroine.

PARALLEL BETWEEN (two similar objects): We all could understand the *parallel between* a river and life itself.

PARALLEL TO, WITH (two or more lines): The railroad tracks ran *parallel to* the highway.

PART FROM (a person or place): Many college graduates are eager to *part from* their home towns.

PART WITH (a possession): A miser does not wish to *part with* his money.

PECULIAR TO (belonging exclusively): The giant panda is *peculiar to* China.

PLAN TO (followed by a verb): We should all *plan to* meet at 8 p.m.

PREFER (one) TO (another): I really *prefer* peaches *to* apples.

PREFERABLE TO: Do you find failing *preferable to* passing this course?

PREPARATORY TO: You should complete a course in typing *preparatory to* taking a computer course.

PREREQUISITE FOR (something required before an allowance): A valid license is a *prerequisite for* driving.

PREREQUISITE OF (a constant requirement): Steady hands are a *prerequisite of* all good surgeons.

PREREQUISITE TO (a requirement prior to transaction): He demanded fifty dollars as a *prerequisite to* the trade.

PRIOR TO (beforehand): We wanted to leave *prior to* the storm.

PRIVILEGE OF (with a gerund): He wanted the *privilege of* sitting in the front seat.

PRODIGAL WITH (extravagant): The treasurer was too *prodigal with* the club's funds.

PROFICIENT IN: My sister is really *proficient in* chemistry.

PROFIT BY (receive benefit): We could all *profit by* studying harder.

After *profit, by* and *from* are often used interchangeably.

PROFIT FROM (gain materially): We should *profit from* the sale of our apple crop.

PROHIBIT FROM: The government tried to *prohibit* us *from* seeing the report.

PROTEST AGAINST: The committee would not hear our *protest against* the election results.

REASON ABOUT (an issue): Let's *reason about* the consequences of our proposed actions.

REASON FOR (an action): The *reason for* assigning the failing grade is obvious.

REASON WITH (a person): Parents sometimes simply cannot *reason with* teenagers.

RECONCILE TO: No one could *reconcile* the cost *to* the quality of the new building.

REGRET FOR: We all had a keen *regret for* our dangerous joke.

REPENT OF: Criminals seldom *repent of* their misdeeds.

REPUGNANT TO: Your actions in the classroom were *repugnant to* your classmates.

REWARDED BY (a person): We were *rewarded by* the president for cleaning the streets.

REWARDED FOR (something done): You should not have to be *rewarded for* doing good deeds.

REWARDED WITH (a gift): Bernice was *rewarded with* a silver bowl for her performance.

SENSITIVE TO: I am highly *sensitive to* changes in the humidity.

SEPARATE FROM: No one could *separate* the milk *from* the cream.

SPEAK TO (communicate a fact): Does anyone here wish to *speak to* the other issue? Ed wanted to *speak to* Matilda.

SPEAK WITH (converse): Students often wish to *speak with* classmates.

STAY AT: We were so tired we all wanted to *stay at* home.

SUBSCRIBE TO: We simply could not *subscribe to* such a plan.

SUBSTITUTE FOR: Water is no *substitute for* wholesome, fresh milk.

SUPERIOR TO: Rubber hoses are *superior to* plastic hoses in winter.

SYMPATHIZE WITH: No one would *sympathize with* the complaining boy.

TALK TO (lecture): The President *talked to* Congress about the tax.

TALK WITH (converse): The principal wanted to *talk with* us students.

TAMPER WITH: It is not wise to *tamper with* recognized success.

TREAT OF (a subject): Does this book *treat of* auto mechanics?

TREAT WITH (a person): The negotiators were willing to *treat with* you about the settlement.

TRY TO (attempt): We were all going to *try to* get an A.

Try and is never correct, unless *to try* is being used in conjunction with an unrelated verb.

>   **Correct:** I think I'll *try to* visit Maureen during my vacation.
>   **Incorrect:** Jessie wants to *try and* get a job at Morris's firm.
>   **Correct:** He was *trying and failing* to win the championship.

UNEQUAL TO: We were all *unequal to* the task proposed for us.

UNMINDFUL OF: He was *unmindful of* the weather when he went hunting geese.

VARIANCE WITH: Your story is at *variance with* the police report.

VARY FROM (one object to another): Obviously, your left foot will *vary from* your right foot.

VARY IN (qualities): These buildings *vary in* color and design.

VARY WITH (tastes): Preferences for paintings *vary with* the individuals surveyed.

VEXED WITH (perturbed): She was *vexed with* her son for tracking in mud on the clean floor.

VIE WITH (compete): Politicians *vie with* one another for publicity.

WAIT AT, ON, IN (a place): *Wait at* the bus station for your parents to arrive. *Wait on* the corner for the bus. *Wait in* the lobby of the hotel.

WAIT FOR (delay): Please *wait for* me to finish this paper.

WAIT ON (serve): The clerk will *wait on* you when she gets an opportunity.

Do not use *wait on* in place of *wait for*.

WORTHY OF: His performance was worthy of an award.

SELECTING THE CORRECT PREPOSITION

Following are numerous sample sentences that demonstrate the correct selection of the preposition:

The children were taught to repent (*for, of*) their wrongdoings.
> **of**

The cuckoo is peculiar (*to, in*) the northern part of that country.
> **to**

This year he was initiated (*into, within*) the fraternity.
> **into**

The child was frightened (*by, at*) the idea of walking home alone.
> **at**

The troops had to contend (*with, against*) a severe winter.
> **against**

How does this product compare (*in, with*) quality?
> **with**

Everyone must adhere (*with, to*) the regulations.
> **to**

The winner was rewarded (*with, by*) a silver cup.
> **with**

Study the script preparatory (*of, to*) entering the tryouts.
> **to**

What kind (*of, of a*) car do you have?
> **of**

It is best to guard (*from, against*) driving when you are sleepy.
> **against**

(*With, To*) which other Byron poem does this selection compare?
> **to**

The mother was concerned (*about, for*) the injured child.
> **for**

He acquiesced (*about, in*) the disputed matter.
> **in**

The clerk would wait (*for, on*) only one customer at a time.
on

Many people subscribe (*to, for*) more than one daily paper.
to

No one likes to part (*with, from*) old friends.
from

Martha lives (*in, on*) Chicago (*in, on*) Michigan Avenue.
in
on

Mr. Reed now lives (*at, in*) a motel.
in

A student should be free (*from, of*) the influences of noise.
of

(*From, Of*) what illness did he die?
of

The automobile collided (*against, with*) a fast-moving train.
with

He did the work in accordance (*to, with*) the suggestion.
with

This portion is unequal (*to, with*) the one on the left.
to

Yesterday for an hour I spoke (*to, with*) the chairman of the committee.
with

What is the necessity (*for, of*) going to court at this time?
of

At a lecture everyone should listen attentively (*with, to*) the speaker.
to

The clerk expressed disdain (*about, for*) complaining customers.
for

The group must desist (*from, of*) further activity of this kind.
from

You must be careful (*about, of*) the company you keep.
> **of**

The victim was accused (*by, of*) his landlord.
> **by**

Do not wait (*for, on*) me because I shall be very late.
> **for**

The dissertation treats (*of, on*) the writings of J. D. Salinger.
> **of**

Draw a line parallel (*with, against*) the first one on the page.
> **with** (or to)

One country must not meddle (*into, with*) the affairs of another.
> **into**

This method is totally foreign (*to, with*) those of my experience.
> **to**

Dr. Jones was disappointed (*by, with*) your not passing the test.
> **with**

That attitude is characteristic (*of, to*) one who has been defeated.
> **of**

Did the delegate abstain (*against, from*) voting?
> **from**

The chairman delivered a protest (*about, against*) the proposal that was offered.
> **against**

A senior usually prefers living off campus (*over, to*) living on campus.
> **to**

The squad leader became impatient (*toward, with*) the malingerer.
> **with**

Everyone should be glad (*for, of*) the opportunity to improve himself or herself.
> **of**

Please confide (*in, to*) me.
> **in**

Everyone should concentrate (*on, with*) the assignment.
> **on**

The entire group agrees (*about, in*) its beliefs.
> **in**

The cause is worthy (*for, of*) your support.
> **of**

Many people are sensitive (*of, to*) certain kinds of pollen.
> **to**

Most people are reluctant to part (*from, with*) their favorite books.
> **with**

Everyone should join (*in, into*) the games.
> **in**

His composition is almost totally free (*from, of*) spelling errors.
> **of**

Mrs. Wilson corresponds regularly (*to, with*) her son.
> **with**

Your work compares favorably (*to, with*) the work of another artist.
> **to**

This testimony should acquit him (*from, of*) the charge.
> **of**

It is better to try (*and, to*) complete the work than to stop now.
> **to**

Is there a necessity (*for, of*) you to be present tomorrow?
> **for**

The child was disappointed (*by, with*) not getting a bicycle.
> **with**

His interests eventually centered (*around, in*) politics.
> **in**

The old lady was accompanied (*by, with*) a nurse.
by

Susan is careless (*of, with*) her appearance.
of

Did he contrast my plan (*against, to*) yours?
to

John is totally independent (*from, of*) his father.
of

Her mother is apprehensive (*about, of*) her welfare.
of

What should we infer (*from, with*) her statements?
from

I dislike parting (*from, with*) my old car.
with

This snake is peculiar (*of, to*) that region.
to

This medicine is a substitute (*for, of*) the other one.
for

He is quite capable (*of, to*) doing the work.
of

The college will prohibit him (*against, from*) doing that work.
from

Are you sad when you part (*from, with*) loved ones?
from

Can the committee agree (*on, to*) an agenda?
on

Is he a person (*in, to*) whom you can confide?
in

I am frightened (*at, by*) the idea of your going home alone.
at

Does he live (*at, in*) Chicago?
> **in**

These boxes vary (*in, with*) sizes and shapes.
> **in**

Will you wait (*for, on*) me (*at, on*) the office?
> **for**
> **at** (or in)

The minister said that one must repent (*of, on*) his sins.
> **of**

We have the privilege (*by, of*) going to the lecture.
> **of**

We usually issue a protest (*against, of*) that kind of proposal.
> **against**

Terri must reconcile herself (*to, with*) the latest changes.
> **to**

Dr. Allen will speak (*to, with*) the assembled students.
> **to**

I can sympathize (*toward, with*) a person who has suffered such a loss.
> **with**

Too many citizens are unmindful (*about, of*) their responsibilities.
> **of**

The professor became vexed (*about, with*) the unruly students.
> **with**

The saleslady will wait (*for, on*) you next.
> **on**

The two plans are at variance (*against, with*) each other.
> **with**

The group arrived prior (*of, to*) the first address.
> **to**

No one can reason (*on, with*) Anthony (*about, on*) the revised itinerary.
> **with**
> **about**

Does he have a reason (*by, for*) objecting?
>   **for**

The student was rewarded (*by, from*) the dean.
>   **by**

Many delegates abstained (*from, on*) voting.
>   **from**

You must separate the good (*and, from*) the bad.
>   **from**

If you are ill, you must stay (*at, in*) home.
>   **at**

The thief tampered (*on, with*) the lock.
>   **with**

What do you infer (*by, from*) his comment?
>   **from**

The secretary is in search (*for, of*) an eraser.
>   **of**

What kind (*of, of a*) story is this one?
>   **of**

He lives (*at, on*) Front Street.
>   **on**

His firm has a monopoly (*of, on*) sales in that territory.
>   **of**

Mary was overcome (*by, with*) the heat.
>   **by**

I prefer the red one (*over, to*) the blue one.
>   **to**

The student is proficient (*at, in*) music.
>   **in**

The soldier was rewarded (*about, for*) his bravery.
>   **for**

He spoke (*to, with*) me about the problem.
with

The new product is superior (*over, to*) the old one.
to

This book does not treat (*of, on*) atomic energy.
of

The student will vie (*against, with*) his classmates for honors.
with

This act is worthy (*for, of*) praise.
of

He studied Shakespeare preparatory (*of, to*) seeing *Hamlet*.
to

One should profit (*by, from*) his mistakes.
from

Red hair is peculiar (*in, to*) that family.
to

He is unmindful (*about, of*) all the chances for error.
of

Did you comply (*to, with*) his request?
with

The evidence will absolve him (*from, of*) suspicion.
of

Do the work in accordance (*to, with*) the instructions.
with

Was he accused (*of, with*) the crime?
of

Jane is adept (*at, in*) music.
in

A politician is usually averse (*of, to*) criticism.
to

Mother was apprehensive (*about, of*) the danger.
>**of**

The professor is a supposed authority (*about, on*) linguistics.
>**on**

I concur (*in, with*) that proposal.
>**in**

This book is different (*from, than*) the other one.
>**from**

Should he be acquitted (*from, of*) the accusation?
>**of**

Everyone was disappointed (*in, with*) the quality of the new material.
>**in**

We were glad (*for, of*) the opportunity to hear him speak.
>**of**

Many students showed hatred (*for, of*) prejudices.
>**for**

The missionary died (*from, of*) his injuries.
>**of**

Was he impatient (*at, with*) me?
>**with**

Two new members were initiated (*in, into*) the club.

>**into**

Postponed Prepositions

You should be alert for postponed prepositions. A *postponed preposition* is one that patterns *after* its object. In the following sentences, the postponed preposition is in italics, and its object is in bold print:

The danger **that** I was warning you *about* is very real.
The situation **which** he has got himself *into* is very embarrassing.
What do you suppose he's *up to*?

Up to may be construed as a two-part preposition, discussed earlier in this section.

Such *postponed prepositions* are frowned upon by many speakers and writers, and you should exercise caution in using them. However, in informal English and in general speaking situations, postponed prepositions seem totally appropriate. The first sentence below is acceptable in *informal* situations; the second sentence seems somewhat inappropriate in informal settings. However, in *formal* situations, just the reverse is true:

Informal: She is the person that I told you about.
Formal: She is the person about whom I told you.
Informal: From now on, ending a sentence with a preposition is something I will not put up with.
Formal: From now on, ending a sentence with a preposition is something up with which I will not put.

In some sentence constructions, the object of the preposition may be absent, as in the following:

She is nearly impossible to get along *with*.

This, of course, is a perfectly acceptable sentence. Recasting it to provide an object of the preposition would result in a sentence similar to this:

To get along *with* **her** is nearly impossible.

But this sentence, you must agree, does not convey the same message the one before it conveys. Postponed prepositions such as in the preceding should be used without fear of censure, despite the strong prejudice that has developed against such uses in formal English. That said, patterns such as those in the following sentences should be avoided, even in most informal situations, because the preposition is superfluous:

Where is the book *at*?
Where is that group going *to*?
The game is over *with*.

In situations involving postponed prepositions, a writer or speaker must choose between strictly formal English—and thus sounding awkward or stilted (or even affectatious)—and less-formal English—and thus sounding somewhat more natural. In these and many other instances, the situations must dictate the standards.

Prepositions and Compound Objects

A real problem for many people is the use of compound objects of the preposition. Basically, the matter is quite simple: Both objects are in the objective case. In the following sentence, the pronouns used as objects of the preposition are in the proper case—the objective case:

We knew the dean was referring to *him* and *me*.

Difficulties seem to arise, however, when the first object of the preposition is a noun and the second is a pronoun, as in this sentence:

We knew the dean was referring to *Jake* and *me*.

The tendency in this case is to use the nominative case for the second object of the preposition:

Incorrect: The judge awarded the prize to Sally and *I*.

To avoid this pesky error, you need only to make two sentences of the one, each having a different object of the preposition:

The judge awarded the prize to *Sally*.
The judge awarded the prize to *me*.

Now that the correct forms are obvious, the two objects may be used together in one prepositional phrase:

Correct: The judge awarded the prize to *Sally* and *me*.

Recognizing Prepositions and Objects of Prepositions

After each of the following sentences, you'll find listed prepositions in that sentence, the object of each preposition, and the word modified by each prepositional phrase:

We looked into the garage and saw a car with stainless-steel wheels.
  into: garage, looked
  with: wheels, car

You should never buy a pig in a poke.
  in: poke, pig

In this class, you cannot pass a test without studying.
  in: class, pass
  without: studying, pass

Abdul found a ruler in the desk at which he was sitting today.
  in: desk, found (this prepositional phrase extends from *in* to the end of the sentence)
  at: which, desk

The hawk in the tree was calling to its mate.
> **in:** tree, hawk
> **to:** mate, calling

In the back of this text, you will find answers to the problems.
> **in:** back, find (this prepositional phrase is actually a combination of all the words from *in* to *text*)
> **of:** text, back
> **to:** problems, answers

The shirt with the green trim appeals to me.
> **with:** trim, shirt
> **to:** me, appeals

When you go to the store, try to find some fresh asparagus.
> **to:** store, go (*to find* is an infinitive phrase, not a prepositional phrase)

"Elegy for Jane" by Theodore Roethke is a poignant poem.
> **for:** Jane, elegy
> **by:** Theodore Roethke, "Elegy for Jane"

For Whom the Bell Tolls is one of Hemingway's best novels.
> **for:** whom, tolls
> **of:** novels, one

Ashley was walking to the store when the rain began to fall.
> **to:** store, walking

Pedro bought a new truck for hauling his farm produce.
> **for:** hauling, truck

The dog with the white paws is named Jake.
> **with:** paws, dog

Felix is the person about whom I was complaining.
> **about:** whom, person

You should never play with a loaded gun.
> **with:** gun, play

CONJUNCTIONS

Conjunctions, like prepositions, are "connectives," joining word groups to the rest of the sentence. Although prepositions have a rather restricted distribution in that they exist solely in a phrase and usually connect the object of the preposition (usually a noun or pronoun) to the sentence, conjunctions may join single words, phrases, or clauses to the rest of the sentence. Several types of conjunctions and their uses are shown in the following sentences:

Carlos *and* James went fishing yesterday.
  (The conjunction joins single words.)

We invited the neighbors *and* their friends to the party.
  (The conjunction joins groups of words.)

Sally did her assignment, *but* Carl went fishing.
  (The conjunction joins independent clauses.)

> An *independent clause* is, essentially, a sentence; that is, although it lacks the capitalization and punctuation of a sentence, it can stand alone, grammatically speaking. You learn more about this and other types of clauses in Part II in the section titled "Clauses."

We didn't go to the picnic *because* we were tired.
  (The conjunction joins a dependent clause to the sentence.)

Neither the parents *nor* the students expected school to be dismissed early today.
  (The two-part conjunction joins word groups.)

A few *adverbial conjunctions,* such as the following, serve to connect independent clauses:

however
nevertheless
moreover
then
therefore
thus
consequently

Here are two examples of adverbial conjunctions in use:

The rain fell all day; *however,* we enjoyed the reunion.
We lost our money; *consequently,* we had to return home.

Categories of Conjunctions

Although conjunctions may be classified in a number of categories and subcategories, we need to examine only three major categories:

- Coordinating conjunctions
- Subordinating conjunctions
- Correlative conjunctions

Coordinating Conjunctions

Coordinating conjunctions connect elements of equal rank in the sentence. The sentence elements may be single words, phrases, or clauses. The seven coordinating conjunctions may be remembered by forming the words *boy fans* or *fan boys* with their initials:

but
or
yet
for
and
nor
so

The coordinating conjunctions are in italics in the sentences that follow. The elements joined by the conjunctions are identified within the parentheses after the sentence:

The dog *and* cat were sleeping peacefully. (words)
She enjoys jogging *but* not swimming. (words)
We were lost, *for* we had never been on this trail before. (independent clauses)
Hoping to earn money *and* to save for school, Einer searched for a summer job. (infinitive phrases)
He knew I was right, *yet* he continued to argue. (independent clauses)

If coordinating conjunctions join pronouns being used as the same part of the sentence, the pronouns must be in the same case:

Incorrect: Sue and *me* went to the concert.
Correct: Sue and *I* went to the concert.

The word *but* is often used as both coordinating conjunction and preposition. If the meaning of *but* is "except," it is used as a preposition:

Conjunction: Mike went to the game, ***but*** I did not.
Preposition: Everyone ***but*** me went to the game. (*But* means "except" in this sentence.)

Use coordinating conjunctions to join grammatical units that are parallel in form. For instance, do not mix words and phrases or different kinds of phrases:

Incorrect: He liked *skiing, swimming,* and *to hike.*
Correct: He liked *skiing, swimming,* and *hiking.*
Incorrect: He liked *to hike* and *swimming* in the lake.
Correct: He liked to hike in the forest and to swim in the lake.

Subordinating Conjunctions

Subordinating conjunctions connect two *clauses* of unequal rank. They begin dependent clauses (usually adverb clauses) and show the relationship of those dependent clauses to the independent clauses of which they are a part. Some of the subordinating conjunctions are the following:

if
because
after
since
when
while
until
unless
although
for (meaning "because")
wherever
than
till
as

Some relative pronouns also function as subordinating conjunctions:

who
whom
whose
which
what
that

In the following sentences, the dependent clauses are in italics and the subordinating conjunctions are in bold print:

While *I was in Texas,* my motorcycle was stolen.
You'll regret your actions **if** *you waste your money.*
The audience waited for the speaker **until** *it grew weary.*
I watched Carl, **whose** *presence upset me.* (In this sentence, the dependent clause is also a relative clause.)
Because *few students elected to take them,* the courses were canceled.

Correlative Conjunctions

Correlative conjunctions function like the other conjunctions. They are distinct from the others, however, in that they pattern in pairs (hence *co,* as in "co-captains," plus *relative,* meaning "related"). The correlative conjunctions are the following:

either . . . or
neither . . . nor
whether . . . or
both . . . and
not only . . . but also

Notice how the correlative conjunctions are used in the following two sentences:

Either you'll clean your equipment *or* you'll have to stay in camp.
Both Nancy *and* John were eager for the play to begin.

Repeat the second *as* when using the correlative conjunction in making comparisons:

Incorrect: A cat is *as* quick, if not quicker than a fox.
Correct: A cat is *as* quick *as,* if not quicker than a fox.

Use *nor,* not *or,* after negative words in conjunctions showing comparisons:

Incorrect: The apartment was *neither* clean *or* furnished.
Correct: The apartment was *neither* clean *nor* furnished.

Recognizing the Various Types of Conjunctions

The following sentences contain examples of various types of conjunctions:

I really wish that I could help you, but I simply cannot.
    but: coordinating

Forget me, because you'll never see me again.
    because: subordinating

The store was closed because the fire destroyed the building.
because: subordinating

If you care to help, I'll assign a task to you.
if: subordinating

Friends and neighbors should respect one another.
and: coordinating

Neither Jane nor Sue had finished the assignment by midnight.
neither . . . nor: correlative

We drank lemonade while we waited for the eclipse.
while: subordinating

Do not leave the building until I give the signal.
until: subordinating

Both Pete and Phil were graduated with honors.
both . . . and: correlative

They complained when they had good reason for doing so.
when: subordinating

The teachers as well as the students enjoyed the demonstration.
as . . . as: correlative

The chairman was reinstated; therefore, it will be business as usual when we meet on Monday.
therefore: adverbial
when: subordinating

Whose house this is I think I know.
whose: subordinating (*Whose* is a relative pronoun serving as a subordinating conjunction.)

You may not leave until the bell rings.
until: subordinating

Whether we win or lose, we'll have played an exciting game.
whether . . . or: correlative

Since you are leaving anyway, take these books to the library.
since: subordinating

Conjunctions and Usage

A few rules govern the use of conjunctions:

- Be careful to use only conjunctions where conjunctions are called for:

  Incorrect: *Except* you pay your bill, you will receive no more credit.
  Correct: *Unless* you pay your bill, you will receive no more credit.

- *Like* should be used as a preposition and not as a conjunction in formal writing:

  Incorrect: We feel *like* we belong here.
  Correct: We feel *as if* we belong here.
  Correct: We feel *that* we belong here.

- Do not use the conjunction *and* before the Latin abbreviation *etc. Etc.* means "and so forth"; therefore, saying "and etcetera" is the equivalent of saying "and and so forth."

- Use *that* before a clause that follows a verb expressing *saying, thinking,* or *feeling.* Avoid pairing it with the preposition *like*:

  Incorrect: The coach feels *like that* we should win this game.
  Correct: The coach feels *that* we should win this game.

- Use *when* after constructions employing *hardly* or *scarcely*:

  Correct: We had hardly arrived *when* the rain began falling.

- In sentences expressing "reason" or "purpose," use *so that* rather than *so* alone:

  Incorrect: We walked *so* we could get some exercise.
  Correct: We walked *so that* we could get some exercise.

- In formal writing or speaking, use *whether,* not *if* to express uncertainty:

  Incorrect: We did not know *if* the professor was coming.
  Correct: We did not know ***whether*** the professor was coming.

  Some writers and speakers maintain that *or not* should always be used after *whether*:

  We did not know *whether or not* the professor was coming to class today.

  Usage is divided on this matter. If you have any doubts about this phrase, include *or not.*

- Use *where* to refer to location. Do not use *where* to mean *that*:

  Incorrect: I read in *TIME where* Congress passed a new law.
  Correct: I read in *TIME that* Congress passed a new law.

INTERJECTIONS

An *interjection* is a word or phrase "injected" into a sentence to express strong feeling or sudden emotion. Because the interjection is not grammatically related to the sentence or any word in a sentence, it is not a true part of speech. In fact, interjections are sometimes used as complete sentences, and often a complete sentence is implied when an interjection is an element attached to independent clauses. The words in italics in the following sentences are interjections:

Ouch! I cut my finger.
Oh! This water is too hot.
Damn! The tire is flat again.
Fine—then I'll do it myself!
Well, what do you have to say for yourself?
Duck! They're throwing acorns at us again.

The interjection *duck* has the meaning of the sentence, "(You) duck your head."

O versus *Oh*

O is an interjection. It is used in very formal direct address, is always capitalized, and is never followed by a mark of punctuation:

O Great Spirit, hear now our prayers.
O wild West Wind, thou breath of Autumn's being . . .

Oh expresses a wish, grief, pain, or surprise and is always followed by a comma or exclamation mark:

Oh, how I wish this semester would end.
Oh, I suppose I'll just stay at home tonight.

Recognizing Interjections

The following sentences contain examples of interjections:

"Help! I'm falling," shouted the skydiver as he leaped from the plane.
    help

Oh, I suppose I could give you the money, since I owe it to you.
    oh

Fine! Just fine! You've ruined the painting.
    fine
    just fine

Work and sleep, sleep and work—shucks, that's all we ever do.
    shucks

Hey, where are the apples and oranges that I brought?
    hey

Well, nobody's perfect; but I'm nearly so.
> **well**

Wow, did you see that crater where the meteor hit the earth?
> **wow**

So! You've been sneaking around behind my back, have you?
> **so**
>
> **have you** (*Have you* is an idiomatic expression used as a means of converting a preceding statement into a question; but, as you can see, it does not have a direct grammatical relationship to the independent clause that precedes it.)

GENERAL OBSERVATIONS ABOUT FUNCTION WORDS

- Unlike content words, such as nouns, verbs, adjectives, and adverbs, *function words,* also called *structure words,* are words that have a grammatical (syntactic) role in a sentence or clause as opposed to a lexical (semantic) meaning. Function words include
  - ◆ Determiners
  - ◆ Prepositions
  - ◆ Conjunctions
  - ◆ Interjections
  - ◆ Auxiliary verbs

- A *determiner* is a word that limits the potential referent of a noun phrase.
- A *preposition* is a word or, in some instances, a word group that relates one sentence element (the *object of the preposition*) to another sentence element.
- Because a preposition must have an object, the preposition and the object of the preposition and any modifiers that pattern with them constitute a *prepositional phrase.*
- One popular way of remembering these prepositional relationships is by remembering this statement: Anywhere a mouse can go, a preposition can go.

- Prepositions often have the same form as adverbs; however, adverbs can be distinguished from prepositions by the fact that adverbs do not pattern with objects.
- For the purposes of this text, only three types of prepositions need be identified:
  - **Simple:** A *simple preposition* is made up of either a simple or a compound word: *up, down, in, into, from, to, with, inside, around, before, upon, along, without,* and so on.
  - **Participial:** A *participial preposition* takes the *ing* form of certain verbs such as *assuming, beginning, barring, considering, following, including, involving, regarding,* and a few others.
  - **Phrasal:** A *phrasal preposition* is a unit of two or more words serving as a single preposition (these types of prepositions are also called *compound prepositions*). Often the phrasal preposition is itself a prepositional phrase.
- Words that are used as prepositions or as single-word adverbs are sometimes linked to verbs to form *verb-adverbial composites* (VACs).
- *Two-* or *three-part preposition*s consist of words such as *together, due, as,* and other words followed by a word that is easily recognized as a preposition.
- The English language employs many expressions that require certain prepositions to show proper relationships. These expressions are, in a sense, peculiar to themselves because of the sometimes seemingly elusive meaning of the preposition.
- A *postponed preposition* is one that patterns after its object.
- When compound objects of the preposition are used, both objects are in the objective case.
- *Conjunctions*, like prepositions, are "connectives," joining word groups to the rest of the sentence.
- Although prepositions have a rather restricted distribution in that they exist solely in a phrase and usually connect the object of the preposition (usually a noun or pronoun) to the sentence, conjunctions may join single words, phrases, or clauses to the rest of the sentence.

- Although conjunctions may be classified in a number of categories and subcategories, we need to examine only three major categories:

  - **Coordinating conjunctions:** *Coordinating conjunctions* connect elements of equal rank in the sentence. The sentence elements may be single words, phrases, or clauses.
  - **Subordinating conjunctions:** *Subordinating conjunctions* connect two *clauses* of unequal rank. They begin dependent clauses (usually adverb clauses) and show the relationship of those dependent clauses to the independent clauses of which they are a part.
  - **Correlative conjunctions:** *Correlative conjunctions* function like the other conjunctions. They are distinct from the others, however, in that they pattern in pairs.

- An *interjection* is a word or phrase "injected" into a sentence to express strong feeling or sudden emotion.
- Because the interjection is not grammatically related to the sentence or any word in a sentence, it is not a true part of speech. In fact, interjections are sometimes used as complete sentences, and often a complete sentence is implied when an interjection is an element attached to independent clauses.

SENTENCE ELEMENTS

The word *grammar* is often used synonymously with the word *syntax*, that is, the way in which words are put together to form phrases, clauses, and sentences. The relationship among words, phrases, clauses, and sentences is a hierarchical one:

- One or more clauses comprise a sentence.
- One or more phrases comprise a clause.
- One or more words comprise a phrase.

Phrases and clauses are relatively easy to define. A *phrase* is a group of words that, together, function as a part of speech (noun, verb, adjective, adverb, preposition, and so on). A *clause* is a sentence or sentence-like construction within another sentence.

 You'll learn more about phrases and clauses later in this part, in the sections titled "Phrases" and "Clauses," respectively.

Sentences are a little more difficult to define; various texts define *sentence* in different ways. The usual definition identifies a sentence as "a group of words containing a subject and predicate and expressing a complete thought."

 A *subject* is a sentence element that represents a person or thing of which something is said. For example, in the sentence, "Alexia began taking ballet lessons at the age of five," *Alexia* is the subject of the sentence; it is being said of her that she "began taking ballet lessons at the age of five." A subject may be a noun, pronoun, or noun phrase, and normally appears before the verb in a sentence. Subjects are covered in more detail later in this part in the section titled "Subjects and Predicates."

 The *predicate* of a sentence makes an assertion or a denial about the subject of that sentence; that is, it represents what is said about the sentence's subject. For example, in the sentence, "Cammy gave up skiing to become a champion snowboarder," *Cammy* is the subject, and "gave up skiing to become a champion snowboarder" is the predicate. Predicates are covered in more detail later in this part in the section titled "Subjects and Predicates."

A standard definition of *sentence* may also include statements about "understood" subjects and predicates. This type of definition is often followed by further explanations of how such constructions as the following are sentences, even though one or more elements seem to be missing:

Stop!
Yes.
John.

The explanation usually given is that parts of the sentence that appear to be missing are really present and "understood"; that is, we can read the sentences above as something similar to the following:

(You must) stop!
Yes, (I agree with you.)
John (is the person).

Readings of the preceding sentences, then, demonstrate that all of them have both subjects and predicates, elements that nearly all grammarians agree that sentences must have. Likewise, nearly all grammarians and others would agree that the following word groups are sentences:

She is in the backyard.
The dog dragged it away.
That color is my favorite color.

These three sentences, however, present problems: Something is obviously missing. Who is the "she" in the first sentence? What is the "it" in the second sentence? What color is "my favorite color" in the third sentence? In other words, how can one logically declare that these three sentences express complete thoughts? Logically, of course, one can't, which seems to nullify the definition of sentence given earlier.

Ironically, we all know what a sentence is; we just have trouble verbalizing what we know. Here's a definition. See how this relates to what you know about sentences:

A *sentence* is a grammatical unit of language, which is recognized by speakers as having relative independence of meaning, which conveys a complete idea or question, and which has a definite beginning and ending.

Much of this definition is, of course, similar to the earlier one; however, *sentence* is defined as a grammatical unit of language, which it certainly is, and as having "relative independence," a phrase meaning that it is moveable—perhaps within the paragraph—without sacrificing its meaning. Further, native speakers of a language recognize the boundaries of a sentence by voice patterns (*intonation contours*), which are represented in writing (*orthography*) by capital letters and periods or other end marks.

This leaves the matter of a sentence's expressing a "complete idea" still unresolved. However, as long as a sentence has only "relative independence," the definition will suffice. Total independence cannot be achieved by any sentence employing pronouns or other words dependent upon previous words for meaning. If the listener understands the antecedent of the word "she" in the sentence, "She is in the backyard," and knows the meaning of the phrase "in the backyard," he or she should have little difficulty comprehending the meaning of the sentence. Any sentence can be seen, then, to be related to other sentences in some way; or, as the definition suggests, they are units of language, not entities existing in isolation.

Types of Sentences

A sentence is classified as being of one of the following basic types:

- Simple
- Complex
- Compound

In addition to being called simple, complex, or compound, sentences are also categorized according to their primary function:

- Declarative
- Interrogative
- Imperative
- Exclamatory

SIMPLE SENTENCES

A *simple sentence* is a sentence that consists of one main clause, with no coordinate or subordinate clause:

> Lloyd and Evelyn went to the World's Fair.
> Sue is an avid knitter.
> Jay negotiates well.
> My sister-in-law teaches at a private school.

 The various types of clauses are discussed in more detail later in this part, under the heading "Clauses."

COMPLEX SENTENCES

A complex sentence contains one main clause; embedded in that main clause are one or more dependent clauses:

> Any woman who has delivered a baby knows that labor is no walk in the park. *(Labor is no walk in the park* is a dependent clause functioning as a direct object; the main clause is *Any woman who has delivered a baby knows that.*)

COMPOUND SENTENCES

Compound sentences contain multiple main clauses, which are often linked by a coordinating conjunction (*but*, *and*, and so on). These should always be separated by a comma; alternatively, a semicolon may be used to unite the two clauses. Clauses may also be linked with a conjunct, such as *however*, *therefore*, and the like.

> Bethany cut grass, and Helena raked the leaves.
> Murgatroyd writes the letters; Chelsea licks the envelopes.
> I paid a fortune to furnish my apartment; however, I did not like the results.

 In addition to simple compound sentences, such as the ones listed above, there are compound-complex sentences, in which at least one of the main clauses contains one or more dependent clauses (shown in italics below):

> Cycling in Boulder is fantastic; *since I started living there five years ago,* I've logged thousands of miles.
> My visit to Jamaica was relaxing; everyone knows that *Jamaicans are laid back.*

DECLARATIVE SENTENCES

A *declarative sentence* (also called a *declarative*) is one whose primary role is to make a statement. The following sentences are examples of declaratives:

> Edwina drives race cars for a living.
> Dogs dislike fleas.
> My favorite movie is *Rocky.*

INTERROGATIVE SENTENCES

The primary role of the interrogative sentence is to ask a question:

> Will we arrive soon?
> Has Victor ever visited Las Vegas?
> Do you prefer wine or beer?

IMPERATIVE SENTENCES

An imperative sentence is one that gives an order or issues a command:

Stand up.
Walk this way.
Stop immediately.

EXCLAMATORY SENTENCES

Exclamatory sentences convey a strong emotion. These types of sentences, which often contain no verb, sometimes consist of the word *what* or *how* followed by a noun phrase.

How wonderful you look!
Please go!
What big eyes you have!

GENERAL OBSERVATIONS ABOUT TYPES OF SENTENCES

- A sentence is classified as being of one of the following types:
  - **Simple:** A *simple sentence* is a sentence that consists of one main clause, with no coordinate or dependent clause.
  - **Complex:** A *complex sentence* contains one main clause; embedded in that main clause are one or more dependent clauses.
  - **Compound:** *Compound sentences* contain multiple main clauses, which are often linked by a coordinating conjunction (*but*, *and*, and so on). Alternatively, a semicolon may be used to unite the two clauses. Clauses may also be linked with a conjunct, such as *however*, *therefore*, and the like.
- In addition to being called simple, complex, or compound, sentences are also categorized according to their primary function:
  - **Declarative:** A *declarative sentence* (also called a *declarative*) is one whose primary role is to make a statement.
  - **Interrogative:** The primary role of the *interrogative sentence* is to ask a question.
  - **Imperative:** An *imperative sentence* is one that gives an order or issues a command.
  - **Exclamatory:** *Exclamatory sentences* convey a strong emotion. These types of sentences, which often contain no verb, sometimes consist of the word *what* or *how* followed by a noun phrase.

Sentence Patterns

One recent approach to understanding English sentences asks you to recognize the various patterns upon which English sentences are based. Fortunately for students of English grammar, you need to concern yourself with only nine basic patterns. These basic sentence patterns are combined in various ways to generate (or construct) longer sentences. But no matter how long a sentence is, it is still based on one pattern, or a combination of two or more basic patterns. It follows, then, that if you learn to recognize these patterns (you already *know* them; you use them in your speech), you will more easily and quickly grasp the basics of the English sentence. Here, in simplified form, are the nine basic patterns of the English sentence:

- **Pattern 1:** Noun + Verb$_{to\ be}$ + Adjective

  The grass is green.

- **Pattern 2:** Noun + Verb$_{to\ be}$ + Adverb

  My bedroom was upstairs.

  The single-word adverb in this sentence pattern may be replaced by a prepositional phrase with a "there" or "then" meaning, as in this sentence:

  Mother was *in the garden.*

- **Pattern 3:** Noun$_1$ + Verb$_{to\ be}$ + Noun$_1$

  Some dogs are good hunters.

- **Pattern 4:** Noun + Intransitive Verb

  The shadows deepened.

- **Pattern 5:** Noun$_1$ + Transitive Verb + Noun$_2$

  The cat caught the mouse.

- **Pattern 6:** Noun$_1$ + Transitive Verb + Noun$_2$ + Noun$_3$

  My brother gave his wife some flowers.

  or

  Noun$_1$ + Transitive Verb + Noun$_2$ + *to* + Noun$_3$

  My brother gave some flowers to his wife.

- **Pattern 7:** Noun$_1$ + Transitive Verb + Noun$_2$ + X, wherein X equals any one of several possibilities:

    - Another noun or a pronoun

        We elected Mabel president.

    - An adjective

        They considered Sam handsome.

    - A pronoun

        The FBI thought Jerry me.

    - An adverb of place

        We imagined him downstairs.

    - Verb, present participle

        We found the child crying.

    - Verb, past participle

        The boys found their clothes pressed.

    - Prepositional phrase

        They considered him in their way.

    - Infinitive phrase with *to be*

        Everyone considered Ella to be a friend.

    In the Pattern 7 sentence (Noun$_1$ + Transitive Verb + Noun$_2$ + X), the X may also represent a combination of sentence elements, such as a verb *and* a prepositional phrase.

- **Pattern 8:** Noun + Linking Verb + Adjective

    The milk smells bad.

- **Pattern 9:** Noun + Linking Verb + Noun$_2$

    Marie remained president until the election.

PATTERNS 1, 2, AND 3: SENTENCES WITH THE VERB *TO BE*

Students of English grammar must be familiar with the various forms of the verb *to be*. They are the following:

be
been
am
are
is
was
were

Most basic grammar books describe how these forms of the verb pattern with *has* and *have*—in other words, these books show the *conjugation* of the verb *to be*. But for purposes of this book, you need only to recognize sentences with *to be* as the main predicate (verb). Here are examples of sentences with patterns discussed earlier in this part (patterns 1, 2, and 3):

Noun$_1$ + Verb$_{to be}$ + __
    These apples are delicious. (Noun + Verb$_{to be}$ + Adjective)
    The dog is outside. (Noun + Verb$_{to be}$ + Adverb)
    That woman is a senator. (Noun$_1$ + Verb$_{to be}$ + Noun$_1$)
        (The subscript numerals indicate that *woman* and *senator* refer to
        the same entity, in this case, the woman who is the senator.)

Of course, more elements may be added to the sentences; but no matter how many elements are added, the basic pattern remains the same. Note this sentence:

The old steer with the crooked horn was really mean.

The pattern is still Noun (steer) + Verb$_{to be}$ (was) + Adjective (mean).

To determine whether a confusing sentence may be a pattern 1 or a pattern 2, insert the word *very* before the third element. If the sentence seems natural, it is probably a pattern 1 sentence. If it seems unnatural, it is probably a pattern 2 sentence:

The sky is (very) blue today. (pattern 1: Noun + Verb$_{to be}$ + Adjective)
The baby is (very) outside this afternoon. (pattern 2: Noun + Verb$_{to be}$ + Adverb)

Sometimes a sentence may have a "there" or "then" phrase that takes the place of the single-word adverb; however, the sentence pattern remains Noun$_1$ + Verb$_{to be}$ + Adverb:

The old books were *in the attic.* (there)
The meeting will be *at 6 o'clock.* (then)

PATTERNS 8 AND 9: SENTENCES WITH LINKING VERBS

Linking verbs are similar to the verb *to be* in that they show a relationship between an element in the predicate and the subject of the sentence. They do not, however, convey action from one to the other as transitive verbs do, nor do they show a subject in action as intransitive verbs do. Many of the linking verbs relate to the senses, such as the following:

smell
look
taste
appear

Refer to the section titled "Linking Verbs" in Part I, "Parts of Speech," for more information about linking verbs.

Examine the linking verbs in these sentences:

Noun$_1$ + Linking Verb + __
This food *smells* bad. (Noun + Linking Verb + Adjective)
The smaller fighter *appeared* winner of the bout. (Noun$_1$ + Linking Verb + Noun$_1$)
The workers *look* tired. (Noun + Linking Verb + Adjective)

Notice that these verbs, unlike the verb *to be*, do not make the same type of positive assertions about the subjects of the sentences. Whereas the verb *to be* states that the subject *is* in a certain state or condition, linking verbs *suggest* that relationship but affirm another—appearance, odor, taste, sound, and so on. Compare these pairs of sentences, the first with the verb *to be* and the second with a linking verb:

The stew *was* good. (Noun + Verb$_{to be}$ + Adjective)
The stew *looked* good. (Noun + Linking Verb + Adjective)

The sergeant *is* the leader of the troops. (Noun$_1$ + Verb$_{to be}$ + Noun$_1$)
The sergeant *appears* leader of the troops. (Noun$_1$ + Linking Verb + Noun$_1$)

Obviously, you can easily detect whether or not a sentence has the verb *to be* as its main predicate. Likewise, you can quickly determine whether or not a sentence has a linking verb as its predicate. If the verb in question can be replaced by a form of the verb *to be*, it is probably a linking verb. Likewise, any verb that may be substituted for *seems* in a sentence such as "These boards *seem* rotten" without varying the meaning of the sentence is probably a linking verb.

A variety of linking verbs exists in English, some not often considered to be linking verbs. Some common ones are the following:

grow
remain
taste
feel
sound
smell
get
continue
become
go

Other linking verbs sometimes not understood to be linking verbs are these:

worked
stood
went
ran
proved

Notice these sentences:

The knot in my shoelace *worked* loose.
The crowd *grew* tired of waiting for the speaker.
The horses *went* wild at the sight of the lion.
The well *ran* dry from the lack of rain this spring.
The gunman *proved* true to the code of the West.

You should be careful when working with sentences containing these kinds of linking verbs so that you don't confuse them with pattern-4 sentences, Noun + Intransitive Verb, as in these sentences:

The carpenter *worked* slowly and carefully.
The children *grew* quickly.
The dog *went* into the woods.

These three sentences do not have an adjective following the verb, unlike the preceding five sentences, which do. Note, too, that the verbs in these sentences can't be replaced by a form of the verb *to be* and still make sense.

In all of the preceding sentences containing linking verbs, the linking verbs relate the subject to a *predicate adjective* (an adjective in the predicate that modifies the subject of the verb). A few linking verbs may relate a predicate noun to the subject of the verb in the same way, as in these sentences:

My uncle *remained* sheriff until the election. (Noun$_1$ + Linking Verb + Noun$_1$)
Elizabeth *became* an ambassador to Iceland.
The boys *stayed* close friends until graduation.
Books *make* fine gifts for college students.

Again, you should not mistake sentences of this pattern with sentences of a different pattern:

The governor *stayed* the execution until midnight.
Don't *make* a mess on the clean floor.

UNDERSTANDING SENTENCE PATTERNS

Each sentence in this section is followed by its associated sentence pattern:

That rifle is certainly an antique.
Pattern 3 (Noun$_1$ + Verb$_{\text{to be}}$ + Noun$_1$)

Bake those cookies a nice golden brown.
Pattern 7 ([Noun$_1$] + Transitive Verb + Noun$_2$ + Adjective)

The sailor gave the scouts a lesson in knot tying.
Pattern 6 (Noun$_1$ + Transitive Verb + Noun$_2$ + Noun$_3$)

The baby played outside nearly all day.
Pattern 4 (Noun$_1$ + Intransitive Verb)

The crew paved the road all the way to Elm Street.
Pattern 5 (Noun$_1$ + Transitive Verb + Noun$_2$)

The senator declared the charges totally false.
Pattern 7 (Noun$_1$ + Transitive Verb + Noun$_2$ + Adjective)

Some birds are excellent fishers.
Pattern 3 (Noun$_1$ + Verb$_{\text{to be}}$ + Noun$_1$)

That board is too long to be of any use.
Pattern 1 (Noun$_1$ + Verb$_{\text{to be}}$ + Adjective)

The bridge appeared too weak to hold us all.
Pattern 8 (Noun$_1$ + Linking Verb + Adjective)

The rescuers found the survivors disoriented.
Pattern 7 (Noun$_1$ + Transitive Verb + Noun$_2$ + Adjective)

The door came loose during the heavy wind.
Pattern 1 (Noun$_1$ + Verb$_{\text{to be}}$ + Adjective)

We found the kite torn by the branches of the tree.
Pattern 7 (Noun$_1$ + Transitive Verb + Noun$_2$ + Verb + Prepositional Phrase)

From a distance, we thought Jerry him.
Pattern 7 (Noun$_1$ + Transitive Verb + Noun$_2$ + Pronoun)

Give the quarterback the ball.
Pattern 6 ([Noun$_1$] + Transitive Verb + Noun$_2$ + Noun$_3$)

We are the world.
Pattern 3 (Noun$_1$ + Verb$_{\text{to be}}$ + Noun$_1$)

We found the puppy under the back porch.
Pattern 5 (Noun$_1$ + Transitive Verb + Noun$_2$)

The cat's basket is in the cellar.
Pattern 2 (Noun$_1$ + Verb$_{\text{to be}}$ + Adverb)

We found Marie an apartment for the semester.
Pattern 6 (Noun$_1$ + Transitive Verb + Noun$_2$ + Noun$_3$)

They discovered the visitors to be charlatans.
Pattern 7 (Noun$_1$ + Transitive Verb + Noun$_2$ + Infinitive Phrase with *to be*)

The minister gave the congregation a stern sermon.
Pattern 6 (Noun$_1$ + Transitive Verb + Noun$_2$ + Noun$_3$)

The milk in the carton smells sour to me.
Pattern 8 (Noun$_1$ + Linking Verb + Adjective)

The flowers seemed a virtual rainbow of colors.
Pattern 9 (Noun$_1$ + Linking Verb + Noun$_1$)

My neighbor gave my little brother a summer job.
Pattern 6 (Noun$_1$ + Transitive Verb + Noun$_2$ + Noun$_3$)

We found the president unresponsive to our request.
Pattern 7 (Noun$_1$ + Transitive Verb + Noun$_2$ + Adjective)

The rescuers heard the victim sobbing.
Pattern 7 (Noun$_1$ + Transitive Verb + Noun$_2$ + Present Participle)

The chairman was the only dissenting speaker.
Pattern 3 (Noun$_1$ + Verb$_{to be}$ + Noun$_1$)

The club members made Richard sergeant-at-arms.
Pattern 7 (Noun$_1$ + Transitive Verb + Noun$_2$ + Noun$_2$)

They thought him sufficiently competent.
Pattern 7 (Noun$_1$ + Transitive Verb + Noun$_2$ + Adjective)

The coach found the team members depressed about the loss.
Pattern 7 (Noun$_1$ + Transitive Verb + Noun$_2$ + Past Participle)

Fortunately, we saved some money for the trip home.
Pattern 7 (Noun$_1$ + Transitive Verb + Noun$_2$ + Prepositional Phrase)

The witness appeared frightened of the jury.
Pattern 8 (Noun$_1$ + Linking Verb + Adjective)

The suspect lied to the police.
Pattern 4 (Noun$_1$ + Intransitive Verb)

Some books are really difficult to read.
Pattern 1 (Noun$_1$ + Verb$_{to be}$ + Adjective)

Generally, students are people who are intellectually curious.
Pattern 3 (Noun$_1$ + Verb$_{to be}$ + Noun$_1$)

All the wedding guests were downstairs.
Pattern 2 (Noun$_1$ + Verb$_{to be}$ + Adverb)

Few people are natural leaders.
Pattern 3 (Noun$_1$ + Verb$_{to be}$ + Noun$_1$)

All the little kittens were in the old barn.
Pattern 2 (Noun$_1$ + Verb$_{to be}$ + Adverb)

GENERAL OBSERVATIONS ABOUT SENTENCE PATTERNS

- One recent approach to understanding English sentences asks you to recognize the various patterns upon which English sentences are based, of which there are nine. These basic sentence patterns are combined in various ways to generate (or construct) longer sentences.
- Sentences containing the verb *to be* display one of the following patterns:

  - Noun + Verb$_{\text{to be}}$ + Adjective
  - Noun + Verb$_{\text{to be}}$ + Adverb
  - Noun$_1$ + Verb$_{\text{to be}}$ + Noun$_1$

- *Linking verbs* are similar to the verb *to be* in that they show a relationship between an element in the predicate and the subject of the sentence. They do not, however, convey action from one to the other as transitive verbs do, nor do they show a subject in action as intransitive verbs do.
- Many linking verbs relate to the senses, such as *smell, look, taste,* and *appear*.
- You can quickly determine whether or not a sentence has a linking verb as its predicate. If the verb in question can be replaced by a form of the verb *to be*, it is probably a linking verb. Likewise, any verb that may be substituted for *seems* without varying the meaning of the sentence is probably a linking verb.

Sentence Parts

A sentence may be comprised of many parts. Some of these parts, such as the following, are required:

- Subjects and predicates
- Punctuation

Others are not required, but frequently appear in sentences nonetheless:

- Direct objects
- Indirect objects
- Complements
- Appositives

- Sentence modifiers
- Phrases
- Clauses

These sentence parts may be in the form of single words (nouns, verbs, adjectives, adverbs, or any of the other parts of speech discussed in Part I), or may be *phrases* or *clauses*.

SUBJECTS AND PREDICATES

Most students of English have been told that the English sentence comprises two parts, a *subject* and a *predicate*. Although it seems it would be simple to identify these basic parts of a sentence, sometimes identifying the subject and predicate can be confusing.

Identifying the Subject of a Sentence

With some sentences, answering a simple "who?" or "what?" question identifies the simple subject of the sentence:

Richard finished the examination.
(Who finished the examination? *Richard. Richard* is the subject of this sentence.)

The current was too swift for us to go fishing in the river.
(What was too swift? The *current. Current* is the subject.)

The big dogs that were in the barnyard seemed friendly.
(What seemed friendly? The *dogs. Dogs* is the subject.)

The single most important word in the group of words in which the subject is located is the *simple subject*. The *complete subject* is the simple subject along with all the words that *pattern* with it—that is, are grammatically tied to the subject rather than to the predicate. These related words may be single words, phrases, or clauses. For example, in the third sentence above, the complete subject is *the big dogs that were in the barnyard*.

 You can also determine the subject in some sentences by noting which word or group of words alternates positions with another part of the sentence when a sentence that is a statement is converted to a sentence that is a question.

Betty *has answered* all the questions on the examination.
Has **Betty** *answered* all the questions on the examination?

Because no words pattern with *Betty,* that word alone is the subject of the sentence, and all the other words are the predicate. To test this theory, try the phrase *My friend Betty* instead of just *Betty* in the sentences above.

Identifying the Predicate of a Sentence

The *predicate* of a sentence is all the words that do not pattern with the subject, as long as the entire sentence (or clause, as you'll see later in this part in the section titled "Clauses") fits into one of the patterns discussed previously, in the section titled "Sentence Patterns." If a pattern is inverted, you can still ask the "who" or "what" questions; but you will not find the subject located at the beginning of the sentence string:

Out in the field stood the horse and cow.

Who or *what* stood out in the field? The *horse* and *cow*. The phrase, *the horse and cow*, is, then, the subject of the sentence. Note, too, the inverted position of *stood* and *the horse and cow* when the statement is converted to a question. (In this example, the form of the verb is changed from *stood* to the basic verb form *stand*; and an auxiliary or "helping verb" is added, as one often is in questions.)

Out in the field *stood* **the horse and cow.**
Did **the horse and cow** *stand* out in the field?
or
Had **the horse and cow** *stood* out in the field?

PUNCTUATION

Punctuation is a mechanical aid to accurate written communication and exists in its present form for two reasons:

- The need for clarity of thought and expression
- Custom

Although custom is a fine reason for the perpetuation of a linguistic standard, the most important reason for the existence of punctuation is clarity of expression. For example, examine the following two letters, created by Gloria Rosenthal for *Games Magazine* (© Games Magazine 1984. Reprinted with permission.). Both letters use the exact same words in the exact same order, but punctuate those words differently:

Dear John,
I want a man who knows what love is. All about you are generous, kind, thoughtful people who are not like you. Admit to being useless and inferior, John. You have ruined me. For other men, I yearn. For you, I have no feelings whatsoever. When we're apart, I can be forever happy. Will you please let me be?
Yours,
Marcia

Dear John,
I want a man who knows what love is all about. You are generous, kind, thoughtful. People who are not like you admit to being useless and inferior, John. You have ruined me for other men. I yearn for you. I have no feelings whatsoever when we're apart. I can be forever happy. Will you please let me be yours?
Marcia

As you can see, the message in the first letter is the exact opposite of that in the second letter—simply because the punctuation is different.

Bear in mind that a number of punctuation *styles* exist:

- Closed (formal)
- Open (informal)
- Newspaper (generally utilizes a variety of the open style)

For example, when punctuating items in a series, a writer may elect to omit the comma between the last two items if no lack of clarity results:

Closed: The three brothers were named Tim, Jim, and Kim.
Open: The three brothers were named Tim, Jim and Kim.

The punctuation guide presented in this section represents closed punctuation, however, meaning that when options exist, the rules reflect a more formal approach to style.

 Various publications may employ different styles, some of which may be unique to a single journal or newspaper; but in general, most publications subscribe to a common set of conventions relative to punctuation. However, you should check a style guide or several editions of a publication if you intend to submit material to a particular journal or magazine to be certain your punctuation style conforms to the style employed by the journal.

This section is divided to cover the two basic types of punctuation:

- Terminal punctuation
- Internal punctuation

Terminal Punctuation

Terminal punctuation is that punctuation that brings something, such as a sentence or an abbreviation, to an end. The various types of terminal punctuation include the following:

The period (.)
The question mark (?)
The exclamation mark (!)
The interrobang (‽)

The Period (.)

A period is used in the following circumstances:

- After a declarative sentence

    John Kennedy was elected President in the fall of 1960.

- After an imperative sentence that is a polite request

    Please close the door as you leave.

- After an indirect question

    He asked whether or not I had called.

- After a polite request that is put in the form of a question

    Will you please sign this contract and return it to me.

 In many circumstances, such as in business letters, either a period or a question mark may be used as end punctuation after polite requests.

- After each initial in a proper name and after most abbreviations

    S. I. Hayakawa
    Dr.
    M.A.
    Ph.D.
    LL.D.
    P.S.
    etc.
    i.e.
    Ms.
    U.S.A.
    A.M.
    B.S.
    D.Litt.
    Mr.
    Jr.
    B.C.

 Abbreviations occur without spaces between letters except for initials in proper names—for example, George H. W. Bush.

 Use no periods after the initials of radio or television call letters, network call letters, government agencies, and the terms *SOS* and *IOU*.

- As a decimal point

  His temperature is 98.6 degrees.
  This book costs $32.95.
  The answer to the problem is 88.5 percent.

- After each numeral or letter division in an outline except those enclosed in parentheses

The Question Mark (?)

A question mark is used in the following circumstances:

- After a direct question

  Did the committee really agree to the proposal?

- After each incomplete question in a series

  What have you done with your books? your papers? your pen?

- In parentheses to indicate historical doubt or uncertainty

  William Kidd (Captain Kidd) lived from 1645(?) to 1701.

The Exclamation Mark (!)

An exclamation mark is used in the following circumstances:

- After a strong interjection

  Help! The boat is sinking!

- After phrases or sentences that show strong emotions

  What a beautiful view!
  Call the guards!

 Avoid using the exclamation point for emphasis, irony, or humor.

  Incorrect: He walked bravely (!!) into the room to take the examination.

The Interrobang (‽)

Use the interrobang after an exclamatory question to which an answer is not expected:

  Now, who could have done this‽

 Most punctuation guides and dictionaries no longer recognize the interrobang as a mark of punctuation. You are certainly justified in selecting an alternate form of end punctuation, such as *?!* used by some.

Internal Punctuation

Internal punctuation separates, divides, and points out elements within an expression, thereby developing clarity and specific identity. Internal punctuation includes such marks as the following:

The comma (,)
The semicolon (;)
The colon (:)
The hyphen (-)
The em dash (—)
The en dash (–)
Parentheses (())
Brackets ([])
The ellipsis (. . . or . . . .)
Quotation marks ("" and '')
The apostrophe (')
Italics

The Comma (,)

Use commas to separate words, phrases, and clauses written in a series. The comma should appear before the conjunction that connects the last two items.

Marian has visited Seattle, Tacoma, and Walla Walla.
The policeman searched under the house, in the attic, and in the garage.
The president is in his office, the dean is out of town, and the registrar is in the auditorium.

 If all the items in a series are joined by a conjunction, do not use commas.

He asked for coats and hats and shoes.
We prefer apples or peaches or pears for this basket.

Within a series of main clauses separated by semicolons, use commas to indicate the omission of verbs.

The president is in his office; the dean, out of town; and the registrar, in the auditorium.

Use commas to set off expressions that interrupt the sentence:

- Appositives with their modifiers are set off with commas.

Cronk, the captain of the team, played a good game.
We visited Rosemary, my favorite cousin.

When an appositive is only one word showing family relationships, omit the commas.

My brother David has recently moved to Lincoln.

See the section titled "Appositives" later in this part for more information about them.

- Words of direct address are set off by commas.

Jean, please help me wash the car.
I do believe, Lynne, that you are right.

- Parenthetical expressions are set off by commas.

You are, on the contrary, not studying seriously.
On the other hand, we shall continue to strive for success.

- Certain words, such as *well, yes, no, why,* and so on, when used at the beginning of a sentence as a *starter* or *stammering expression,* are followed by a comma.
- In dates and addresses, every item after the first is enclosed by commas.

Is 261 Parklane Drive, Murray, Kentucky, the correct address?
Yes, August 3, 1964, was the date of his arrival.

When the month appears *immediately before* the year, no comma is used:

During April 1991, he revealed his invention.
The discovery was made on 22 June 1936.

- A nonrestrictive clause is set off by commas.

Dr. Miller, who is retiring soon, was honored at the banquet.
Miss Allen's car, which is quite old, is a conversation piece around campus.

Restrictive and nonrestrictive clauses are covered in more detail later in this part in the section titled "Restrictive Versus Nonrestrictive Clauses."

- A nonrestrictive participial phrase is set off by commas.

The players, tired from many rehearsals, left early.

Additionally, commas should be used in the following circumstances:

- Before *and, or, for, but*, and *nor* when these words join main clauses unless the comma has been used for another purpose within one or more of the main clauses.

  > The employees asked for an increase in salary, but the manager did not grant it.
  > The babies in the day care require constant attention, love, and nurturing but are a joy to care for.

- Before *for, as,* and *since* when these words introduce clauses of reason; before *though* and *although* when these words introduce clauses and mean "in spite of"; and before *while* when it means "but,"

  > We chose to remain at home, since we could not get good seats.
  > Mr. Williams climbed the stairs, although the doctor had warned him not to do so.
  > He was rewarded, while his teammates were not.

- After the following conjunctions when they join independent clauses:

  > hence
  > thus
  > then
  > still
  > accordingly
  > also
  > besides
  > however
  > moreover
  > otherwise
  > therefore

  In this use, these words are preceded by a semicolon:

  > Dr. Copps has taught for more than forty years; however, she has no plans to retire.

- After an introductory adverb clause, an introductory participial phrase, a succession of introductory prepositional phrases, or an introductory infinitive phrase not used as the subject of the sentence.

  > While the weather was warm, we went swimming every day.
  > Standing quietly in the corner, the child waited for his mother.

> On top of the mountain in that country, we found some relics.
> To win easily in this contest, you must have a special talent.

- After the salutation of a *friendly* letter and after the complimentary close of any letter.

  > Dear Mother,
  > Yours sincerely,
  > Very truly yours,

- Between coordinate adjectives; that is, adjectives alike in usage, between which the word *and* may be used as a sensible alternative.

  > The drum major was a tall, dark young man.
  >   (*And* would fit between *tall* and *dark* but not between *dark* and *young*.)

Adjectives indicating size, shape, color, age, material, religion, or national origin are not separated by commas.

  > The hermit lived in a little old wooden shack near the river.
  > The gigantic rectangular American flag was a sight to behold.

- To set off a direct quotation, except when the sense of the sentence requires a question mark or an exclamation mark.

  > "Yes, this is the assignment," replied Dr. Jones.
  > "What was your reply to that question?" asked Fred.

- To separate proper nouns that refer to different persons, places, or things.

  > To Tom, Jim was always very kind.
  > In January, Russia called for the meeting.
  > To England, America has always been a strong ally.

- After *etc., viz., i.e.,* and *namely*.

  > The patient asked for three things; namely, a television set, several magazines, and a radio.

- To separate two identical or closely similar words, even if the sense or grammatical structure does not require such separation.

  > Whatever it was, was not what we asked for.

- To separate two unrelated numbers.

  > In 1990, 3,245 professors attended the convention.

- Before *of* in connection with residence.

  We visited Mr. and Mrs. Cousins, of Louisville.

- To set off words, phrases, or other modifiers that are out of their natural order in the sentence.

  The young child, ill and sleepy, whimpered as he sat with his mother.

- To set off a clause that changes a statement into a question or an exclamation.

  The morning paper did arrive already, didn't it?
  Those explosions were surely loud, weren't they?

- After digits indicating thousands.

  1,254
  115,589
  22,674
  4,789,654

- To set off a title or a degree following a proper name.

  William Darnton, Jr., was the first speaker.
  Joseph N. Colley, Ph.D., is the dean.

 No comma is employed between a name and Roman numeral designating generations:

  Henry Ford III became president of the Ford Motor Company.

- After a surname when it precedes a first name (if the reversed name is within a sentence, two commas are required).

  The book is listed under the name of Grise, G. C.
  Write the name Grise, G. C., at the top of the card.

- To separate contrasted coordinate elements.

  The child's name is Mary, not Susan.
  The bandit struck wildly, but forcefully.

- To separate an absolute expression from the rest of the sentence.

  The storm having come, we lowered the sails.
  On the deck of the ship, the storm having passed, he saw the rain-soaked decorations from the celebration.

- After *Whereas* and *Resolved* in a formal resolution.

    Whereas, He has performed his duties in a most commendable manner . . .
    Resolved, That . . .

- Wherever it is necessary to prevent misreading.

    Ever since, she has prepared her assignments well.
    Inside, the workmen were holding a meeting.

The Semicolon (;)

Semicolons are used in the following circumstances:

- Between *main clauses* that are not joined by *and, or, for, nor, but, so,* or *yet.*

    You have presented a valid reason for your request; nevertheless, we find that we are unable to honor it.

- Between main clauses that are joined by *and, or, for, but, nor, so,* and *yet* if there is a comma within any one of the main clauses.

    If you are able, come to the first meeting; but I cannot promise any startling results.

- Between the *items in a series* if any one of the items contains commas.

    Mr. Snider, owner of the store; Mr. Henry, an eminent attorney; and Miss Wilson, a retired nurse, were elected to the board.

- Before such explanatory words and phrases as *namely, for example, in fact,* and *that is.*

    Choose a very narrow subject for your research; for example, one period in the author's life.

The Colon (:)

Colons are used in the following circumstances:

- After the salutation of a business letter.

    Dear Dr. Tucker:
    Gentlemen:
    Madam:

- Before a list of any kind that is introduced formally by such words as *the following* or *as follows,* by a number, or by any other "pointing out" expression.

> Dr. Standard made the following observation: "The time has come when a general college education is almost as common as a high-school education was 20 years ago."
> In his pockets, the little boy had four things: a pocket knife, a piece of string, a rusty washer, and a large marble.

Do not use a colon after a linking verb or the verb *to be.*

> **Incorrect:** The things we took with us are: a tent, a camp stove, some food, and sleeping bags.
> **Correct:** The things we took with us are a tent, a camp stove, some food, and sleeping bags.

Do not use a colon after a preposition.

> **Incorrect:** These books are for: Mary, James, and Frankie.
> **Correct:** These books are for Mary, James, and Frankie.

- Before a long and formal statement.

> To the witches, Banquo said: "If you can look into the seeds of time and tell which grain will grow and which will not. . . ."

- Between main clauses when the second clause explains or restates the first.

> This coat is the most durable kind: It is reinforced with double stitching and has a nylon lining.

The first word of the second clause should begin with an uppercase letter if it is preceded by a colon and is an independent clause.

- Between numbers expressing the time by the clock, between the volume and page number of a magazine, between chapter and verse of a Bible passage, and between the title and subtitle of a book when the subtitle explains the title.

> 5:30 a.m.
> *Harper's* 198:56–64
> John 3:16
> Their book is *A Various Language: Perspectives on American Dialects.*

The Hyphen (-)

Hyphens should be used in the following situations:

- Between words that act as a single adjective modifier (including coined ones) preceding the word being modified.

  > well-cared-for building
  > 40-yard line
  > poverty-stricken children
  > holier-than-thou attitude
  > up-to-date accounts

 Similar words used in the predicate to modify the subject are not hyphenated.

 The hyphen should be omitted from compounds when the first word is an adverb form ending in *ly*.

  > He had to jump from the slowly moving train.

- In two-word fractions only when the fraction is a single adjective that modifies directly.

  > He was elected by a two-thirds majority.
  > Two thirds of the food has been eaten already.

- In numbers from *twenty-one* through *ninety-nine*.
- After a prefix that has been attached to a proper noun.

  > un-American
  > pro-British
  > pre-Cambrian

- After *self* and *all* when these words are prefixed to nouns.

  > self-control
  > all-American
  > self-defense

- In compound titles containing *vice, ex,* and *elect*.

  > President-elect Smith
  > Vice-President Adams
  > ex-President Carter

- In words when there may be doubt as to meaning.

  > They re-acted the entire ceremony.
  > She reacted to the call.
  > I plan to re-tire my car soon.
  > We re-created Monet's garden in our backyard.

- When the joining of a prefix with the root causes an awkward combination of letters.

  co-operation
  re-enter
  re-echo
  de-emphasize

Consolidate a prefix and a root word unless the root word begins with the last letter of the prefix or with *w*.

  coeducational
  re-establish
  nonessential
  semi-invalid
  postgraduate
  co-worker

- To show the *omission* of a connecting word.

  the Anglo-Saxon people (*and* is omitted)

Additionally, a hyphen should be used to divide a word at the end of a line. When doing so, however, the following rules should be observed:

- Divide a word between pronounceable parts only. One-syllable words should never be divided.
- A word having double consonants should be divided between the consonants.
- Do not divide proper names, or separate title, initials, or first name from a last name.
- Do not divide a word so that a single letter stands alone. If possible, do not divide a word so that only two letters are carried over to the next line.
- Words having prefixes and suffixes should be divided between the prefix and the root of the word or between the root of the word and the suffix.

The Em Dash (—)
Em dashes should be used in the following situations:

- To indicate an important break in thought or in sentence structure.

  The title—if it has a title—cannot be found on this page.
  Books, paper, pens—these are essential materials.

- To set off an appositive that is a series.

   The winners—Allen, Susan, and Dan—have entered the finals.

- To mean *namely, in other words, that is,* and similar expressions that precede explanations.

   The umpire had it in his power to prevent the trouble—he could have stopped the game.

- To indicate speech that is broken or faltering.

   "I—I'm not sure exactly where I—left the book," he stammered.

- After an incomplete sentence (the em dash should be used without a period).

   She murmured, "When I saw the giant mushroom cloud in the sky—"

 Four spaced periods may be used in place of the em dash in this situation. See the section titled "The Ellipsis" later in this part.

 In typing, an em dash is constructed of two hyphens.

The En Dash (–)

En dashes should be used in the following situations:

- To connect continuing (that is, inclusive) numbers, as in dates, time, or reference numbers.

   1997–2001
   13 May 1996–1 August 1999
   8:00 a.m.–5:00 p.m.
   pp. 11–40

 If a preposition, such as *from* or *between,* is used to introduce the range of numbers, an en dash should not be used. Instead, *to* should be used with *from,* and *and* should be used with *between*:

   Correct: from 11:00 a.m. to 2:00 p.m.
   Incorrect: from 11:00 a.m.–2:00 p.m.
   Correct: between May and August
   Incorrect: between May–August

 When the concluding date of a range denoting duration of time has not yet been determined, as in the case of dates denoting the life span of a person who is still living, a single en dash is used after the first date in the range:

   Barbara Smythe (1947–)

- A single period or season spanning parts of two successive calendar years may be indicated by an en dash.

  fiscal year 2000–2001
  winter 1999–2000

- In cases of compound adjectives, an en dash is used in place of a hyphen when one element of the adjective is an open compound or when multiple elements are hyphenated compounds.

  New York–Boston train
  half-chocolate–half-vanilla milkshake

 In typing, a hyphen is used in place of an en dash.

Parentheses (( ))

Parentheses should be used under the following conditions:

- To enclose parenthetical material that is only remotely connected with the content.

  This punctuation (I am convinced it is important) should be studied carefully.

- To enclose references, directions, and incidental explanatory matter.

  Communism (see Book I) was the second topic.
  Senator Morton (R., Ky.) was the chairman of the committee.

- To enclose figures repeated to ensure accuracy.

  He paid sixty dollars ($60) for those shoes.

- To enclose figures or letters used to mark divisions or enumerations that run into the text.

  The reasons for his resignation were three: (1) advanced age, (2) failing health, (3) a desire to see more of the world.

Additionally, you should use a question mark within parentheses after a word or a statement of which the accuracy is questionable:

Chaucer was born in 1340 (?) and died in 1400.

Brackets ([ ])

Brackets should be used under the following conditions:

- To enclose explanations within parentheses or in quoted material when the explanation is not part of the quotation.

> The President criticized his own party ("We must reorganize it [the Republican Party] before next November") and then pointed out the mistakes made in earlier years.
> This is an excerpt from Dr. Swanson's address of acceptance: "I am honored by it [the appointment], but I am also keenly aware of the many responsibilities that I shall assume today."

- To rectify a mistake such as may appear in a book or other manuscript.

> "The French [English] dramatist Shakespeare will live forever."

Additionally, you should use a bracketed [sic] to show that an error in a quotation is not an error in quoting:

> Mr. Laurence wrote as follows: "I am enclosing the monie [sic] that I promised you when you were here."

The Ellipsis (. . . or . . . .)

An ellipsis mark should be used to indicate an omission from a quotation. To indicate an omission within a sentence, use three periods. To indicate an omission at the end of a sentence, employ the original mark of punctuation and then three periods.

> Sharon wrote that she had met "an unusually brilliant young man . . . whose ancestors came over on the Mayflower . . . ."

 Do not use ellipsis marks before or after quoted words or word groups incorporated into your sentence:

> Juan said he had an "unfortunate incident" as he traveled in Spain.

If internal punctuation occurs where an ellipsis begins, include that mark of punctuation before the ellipsis mark. If the omitted words occur at the beginning of a quotation, do not employ the ellipsis mark:

> He clearly stated that he "would never, . . . consent to the agreement; but who would even request such an action? . . ."

 Some authors prefer to put the end punctuation after the ellipsis mark if the omitted material carries to the end of the sentence:

> Lady Macbeth asked, "Why did you bring these daggers . . .?"

Quotation Marks (" " and ')

Quotation marks are used only for quotations that employ the exact words from some source (either spoken or written), but not for indirect quotations in which a source's ideas are used but not the exact words. Here are a few guidelines to remember when using quotation marks:

- Use double quotation marks to enclose a direct quotation.

  > What he said is, "I shall never be able to do this work."

- Use double quotation marks to enclose slang expressions, epithets, and nicknames used in formal writing.

  > The professor said that our idea is "far out."
  > Lou Gehrig is often referred to as the "Iron Horse."
  > His younger brothers have always called him "Pat."

- Use double quotation marks to enclose borrowed material.

  > Much it grieved Charles to think "what man has made of man."

- Use double quotation marks to enclose words or expressions used in a particular way. Such expressions may be coined, technical, or ironic.

  > We must develop more "stick-to-itiveness."
  > Did you say that you wish to "up" the bid?
  > The champion has gone home to the "protection" of his mother.

- Use double quotation marks to enclose the titles of songs, short stories, chapters, articles, poems, booklets, and radio and television programs that are single episodes in a series.

  > Have you read Poe's "The Raven"?
  > He enjoyed today's episode of *The Twilight Zone* entitled "It's a Good Life."

 See the section titled "Italics" later in this part for information about punctuating television episodes and programs.

- Use single quotation marks to enclose a quotation within a quotation.

  > Beullah told us, "He began by saying, 'I shall always remember this day.' "

Other marks of punctuation, when used with quotation marks, are placed according to the following principles:

- Commas and periods are always placed inside the closing quotation marks, with one exception: When citing a reference, the quotation is enclosed in quotation marks, the source is enclosed in parentheses, and then a period is placed at the end of the sentence:

> After reviewing, he stated, "The data are quite clear" (Carlane 141).

- Semicolons and colons are always placed outside the closing quotation marks.
- Question marks and exclamation marks are placed inside the closing quotation marks if they belong with the quotation; otherwise, they are placed outside.

> Quietly she asked, "May I go along with you?"
> Was it she who said, "I have no desire to quit"?
> Was it she who asked, "May I have my pen back?"

Only one mark of end (terminal) punctuation is used at the end of a sentence.

- When a quoted passage consists of more than one paragraph, place quotation marks at the beginning of each paragraph and at the end of the entire passage, not at the end of each paragraph.

For dialogue (two or more persons carrying on a conversation), begin a new paragraph with each change of speaker.

The Apostrophe (')

The apostrophe is used in forming most possessives. To form the possessive case of a singular noun, first write the noun; then add an apostrophe and an *s*.

> Father's opinion
> Mr. Jones's car
> a man's coat
> the princess's coat
> Gus's hat
> Ebby's travels

To form the possessive case of a plural noun, first write the plural form of the noun; next, add an apostrophe if the plural form ends in *s*; otherwise, add an apostrophe and an *s*.

> the dogs' trainers
> children's games
> women's fashions
> mice's tails
> the two Charleses' cars

In certain "tongue-twister" words, acceptable shortcuts may be taken. For instance, the possessive form of Jesus (Jesus's) may be written Jesus' and then pronounced "Jesus."

In Jesus' name we pray . . .

To determine whether this shortcut is appropriate, examine the word in question. If the word is one syllable, add an 's; if a word is of more than one syllable or ends with a "z" sound, add an apostrophe only.

Jess's mother answered the phone.
My nieces' kittens were fluffy and white. (*Nieces* is intended to be plural in this sentence.)

 Do not use an apostrophe on signs or plaques to indicate a family's residence:

Incorrect: THE SMIDGEON'S

The indefinite pronouns *one, everyone, everybody*, and the like form their possessive case in the same way as do nouns.

one's chances
everybody's opportunity

Personal, interrogative, and relative pronouns in the possessive case (*his, its, ours, hers, yours, whose, theirs*) do not require an apostrophe.

In compound words, words followed by *else*, names of business firms, and words showing joint possession, only the last word is made possessive in form.

his mother-in-law's visit
Dun and Bradstreet's publication
Jack and Tom's responsibility
someone else's book

When two or more persons possess something individually, each of the names is possessive in form.

Jack's and Tom's sweaters
Barry's and Barbara's eyes

The words *minute, hour, day, week, month,* and *year,* when used as possessive adjectives, require an apostrophe. Words indicating amount in dollars and cents, when used as adjectives, also require apostrophes.

a minute's work
five minutes' work
a day's rest
three days' rest
one cent's worth
five cents' worth
a dollar's worth
ten dollars' worth

Besides possession, various semantic relationships exist between one noun and a following noun that are expressed through the use of the apostrophe:

- Characterization or description

  horse's gait
  sailor's walk
  boys' sneakers
  women's garments
  bird's flight
  master's degree (but Master of Arts degree)

- Origin

  Hemingway's novels
  Joyce's short stories
  Poe's poems

- Measure

  Time: a day's journey; a night's work
  Value: a dime's worth; a quarter's worth
  Distance: a hair's breath; a stone's throw

- Subject of an act

  athlete's leap
  umpire's decision
  bird's flight

- Object of an act

  team's penalty
  child's scolding
  author's critics

Additionally, apostrophes are used in the following circumstances:

- To indicate where letters have been omitted in a contraction (a *contraction* is a word made up of two words combined into one by omitting one or more letters)

can not	can't
they have	they've
does not	doesn't
is not	isn't
would not	wouldn't
we have	we've
he is	he's
I have	I've
they are	they're
I am	I'm
will not	won't
you are	you're
are not	aren't

- To indicate the omission of letters in words in dialect and to indicate missing numbers in a date

    I'm goin' to see 'im now.
    It all happened in '63.

An apostrophe with an *s* should be used to form the plurals of letters, numbers, symbols, and words referred to as words.

He listed on his paper these things: four *m*'s, seven *4*'s, two *+*'s, and five *but*'s.

 To show possession by inanimate objects, avoid the use of an apostrophe. Instead, use the "of phrase":

leg of the table
head of the stairs
back of the bus
top of the house
arm of the sofa

The *of* structure should also be used when referring to the title of a work of art:

Correct: The star of *Logan's Run*
Incorrect: *Logan's Run*'s star

Italics (Underlining)

Use italics (indicated by underlining on standard typewriters) for names of books, magazines, newspapers, long plays, long poems (book length), motion pictures, musical productions, works of art, ships, aircraft, and trains. The words *A*, *An*, and *The* written before a title are italicized only when they are part of the title. Before the names of magazines and newspapers, these three words are not underlined (italicized) within a sentence.

> He is reading *Catcher in the Rye*.
> Do you subscribe to the *Saturday Review*?
> President Truman's plane was *The Sacred Cow*.
> He has a miniature of *Venus de Milo*.
> Did you see the motion picture version of *Gone With the Wind*?
> Indeed, it was Shakespeare who wrote *Twelfth Night*.

 The matter of using quotation marks or underlining when punctuating the titles of television series and the titles of episodes within those series has created a bit of confusion at times. A logical manner in which to proceed is to put the titles of weekly, titled episodes within quotation marks and then underline or italicize the name of the series. This is becoming more and more common.

> Did you see the *Star Trek* episode, "The City on the Edge of Forever"?

Italics should also be used for words, letters, figures, and symbols referred to by name.

> The word *Mississippi* has four *s*'s.
> Doesn't his license plate have a *7* in it?
> The entire composition has only one *and* in it.
> Press the *#* button on your phone.

 In this particular group, words may be typed in upper case without the italics.

 Use italics for foreign words and phrases, but note that many words and phrases of foreign origin have been absorbed into the English language and are no longer italicized. When you are in doubt about the acceptability of a word, consult a recent dictionary. If the word appears in the main section and is not set off in any way, it should not be italicized. If, however, the word appears in a special section that treats of foreign words and phrases or if it is set off in the main section, it should be italicized.

Finally, you should use italics to lend emphasis. (Again, such an expression may be typed in uppercase without the italics.)

Unfortunately, this was indeed *not* the correct story for today's assignment.

Examples of Correctly Punctuated Sentences

Following are several sentences that contain correct punctuation:

Our professor is Dr. J. L. Jerome, Ph.D., associate professor of English.

His address—at least as far as it is known—is 1703 Parklane Drive, Murray, Kentucky.

Help! I'm drowning!

Send your letter to 1000 Oak Street, Tulsa, Oklahoma, if you want a reply.

Jane has lived in Yuma, Arizona; Ingalls, Michigan; Nome, Alaska; and Austin, Texas.

As I told you yesterday, six cows, three hogs, and two professors are for sale—cheap.

"No," she said. "Let's go see St. Nick." (Alternatively: "No." She said, "Let's go see St. Nick.")

The runners, suffering from the heat, decided not to finish the race. (No commas are needed if some of the other runners finished the race.)

Did Mother say, "Let's go on a picnic"?

Who said, "Can you hear me?"

I arrived late; therefore, I did not receive a handout.

The dog, hungry and wet, scratched at my door.

I was really ill: I had a bad case of the plague.

He had a choice: He could have chosen red or green.

He, President Nixon, was forced out of office for no good reason.

There are four *s*'s in *Mississippi*.

She stated that she was "perturbed" about the results of the test.

The usher did not know what to do with the women's coats that he found.

Mother told us the following: "Dad said you can go to the fair 'over my dead body.'"

Joan stammered, "Well, I'll be . . . ."

"I'll receive the report tomorrow," said President Bush.

Chaucer was born in A.D. 1340 (?) and died in A.D. 1400.

In father's opinion, our neighbors are—to use his word—"idiots."

That soon-to-be-painted lighthouse is a true landmark.

Melville's *Moby Dick* is one of the great books of American literature.

DIRECT OBJECTS

A major sentence element contained in many predicates is the *direct object*, which occurs in sentences that have *transitive verbs*. A transitive verb is a verb that requires a direct object to give the sentence a sense of completeness.

> Sentence Pattern: Noun$_1$ + Transitive Verb + Noun$_2$

 Refer to the section titled "Transitive Verbs" in Part I for more information about them.

Note these word groups:

> The small boy found
> The old mule could not carry

Neither "sentence" conveys a sense of completeness. But if certain nouns are added, the sentences would seem normal:

> The small boy found *a silver coin.*
> The old mule could not carry *the heavy load of wood.*

The nouns that have been added are identified as *direct objects*.

Identifying Direct Objects

To identify direct objects, you may ask the "what question" (or the "who question") in conjunction with the verb. In the first sentence above, *what* did the small boy find? *A silver coin. A silver coin* is the complete direct object, while *coin* is the simple direct object. In the second sentence above, *what* couldn't the old mule carry? *The heavy load of wood. The heavy load of wood* is the complete direct object and *load* is the simple direct object. (*Load*, not *wood*, is the simple direct object, as prepositional phrases are seldom either subjects or direct objects.)

In the following sentences, you can identify various sentence elements: the complete subject, the simple subject, the predicate, and, within the predicate, the verb, the complete direct object, and the simple direct object:

> The boy and his companion found a *buried treasure.*
> **Complete Subject:** The boy and his companion
> **Simple Subject:** boy, companion
> **Predicate:** found a buried treasure
> **Transitive Verb:** found
> **Complete Direct Object:** a buried treasure
> **Simple Direct Object:** treasure

The little kitten quietly drank the warm milk.
Complete Subject: The little kitten
Simple Subject: kitten
Predicate: quietly drank the warm milk
Transitive Verb: drank
Complete Direct Object: the warm milk
Simple Direct Object: milk

The senator read the speech to his audience.
Complete Subject: The senator
Simple Subject: senator
Predicate: read the speech to his audience
Transitive Verb: read
Complete Direct Object: the speech
Simple Direct Object: speech

The black bears ate the berries in the wooden crate.
Complete Subject: The black bears
Simple Subject: bears
Predicate: ate the berries in the wooden crate
Transitive Verb: ate
Complete Direct Object: the berries in the wooden crate
Simple Direct Object: berries

She wrote the letter on her computer.
Complete Subject: She
Simple Subject: She
Predicate: wrote the letter on her computer
Transitive Verb: wrote
Complete Direct Object: the letter
Simple Direct Object: letter

Every student in the class did the first three exercises.
Complete Subject: Every student in the class
Simple Subject: student
Predicate: did the first three exercises
Transitive Verb: did
Complete Direct Object: the first three exercises
Simple Direct Object: exercises

The hawk caught the mouse in its strong talons.
Complete Subject: The hawk
Simple Subject: hawk
Predicate: caught the mouse in its strong talons
Transitive Verb: caught
Complete Direct Object: the mouse
Simple Direct Object: mouse

The students found the buses in the parking lot.
Complete Subject: The students
Simple Subject: students
Predicate: found the buses in the parking lot
Transitive Verb: found
Complete Direct Object: the buses in the parking lot
Simple Direct Object: buses

The old cow chewed its cud contentedly.
Complete Subject: The old cow
Simple Subject: cow
Predicate: chewed its cud contentedly
Transitive Verb: chewed
Complete Direct Object: its cud
Simple Direct Object: cud

INDIRECT OBJECTS

Indirect objects are those parts of the predicate that occur in sentences containing direct objects and that are closely related to the direct objects by identifying the person/thing to whom or for whom something is done or given, or of whom a question is asked. Indirect objects are usually nouns or pronouns.

Sentence Pattern: $Noun_1$ + Transitive Verb + $Noun_2$ + $Noun_3$

The following sentence has a direct object but not an indirect object:

The pony pulled the little cart.

Cart is the direct object, because it was the thing the pony pulled.

In a sentence containing an indirect object, you can use only certain verbs, such as the following:

give
tell
buy
send
write
teach
get
bring

Notice that all these verbs suggest the "giving" idea. The sentences that follow contain indirect objects, which are italicized. Note that indirect objects occur before the direct objects:

> The boy gave the thirsty *puppy* a drink.
> The scout leader told the young *scouts* a frightening story.
> Don't tell *me* your troubles!

Notice how the direct object and indirect object are related in each of the sentences. In the first sentence, you determine what was given—a drink. *Drink* is the direct object. To determine the indirect object, you determine *to whom* that drink was given, in this case *the thirsty puppy.* Therefore, *puppy* is the simple indirect object. Each of the other sentences may be analyzed in much the same way. In the second sentence, the leader told a story. To whom did he or she tell the story? To the young scouts. *The young scouts* is the indirect object, while *scouts* is the simple indirect object. In the third sentence, *you* is the understood subject of the verb *tell. Troubles* is the direct object. To whom were the troubles told? To me. Thus, *me* is the indirect object.

 Sentences such as the preceding ones that express requests, commands, or instructions, and begin with a verb and have no apparent subject, are called *imperative sentences*. The subject of such sentences is an "understood *you*." For more information, refer to the section titled "Imperative Sentences" earlier in this part.

 Another way to locate the indirect object in a sentence is to recast the sentence to include a prepositional phrase starting with *to.* "Don't tell me your troubles!" becomes "Don't tell your troubles to me!"; *me* is the indirect object.

The following sentences further illustrate subjects, verbs, direct objects, and indirect objects:

> The children brought their mother some wild flowers.
> **Complete Subject:** The children
> **Simple Subject:** children
> **Predicate:** brought their mother some wild flowers
> **Transitive Verb:** brought
> **Complete Direct Object:** some wild flowers
> **Simple Direct Object:** flowers
> **Complete Indirect Object:** their mother
> **Simple Indirect Object:** mother
>
> Can you give me directions to the stadium?
> **Complete Subject:** you
> **Simple Subject:** you

Predicate: can give me directions to the stadium
Transitive Verb: give
Complete Direct Object: directions to the stadium
Simple Direct Object: directions
Complete Indirect Object: me
Simple Indirect Object: me

The class gave Professor Allen a book and a card.
Complete Subject: The class
Simple Subject: class
Predicate: gave Professor Allen a book and a card
Transitive Verb: gave
Complete Indirect Object: a book and a card
Simple Direct Object: book, card
Complete Indirect Object: Professor Allen
Simple Indirect Object: Professor Allen

The postman gave me Mother's package.
Complete Subject: The postman
Simple Subject: postman
Predicate: gave me Mother's package
Transitive Verb: gave
Complete Direct Object: Mother's package
Simple Direct Object: package
Complete Indirect Object: me
Simple Indirect Object: me

The professor gave the class a long assignment.
Complete Subject: The professor
Simple Subject: professor
Predicate: gave the class a long assignment
Transitive Verb: gave
Complete Direct Object: a long assignment
Simple Direct Object: assignment
Complete Indirect Object: the class
Indirect Object: class

We gave our father a book for Christmas.
Complete Subject: We
Simple Subject: We
Predicate: gave our father a book for Christmas
Transitive Verb: gave
Complete Indirect Object: a book for Christmas
Simple Direct Object: book
Complete Indirect Object: our father
Simple Indirect Object: father

COMPLEMENTS

A *complement*, which may be a noun, adjective, pronoun, or phrase, is added to a verb to complete the predicate of a sentence. The complement provides information about a clause's subject or object.

There are four main types of complements:

- Object complement
- Subject complement
- Adverbial complement
- Adjectival complement

Object Complements

Sentences that correspond to the following pattern have a sentence element known as an *object complement*. In effect, an object complement describes or "completes" the direct object, usually by adding a noun or adjective immediately after the direct object.

Sentence Pattern: $Noun_1$ + Transitive Verb + $Noun_2$ + X

The words in bold print in the following sentences are direct objects; the words in italics are object complements. Note how the object complements relate to the direct objects and complete the idea of the action of the verb:

Our neighbors painted their **house** *green*.
The student council elected **me** *president*.

When a sentence containing an object complement is made passive, only the direct object may become the subject of the verb in the passive voice, as in this passive form of the preceding second sentence:

I was elected president by the student council.

Only a very limited number of verbs may be used in sentences containing an object complement, including the following (and a few others):

appoint
believe
call
choose
consider
declare
elect
feel
find

get
imagine
keep
make
nominate
prove
suppose
think

These verbs suggest a "to be" meaning after the direct object, but bear in mind that the verb *to be* is not stated:

We all thought George [*to be*] honest.

Understanding object complements enables you to make correct choices of modifiers and pronouns, because both relate to the object. The following sentences exemplify a common problem: Which is the correct form?

Shut the door (tight, tightly).
The dean thought Fred (me, I).

Because the word in parentheses in the first sentence modifies door—a noun—the adjective form *tight* is the correct form. Consider a similar sentence:

Paint the door (white, whitely).

Obviously, *whitely* is incorrect. We know the door will be white.

In the second sentence, the pronoun that relates to *Fred* is in the same case as *Fred*—the objective case, because *Fred* is the direct object. The correct choice, therefore, is *me*.

 Some speakers, thinking *I* sounds more "elegant" than *me* in such constructions, mistakenly employ the nominative case in these and similar constructions. Be careful.

Subject Complement

A *subject complement* is an adjective, noun, or noun phrase that is linked to a subject by the verb *to be* or by other copulative verbs such as the following:

become
turn
look
appear
seem
feel
sound

Refer to the section titled "Copulative Verbs" in Part I for more information about them.

Sentence Pattern: Noun$_1$ + Verb$_{to\ be}$ + ___

The words in bold print in the following sentences are subjects; the words in italics are subject complements. Note how the subject complements relate to the subjects:

Benedict Arnold turned *traitor* during the Revolutionary War.
Susan was *upset* about her grade.
Julie is my close *friend*.

In the relatively few instances where the subject complement is a pronoun, the pronoun must be in the nominative case, just as it is after a form of the verb *to be*:

The treasurer was *she* whom we elected.
The treasurer remained *she* whom we elected.

Adverbial Complements

Adverbial complements function as adverbs and are necessary to complete the meaning of the sentences that contain them. They are similar to subject complements, but usually convey the meaning of location, direction, progression, duration, condition, circumstance, or purpose.

Sentence Pattern: Noun$_1$ + Verb$_{to\ be}$ + Adverb

Several examples of these meanings are demonstrated in these sentences:

These flowers are *for Roweena*. (purpose)
My term paper is *in its final stage*. (condition)
The entire project is *on schedule*. (progression)
The warranty is *for thirty days*. (duration)
The entire delegation is *under surveillance*. (circumstances)

Adverbial complements differ from simple adverbs and adverb phrases in that simple adverbs and adverb phrases are usually not essential elements of a sentence. The sentences below demonstrate the differences between adverb phrases and adverbial complements:

The new recruits were *in their barracks*. (adverbial complement)
The new recruits were standing *in the rain*. (adverb phrase)

I have a package *in my car*. (adverb phrase)
The package is *in my car*. (adverbial complement)

To distinguish between the two types of constructions, simply re-read the preceding sentences, omitting the phrases in italicized print. In the first and fourth sentences, the highlighted phrases are essential elements of the sentences.

Although adverbial complements are usually short prepositional phrases, single-word adverbs may function as adverbial complements:

The book is *there*.
The money is *here*.
Our final examination is *tomorrow*.

Adjective Complements

In some sentences, a construction identified as an *adjective complement* may occur. This type of complement restricts or completes the meaning of an adjective in a sentence.

Sentence Pattern: Noun$_1$ + Verb$_{to\ be}$ + Adjective + Adjective

Notice the adjective complements in the sentences below. The adjective complements are italicized.

I am happy *that you won the game*.
The farmer was reluctant *to plant sweet peas*.
The boys grew tired *of waiting*.
I am afraid *that we are lost*.

Identifying the Various Types of Complements

Following are some sample sentences that make use of complements:

Seeing is believing.
Subject: Seeing
Verb: is
Complement: believing (subject complement)

The wanderers looked exhausted from their experience.
Subject: wanderers
Verb: looked
Complement: exhausted (subject complement)
Complement: from their experience (adjective complement)

The wind remained steady all night.
Subject: wind
Verb: remained
Complement: steady (subject complement)
Complement: all night (adjective complement)

Some loggers are concerned about the environment.
Subject: loggers
Verb: are
Complement: concerned (subject complement)
Complement: about the environment (adjective complement)

Jealousy is a foolish emotion.
Subject: jealousy
Verb: is
Complement: emotion (subject complement)

All the cargo was in the ship's hold.
Subject: cargo
Verb: was
Complement: in the ship's hold (adverbial complement)

The farmer painted his new barn yellow.
Subject: farmer
Verb: painted
Direct Object: barn
Complement: yellow (object complement)

Our club elected Mary president.
Subject: club
Verb: elected
Direct Object: Mary
Complement: president (object complement)

I have made Ronald the captain.
Subject: I
Verb: have made
Direct Object: Ronald
Complement: captain (object complement)

Renee is a very fine singer.
Subject: Renee
Verb: is
Complement: singer (subject complement)

APPOSITIVES

An *appositive* is a word, phrase, or clause usually located after a nominal (a noun, noun phrase, or noun substitute) to identify, explain, or describe the nominal. Although adjectives may be used in apposition, appositives are usually nouns and pronouns. The following sentences contain appositives, which are set off within commas and are in italics.

> The editor of the paper, *Mr. Parker*, spoke to our group, *the senior English class.*
> We spoke with the director, *the man responsible for the mix-up.*
> Sally gave the cat, *a family pet*, a good home.

Appositives usually do not cause speakers or writers any problems unless pronouns are involved. When such is the case, you must remember that the case (or form) of the pronoun is determined by the use of the nominal with which the pronoun is in apposition, as in these sentences:

> The swimmers, John and *he*, were ready for the competition.
> (*He* patterns with the subject of the sentence and is, therefore, in the nominative case.)

> The winners were the two seniors, Mary and *she*.
> (*She* patterns with a subject complement [seniors] and is, therefore, in the nominative case.)

> They watched the two cyclists, Carlos and *me*.
> (*Me* patterns with the direct object and is thus in the objective case.)

> The professor gave the two students, Peggy and *him*, some extra problems to work.
> (*Him* patterns with the indirect object and is, therefore, in the objective case.)

SENTENCE MODIFIERS

Certain types of adverbials may be employed as *sentence modifiers*. Usually set off by commas, these modifiers relate to the entire sentence, not to any separate element within the sentence.

Adverbials, which are optional elements in sentence or clause structure, come in three forms: *adjuncts, conjuncts,* and *disjuncts.*

- *Adjuncts* are integrated to some degree in the sentence or clause structure, and typically inform as to space, time, process, or focus.

  > in my neighborhood
  > next week
  > easily
  > primarily

- *Conjuncts*, which are mainly adverbs or prepositional phrases, indicate logical relationships between sentences or clauses.

   therefore
   however
   nonetheless
   on the other hand

- *Disjuncts* are of type style or content.

   - *Style disjuncts*—which may be adverbs, prepositional phrases, finite clauses, and non-finite clauses—comment on the act of speaking or writing.

      truthfully
      in short
      frankly speaking
      since you mentioned it

   - *Content disjuncts*, on the other hand, evaluate or comment on the truth of what is said.

      probably
      unfortunately

For the purposes of comparison, examine the sentence that follows. This sentence employs the adverbs *naturally* and *gracefully* as modifiers of the verb *ran*:

The boy ran naturally and gracefully.

In the next sentence, however, *naturally* cannot be associated with *ran* and still have the sentence retain the meaning that seems to be intended:

Naturally, my sister ran for the presidency of the club.

In this sentence, the word *naturally* modifies the entire sentence. As another example, consider this sentence:

Because the door was locked, the thief crawled through the window.

The introductory adverbial clause, *Because the door was locked*, does not tell the reader why the thief crawled. Rather, it tells the reader why the thief crawled *through the window*. The thief crawled, presumably, because the window was too low and too small to have enabled the thief to *walk* through. He *crawled through the window* because the door was locked.

Various types of sentence modifiers exist:

- Single-word adverbials

  Strangely, the moon seemed to rise in the west.
  (The moon did not *rise* strangely.)

- Clause adverbials

  Because the table was dirty, we ate at the counter.

- Prepositional phrases

  In fact, we made some serious errors.
  (The errors were not errors of fact.)

- Absolute phrases

  The rain having stopped, we went on our picnic.

- Infinitive phrases

  To summarize, we need a new committee.

- Participial phrases

  Knowing the dog's temper, we circled the barn at a respectable distance.

- "-ever" clauses

  Whoever she is, I will marry her.

Sentence modifiers such as those previously shown may also be placed after or within the sentences they modify. For example, examine the following:

We need, to summarize, a new committee.

Notice the essential commas in the preceding sentence. If the commas are omitted, the "We" of the sentence would be summarizing a new committee, whatever that means. On the other hand, if the sentence modifier is placed *after* the sentence without being separated by a comma, the sentence takes on still another meaning:

We need a new committee to summarize.

The following sentences contain sentence modifiers, which are italicized:

My uncle was, *understandably*, upset about the damage to his car.
As I was saying, not enough people vote in our elections.
Since the mail hadn't arrived, we didn't receive an invitation.

We can, *in retrospect*, see where we made the greatest errors.
We missed the concert *because of the flat tire.*
The boat did not sail, *the crew having gone on strike.*
Before we know it, the semester will be gone.
We need new officers, *to put the matter briefly.*
Knowing where the fish were, we caught many nice bass.

PHRASES

The traditional definition of a *phrase* is somewhat as follows: A phrase is a group of words not containing a subject and predicate and used as a single part of speech. While certain aspects of that definition may be subject to some dispute, the definition is functional and adequate for purposes of this book; but we must remember that phrases (the groups of words) may contain modifying *clauses*, which, by definition, contain subjects and verbs. The various types of phrases include the following:

- Noun phrases
- Prepositional phrases
- Verbals

Noun Phrases

Noun phrases (which, for purposes of this book, may be a noun without any other words patterning with it) may be used in a sentence just as a noun is used. That is, a noun phrase can be used in a sentence as the subject, direct object, indirect object, subject complement, object complement, object of a preposition, object of an infinitive, subject of an infinitive, and so on. Notice the example of two noun phrases in the following sentence:

The boy who was here is my nephew.

On the most superficial level, the sentence contains two noun phrases, one (*the boy*) with a modifying clause (*who was here*) and one (*my nephew*) without such a clause. To determine the extent of the first noun phrase, you must identify the head word of the phrase (usually called the *noun head*) and then include all the modifiers of the noun head—all the single words, phrases, and clauses that pattern with that head word. The head word of the first noun phrase in the preceding example is *boy.* The words that pattern with *boy* are *the* and *who was here.* In the second phrase, *nephew* is the noun head, and *my* is the only other word in the phrase.

Examine the noun phrases in italics in the following sentences. The noun heads of the target phrases are in bold print:

Try to find *the little* **boy** *with the wet feet.*
We do our shopping *in the little* **store** *on the corner.*
The **students** *who were absent* missed *the final examination.*

Other noun phrases in the preceding examples are *the wet feet, the corner, the final examination,* as well as pronouns.

Prepositional Phrases

A *preposition* is a word that functions as a connector between sentence elements. The element that it connects and patterns with is usually a noun and is identified as the *object of the preposition.* The preposition itself is "pre-positioned" (thus "preposition") between the object and the word the object is related to. Take the following sentence as an example:

The kitten *with the white paws* is named Fluffy.

In this sentence, the preposition *with* shows a relationship between *kitten* and *paws.* The prepositional phrase serves as an adjective indicating which kitten is named Fluffy.

Prepositional phrases may also serve as adverbs, as in this sentence:

The scouts hurried *to their campsite.*

Because adverbs indicate where, when, why, under what conditions, and to what extent, and because *to their campsite* tells where they hurried, the prepositional phrase is an adverbial prepositional phrase, or to keep the designation simple, an adverbial phrase.

A prepositional phrase contains a preposition and the object of the preposition, which is usually a noun, and all the modifiers of the noun. Those modifiers may themselves be prepositional phrases; thus we often find sentences such as this:

The rooms in the old building with the sagging roof were dark and damp.

The first prepositional phrase is *in the old building with the sagging roof.* The preposition is *in*; its object is *building. Building* has itself a modifying prepositional phrase: *with the sagging roof. With* is the preposition; *roof* is the object of the preposition.

Remember that objects of prepositions are in the objective case. Fortunately, English does not have a separate form (or case) for nominative and objective uses of nouns. Pronouns do have separate cases, however; therefore, you must remember to use the objective case of the pronoun where the pronoun is the object of the preposition. Notice the following:

No one could distinguish *between* **him** and **me.**
Route your report *through* **Mildred** and **her.**

Occasionally, prepositional phrases may be used in somewhat unusual ways, for example as subjects of sentences. These usages are somewhat rare, but the construction of the prepositional phrase remains the same:

Over the fence is a home run.
In shallow water is the place to find minnows.

After each of the following sentences, you'll find listed the prepositional phrases within that sentence, the preposition within each prepositional phrase, and the object of each prepositional phrase. If the sentence contains prepositional phrases within prepositional phrases, they will be so noted.

The tree in the meadow is an old oak.
   in the meadow: in (meadow)

We do not trust the bridge across the big river in Tennessee.
   across the big river in Tennessee: across (river)
   in Tennessee: in (Tennessee)

Cows with calves by their sides often remain in one area.
   with calves by their sides: with (calves)
   by their sides: by (sides)
   in one area: in (area)

Shagbark hickories are identified by their hard, peeling bark.
   by their hard, peeling bark: by (bark)

Jeans with designers' names on them are popular with the young set.
   with designers' names on them: with (names)
   on them: on (them)
   with the young set: with (set)

Into the hole ran the mouse with the cat after it.
   into the hole: into (hole)
   with the cat after it: with (cat)
   after it: after (it)

Except for dogs with fleas, I like most animals.
> **except for dogs with fleas:** except (dogs)
> **with fleas:** with (fleas)

The best place for a vacation is in the mountains.
> **for a vacation:** for (vacation)
> **in the mountains:** in (mountains)

During the night, the south wind brought rain and snow.
> **during the night:** during (night)

We hiked through the woods and over the hills until late afternoon.
> **through the woods:** through (woods)
> **over the hills:** over (hills)
> **until late afternoon:** until (afternoon)

Verbals

The three types of phrases to be discussed in this section—infinitives, gerunds, and participles—are known as *verbals* because they incorporate verb forms in their basic constructions. Verbals are employed as grammatical units within sentences, usually as nouns or modifiers, as the following discussions reveal. They are often classified as *nonfinite verbs*, because they are not inflected (do not change form) to indicate person, number, or tense.

Infinitive Phrases

Infinitive phrases, like prepositional phrases, may be used in a number of ways in the English sentence. Fortunately, the infinitive phrase is fairly easy to recognize. First of all, it has as one of its constituents the infinitive from which the phrase gets its name. An infinitive is the word *to* followed by the base form of a verb, such as *run, jump, play, work, buy, see*, etc. Infinitives, then, look like this: *to run, to jump, to play, to buy, to see.*

An infinitive phrase contains an infinitive and words that pattern with it—modifiers, objects, and subjects. Like verbs that are used as predicators in sentences, an infinitive may have objects—in this case called *objects of the infinitive* rather than direct objects.

Note the infinitive phrases and the objects of the infinitives in the following sentences. The phrases are printed in italics, and the objects of the infinitives are in bold print:

My father tried *to find his missing* **wallet**.
To buy a **house** *in the country* was his life-long dream.
She wanted *to play her* **violin** *at a concert in New York*.

Like verbs used as predicators, infinitives may have indirect objects, as the boldfaced words in the following sentences demonstrate:

The professor threatened *to give **us** a test*.
Matilda left *to get **Marty** an ice cream cone*.

Pronouns used as either objects or indirect objects of the infinitive must be in the objective case, unless the infinitive is constructed with the verb *to be*. Such a construction requires special consideration; however, the rules governing it are few and really quite simple:

- If the infinitive *to be* has no subject, the complement of the infinitive is in the *nominative* case:

  The girl with the red shorts was thought to be **she**.
  The winner turned out to be **he** whom we selected.

- If the infinitive *to be* has a subject, its subject and complement are in the objective case:

  They all thought **him** to be **me**.
  The principal believed the **leader** to be **him**.

Insofar as the infinitive has many of the characteristics of the verb, it can pattern in much the same way as a verb—with objects and indirect objects, and with subjects and modifiers. Again, examine the following sentences and note the subjects, objects, and modifiers of the infinitives. The modifiers have been boldfaced for ease of identification; the infinitive phrases are in italics:

We all tried *to finish our work **quickly***.
The club wanted *Bill to construct a shelf **in the hall***.
*To write **well*** was his greatest ambition.
All the students wanted *him to cover **adequately** the material that would be on the test*.

Bill in the second sentence and *him* in the fourth sentence above are subjects of the infinitives in those sentences. Subjects of infinitives are in the objective case, as noted earlier in the discussion of the infinitive with the verb *to be*.

On split infinitives

Some texts inform speakers and writers that you must not "split an infinitive." That rule is a holdover from early studies of English based on observations about Latin. In Latin, infinitives cannot be split, because they are single words, not two words as they are in English. Because splitting the infinitive is still often frowned upon, you probably should avoid doing so as often as possible. But at times, awkward constructions may result, and you must decide whether splitting the infinitive or sounding awkward—or even inane— is the greater error. The infinitives are split in the sentences that follow. How would you avoid doing so?

To better *reflect* nutritional knowledge, the USDA began redrawing the [basic food] chart three years ago. (Slightly modified from *TIME* magazine, July 15, 1991, p. 57.)

We plan *to* completely *remove* partially weakened beams to satisfy the inspector from OSHA.

You could argue, of course, that a different type of construction could be used in place of the infinitive. You could use a participle, for instance, and create this sentence:

Our plan incorporating total removal of partially weakened beams is designed to satisfy the inspector from OSHA.

Such a position is valid; but in order to create sentences with a variety of constructions, you must understand all the options available to a writer and the fine points of using those options. Knowing those options is nearly totally dependent upon knowing sentence parts, including infinitives.

The infinitive phrase is a versatile construction, capable of being used in a number of ways within the sentence: as subject of various constructions, as objects of verbs and verbals, and as modifiers. Notice the sentences that follow. The infinitive phrases are in italics, and the use of the infinitive phrase in each sentence is indicated in parentheses:

The team wanted *to win the final game of the season.* (direct object)
To win the final game was the team's greatest goal. (subject)
The team knew that the game *to win* was the final game. (adjective, telling which game)
The puppy ran *to get the bone.* (adverb, telling why the puppy ran)
My goal is *to get an A in biology.* (subject complement)
His objective, *to climb the mountain,* is unrealistic. (appositive with subject)
We discovered his secret ambition, *to write a novel.* (appositive with direct object)
We laughed as we tried *to open the car door.* (direct object)
The colors *to wear in the summertime* are light colors. (adjective, telling which colors)

The students wanted *to solve as many problems as they could*. (direct object)

You must wear sunglasses *to protect your eyes from the sun's rays*. (adverb, telling why you must wear sunglasses)

Carl's job is *to eliminate needless paperwork*. (subject complement)

To eat much less at mealtime was his latest goal. (subject)

My role, *to play the fool*, was not very enjoyable. (appositive)

The officer knew his task—*to apprehend the criminal*. (appositive)

You should try *to discover answers for yourself*. (direct object)

Students should take a variety of courses *to get a well-rounded education*. (adverb, telling why students should take a variety of courses)

After the following sentences, the infinitive phrases are listed. Also listed are any subjects and objects of the infinitives, if applicable.

Everyone wanted Elizabeth to win the contest.
Infinitive Phrase: Elizabeth to win the contest
Subject of the Infinitive: Elizabeth
Object of the Infinitive: contest

His goal was to bowl a perfect game.
Infinitive Phrase: to bowl a perfect game
Object of the Infinitive: game

The wrench to use to loosen the bolt is missing.
Infinitive Phrase: to use (used as an adjective modifying *wrench*)
Infinitive Phrase: to loosen the bolt (used as an adverb modifying *to use* telling when or under what conditions)
Object of the Infinitive: bolt

The cowboy tried to capture the wild mustang.
Infinitive Phrase: to capture the wild mustang
Object of the Infinitive: mustang

We found Richard to be someone whom we could trust.
Infinitive Phrase: Richard to be someone whom we could trust
Subject of the Infinitive: Richard

The officer threatened to give the driver a traffic citation.
Infinitive Phrase: to give the driver a traffic citation
Object of the Infinitive: citation (*driver* is the indirect object of the infinitive)

In the closet he found the perfect costume to wear to the ball.
Infinitive Phrase: to wear to the ball

To move quietly through the brush takes the skill of a woodsman.
Infinitive Phrase: to move quietly through the brush

Strive to show yourself worthy of any praise you receive.
Infinitive Phrase: to show yourself worthy of any praise you receive
Object of the Infinitive: yourself

The hunters found orange to be visible during cloudy days.
Infinitive Phrase: orange to be visible during cloudy days
Subject of the Infinitive: orange

We all wanted to be in bed before midnight.
Infinitive Phrase: to be in bed before midnight

To do a good job, one must strive to follow instructions.
Infinitive Phrase: to do a good job
Object of the Infinitive: job
Infinitive Phrase: to follow instructions
Object of the Infinitive: instructions

The clothes to wear to a ball game are sports clothes.
Infinitive Phrase: clothes to wear to a ball game
Subject of the Infinitive: clothes

Try to keep calm during emergencies.
Infinitive Phrase: to keep calm during emergencies
Object of the Infinitive: calm

To achieve victory does not always mean to win.
Infinitive Phrase: to achieve victory
Object of the Infinitive: victory
Infinitive Phrase: to win

Gerund Phrases

Another type of verbal is the type known as the *gerund phrase*. Gerund phrases are recognized by two means, one of description and one of function. First, the gerund phrase is recognized by its characteristic verb form with an *ing* ending, although this is not always a sure-fire means of spotting a gerund. In addition to the *ing* ending, the gerund functions in a sentence in a manner similar to that of a noun. For purposes of this book, then, a gerund may be identified as a verb form ending in *ing* and used as a noun. And, of course, because this discussion concerns phrases, other words must be included with the gerund to form the phrase. Notice the gerunds and gerund phrases in the sentences below. The gerunds are bold and the entire gerund phrases are in italics:

> ***Painting** houses* can be very rewarding.
> We all enjoyed ***seeing** the pictures.*
> The team won the game by ***passing** the ball.*

In the first sentence, the gerund phrase functions as the subject of the verb *can be*. In the second sentence, the gerund phrase is the direct object of the verb; and in the third sentence, the gerund phrase is used as the object of the preposition *by*. Basically, the use of the gerund duplicates the use of the noun, although some uses are fairly rare.

In the examples that follow, note the use of the gerund as an indirect object in the first sentence, and as object of the infinitive in the second sentence:

> The boy gave ***flying** his kite* his undivided attention.
> The runners began to find ***hiking** in the park* somewhat boring.

Gerunds may also be used as subject complements (in the first sentence following) and as appositives (in the second and third sentences that follow):

> His favorite pastime is ***building** model airplanes.*
> Her hobby, ***painting** sand pictures,* requires great patience.
> The class finished the assignment, ***finding** gerund phrases.*

To complicate matters a bit, gerunds, like verbs and infinitives, may pattern with their own complements, such as objects and modifiers. The sentences in the group that follows demonstrate various patterns. The gerunds are underlined, and the various associated word groups are in bold print. The entire gerund phrase is in italics:

> The artist enjoyed <u>*painting*</u> ***pictures of the sea.***
>   (*Pictures of the sea* is the object of the gerund.)

> <u>*Working*</u> ***in the hot sun*** was an unpleasant experience.
>   (The gerund phrase is used as the subject of the verb *was*, while *in the hot sun* is an adverbial prepositional phrase telling "where.")

> <u>*Crying*</u> ***hysterically*** is quite distracting.
>   (*Hysterically* is a single word adverb telling "how.")

> We learned the technique by <u>*watching*</u> ***the experts.***
>   (*Watching the experts* is the object of the preposition *by*; *the experts* is the object of the gerund.)

The swimmer enjoys <u>practicing diving</u> **into the new pool.**
(The gerund phrase is the object of the verb *enjoys*, while the gerund, *diving*, is the object of the gerund, *practicing*.)

Your greatest mistake was <u>giving</u> **your roommate your notes.**
(*Notes* is the object of the gerund, *giving*, while *your roommate* is the indirect object of the gerund. The gerund phrase is a subject complement.)

As you can see, if you understand the special relationships that exist between the verb and other parts of the sentence, along with the various uses of nouns, you should have very little difficulty understanding the gerund and its uses in the sentence. Two cautions must be exercised, however:

- You must be careful not to mistake a participle for a gerund. Participles may have the *ing* ending that is also characteristic of gerunds, but participles are used as modifiers, not as noun substitutes. (Participles are discussed in the next section.)
- A gerund without an auxiliary always consists of the *ing* form of the verb; if it has an auxiliary when a past-participial form is used, it will be preceded by an auxiliary ending in an *ing* form:

    Having **worked** *for an attorney* was a valuable experience.

The gerund *worked* has the past-participle form, thus it contains no *ing* ending; however, the auxiliary preceding it, *having*, does have the characteristic *ing* ending. In the following sentence, two auxiliaries are employed in the gerund phrase:

    Having been **found** *guilty* caused his consternation.

In both sentences above, the gerund phrases are subjects of the verb.

SHOWING RELATIONSHIPS AMONG GERUNDS AND ACTORS

To show a relationship between an actor (noun) and a following gerund, always use a possessive pronoun—if a pronoun is used. If a noun is used, always use the possessive form. Notice the following:

His *working late* always bothered his wife.
No one seemed to mind *our* *mowing the lawn on Sunday.*
My *singing so loud* was unappreciated by music lovers.
Roger's *coming late* disturbed the class.

But, again, you must be able to distinguish between a gerund with a possessive pronoun and a participial phrase, as in the following sentences:

We did not appreciate **his** walking through our garden. (gerund phrase)
We saw **him** walking through our garden. (participial phrase)

In the preceding first sentence, the italicized element is a gerund phrase used as a direct object. Thus *his* is the properly employed pronoun form. However, in the second sentence, the pronoun *him* is the object of the verb *saw*. *Walking through our garden* is a participial phrase modifying *him*. The sentence can be read this way:

We saw him. He was walking through our garden.

Here's another example:

We saw the *workers leaning against the building*.

Leaning against the building describes the workers, thus it is a participial phrase, not a gerund phrase.

Recognizing Gerund Phrases

Following are sentences demonstrating the use of gerund phrases. After each sentence, the gerund and object of the gerund (if any) are listed.

Hunting quail was his favorite pastime.
Gerund Phrase: hunting quail (subject)
Gerund: hunting
Object of the Gerund: quail

The scouts enjoyed swimming in the clear, cold water.
Gerund Phrase: swimming in the clear, cold water (direct object)
Gerund: swimming

You will receive recognition for maintaining an *A* average.
Gerund Phrase: maintaining an *A* average (object of the preposition)
Gerund: maintaining
Object of the Gerund: *A* average

Mowing grass on a hot afternoon is not very enjoyable.
Gerund Phrase: mowing grass on a hot afternoon (subject)
Gerund: mowing
Object of the Gerund: grass

Trying to win is not the same as winning.
Gerund Phrase: trying to win (subject)
Gerund: trying
Object of the Gerund: to win
Gerund Phrase: winning (object of preposition)
Gerund: winning

The old artist gave painting landscapes his undivided attention.
Gerund Phrase: painting landscapes (indirect object)
Gerund: painting
Object of the Gerund: landscapes

No one understood his rejecting such an attractive offer.
Gerund Phrase: his rejecting such an attractive offer (direct object)
Gerund: rejecting
Object of the Gerund: offer

We were recognized for keeping our streets free of trash.
Gerund Phrase: keeping our streets free of trash (object of the preposition)
Gerund: keeping
Object of the Gerund: streets

Searching for Civil War relics can be an exciting hobby.
Gerund Phrase: searching for Civil War relics (subject)
Gerund: searching

Some people cannot endure coping with loud roommates.
Gerund Phrase: coping with loud roommates (direct object)
Gerund: coping

The mechanic tried washing his hands in hot, running water.
Gerund Phrase: washing his hands in hot, running water (direct object)
Gerund: washing
Object of the Gerund: hands

By scaling the wall, the explorers were able to see the treasure.
Gerund Phrase: scaling the wall (object of the preposition)
Gerund: scaling
Object of the Gerund: wall

Beware! Seeing is *not* believing.
Gerund Phrase: seeing (subject)
Gerund: seeing
Gerund Phrase: believing (subject complement)
Gerund: believing

Driving recklessly on the streets is against the law.
Gerund Phrase: driving recklessly on the streets (subject)
Gerund: driving

Joe talked of seeing an interesting play while in Paris.
Gerund Phrase: seeing an interesting play while in Paris (object of the preposition)
Gerund: seeing
Object of the Gerund: play

His hobby was building model airplanes.
Gerund Phrase: building model airplanes (subject complement)
Gerund: building
Object of the Gerund: airplanes

We were all accustomed to seeing some students given special consideration.
Gerund Phrase: seeing some students given special consideration (object of the preposition)
Gerund: seeing
Object of the Gerund: students

Vacationing in Hawaii is not economical for anyone trying to save money.
Gerund Phrase: vacationing in Hawaii (subject)
Gerund: vacationing

He tried losing weight by not eating.
Gerund Phrase: losing weight by not eating (direct object)
Gerund: losing
Object of the Gerund: weight
Gerund Phrase: eating (object of the preposition)

He was given a citation for not yielding the right-of-way.
Gerund Phrase: yielding the right-of-way (object of the preposition)
Gerund: yielding
Object of the Gerund: right-of-way

Participial Phrases

The participle of a verb has two basic forms: the *present participle* and the *past participle*.

- The present participle is always the base form of the verb with *ing* added to it—for example, *play + ing, work + ing, go + ing.*
- The past-participle form of regular verbs ends in *ed* and patterns with auxiliaries such as *have* and *had*—for example, *worked, tried, moved, cleaned.*

- Various forms, of course, represent the irregular verbs: *swept, seen, caught, run, rung,* and so on.

A participial phrase, then, is one that contains a participle. Such phrases can function in various ways:

- They can follow noun phrases:

  The plane *now landing at Gate C11* is three hours late.

- They can function like dependent clauses to indicate time, result, reason, and so on:

  While skiing off-piste, Klaus discovered an old mining shack. (time)
  Obscured by the hedge, Grover was not detected by the police officer. (reason)
  Bert tripped, *dropping the jug of milk he carried*. (result)

- They can follow an object and verb of the senses (*see, feel, hear, smell, taste,* and so on):

  I could hear Heidi *playing in her crib*.

In all the preceding examples, the participial phrases act as adjectives; in fact, participial phrases pattern and function exactly as do adjectives. The difference between the two sets of words (adjectives and participles) is in form only (and, of course, the action indicated by the participles). The participles have the characteristic verb form plus the *ing* endings. Following are several sentences with participles, which appear in italics:

Lazily, the *yawning* soldiers returned to work.
We watched the *setting* sun, with feelings of sadness and delight.
We felt the *rising* wind against our *perspiring* bodies.
The *fainting* student fell against the *moving* chair.
The *smitten* student knew his heart was breaking. (*Smitten* is the past participle of *smite*.)
Huffing and *chuffing*, the little train left the *fading* station behind.
The *sleeping* children are resting in the shade of the *spreading* oak tree.
Jogging is *exhilarating* exercise for some ambitious souls.

DISCERNING THE DIFFERENCE BETWEEN GERUNDS AND PARTICIPLES

As noted, participles and gerunds often have the same form, that of the base form of the verb plus the *ing* ending. The difference between the gerund and the participle is in *function* in the sentence: The gerund functions as a noun; the participle functions as an adjective.

Notice the similarities between regular adjectives and participles in this sentence:

The lazy, *sleeping* cat did not see the quiet, *creeping* mouse.

In contrast, a gerund typically acts as a noun, as in the following sentence, of which *snowboarding* is the subject:

Snowboarding is Ethan's favorite activity.

PARTICIPIAL MODIFIERS AND OBJECTS

Because a participle—like gerunds and infinitives—is, in reality, a form of the verb, it too may have modifiers and objects. In other words, participles may be incorporated into their own grammatical units, the *participial phrase*. Notice the modifiers and objects of the participles in the sentences that follow. The participial phrases are written in italics, and the participles are in bold print:

The children, ***sitting*** *quietly,* waited for the teacher.
Finding *a quarter*, the boys headed to the candy store.
Working *in the hot sun*, the laborers soon grew weak.
Not ***worrying*** *about the others*, the guides soon left the stragglers behind.
John, *having **seen** the answers*, received the highest score.

The adjectival function of the participles and participial phrases is apparent in the preceding sentences. Also, the various elements of the participial phrases are generally apparent. In the first sentence, the participle *sitting* has a single modifying adverb, *quietly*. In the second sentence, the participle *finding* has an object, called, logically enough, *the object of the participle*. What was found? A quarter. Thus, *quarter* is the object of the participle. In the third sentence, the participle *working* has a modifying prepositional (adverbial) phrase, *in the hot sun*. The fourth sentence contains a participial phrase with a negative, *not*, preceding it. The fifth sentence contains a participial phrase with the participle in the past-participle form. Although *having* does have the participial *ing* ending, in this sentence it is used as an auxiliary, not as the head word of the participial phrase.

RECOGNIZING PARTICIPIAL PHRASES

Following are several sentences containing participial phrases. Listed with each sentence is the phrase, the participle, and the object of the participle (if any):

My brother, repairing his car at the last minute, was able to enter the race.
Participial Phrase: repairing his car at the last minute
Participle: repairing
Object of the Participle: car

We enjoyed watching the ducks swimming peacefully on the small pond.
Participial Phrase: swimming peacefully on the small pond
Participle: swimming

Repairing the roof with new shingles, the carpenter earned his reward.
Participial Phrase: repairing the roof with new shingles
Participle: repairing
Object of the Participle: roof

The class, anxiously awaiting the professor, talked among themselves.
Participial Phrase: anxiously awaiting the professor
Participle: awaiting
Object of the Participle: professor

Trying to unfasten the window, the burglar awakened the family's dog.
Participial Phrase: trying to unfasten the window
Participle: trying
Object of the Participle: to unfasten the window

Directing traffic with confidence, the rookie officer impressed his sergeant.
Participial Phrase: directing traffic with confidence
Participle: directing
Object of the Participle: traffic

The fire truck, leading the holiday parade, was involved in a mishap.
Participial Phrase: leading the holiday parade
Participle: leading
Object of the Participle: parade

The hunter saw his dog tracking the bear.
Participial Phrase: tracking the bear
Participle: tracking
Object of the Participle: bear

We watched the cat climbing up the curtains.
Participial Phrase: climbing up the curtains
Participle: climbing

The soldiers, quickly loading their rifles, fired at the invaders.
Participial Phrase: quickly loading their rifles
Participle: loading
Object of the Participle: rifles

The old gardener was angry at the squirrels eating his vegetables.
Participial Phrase: eating his vegetables
Participle: eating
Object of the Participle: vegetables

Working with old lumber, the craftsman manufactured beautiful furniture.
Participial Phrase: working with old lumber
Participle: working

Leaving the office early, the workers went to the ball game.
Participial Phrase: leaving the office early
Participle: leaving
Object of the Participle: office

Knowing he was being watched, the spy left a fake message.
Participial Phrase: knowing he was being watched
Participle: knowing
Object of the Participle: he was being watched

Sitting in the shade, the workers ate their lunches.
Participial Phrase: sitting in the shade
Participle: sitting

We all knew the woman singing the song so beautifully.
Participial Phrase: singing the song so beautifully
Participle: singing
Object of the Participle: song

The victim, pretending injury, sat in the street crying.
Participial Phrase: pretending injury
Participle: pretending
Object of the Participle: injury
Participial Phrase: crying

Trapped by the tide, the swimmers drifted off course.
Participial Phrase: trapped by the tide (past-participle form)
Participle: trapped

The person lying in the sun trying to sleep is my brother.
Participial Phrase: lying in the sun
Participle: lying
Participial Phrase: trying to sleep
Participle: trying

Dangling participles

Writers from the early grades of middle school through university have been warned about dangling participles—that is, participial phrases located in the wrong place in the sentence. In effect, it is not placed next to the word (noun) that it modifies. Although the results are often very humorous, such a lapse in style indicates a carelessness on the part of the writer that one can ill afford to convey to a reader.

The sentences that follow contain dangling participial phrases (in italics). Laugh if you wish, but be able to explain what needs to be done to make the sentences say what they were probably meant to say.

Spurting gas all the way, the little old lady slowly drove her car into town.
Changing her diapers, the baby-sitter made the young child warm and comfortable.
After *paying my fine*, the judge told me I was free to leave.
Walking on two wooden legs, the little puppy tripped the unsteady man.
Holding his spear in front of him, the old lion charged the native.
Chased by the hound, the rock pile offered shelter for the frightened rabbit.

NOMINATIVE ABSOLUTE PHRASES

Nominative absolute phrases are not, strictly speaking, participial phrases. In fact, they function differently from participial phrases in the English sentence; however, they do contain participles, and they do function as modifiers. Therefore, students of grammar and usage should be aware of these types of phrases.

In order to understand nominative absolute phrases, you may need a crash course in nominals. A *nominal* names one or more people, places, objects, or events. If you think that the definition of a nominal is rather similar to the definition of a noun, you're absolutely correct. In fact, nouns and pronouns are the most common types of nominals, which are the following:

- Nouns

  Heidi
  laundromat
  letter opener
  Indianapolis 500

- Pronouns

  he
  her
  who
  it

- Noun phrases

  the man in the airplane

- Noun clauses

  whether she is absent

- Gerunds and gerund phrases

  seeming composed

- Infinitives and infinitive phrases

  to seem composed

A nominative absolute phrase, then, is a phrase without a finite verb that modifies the whole sentence.

The game being over, the crowd left the stadium.

Take the two sentences that follow. The first contains a participial phrase; the second contains a nominative absolute phrase. Note the differences in structure and relationship to the main clause of each:

Being the leader, I was responsible for the group.
The leader being absent, I was responsible for the group.

The first sentence could be reconstructed in this manner:

I was the leader. I was responsible for the group.

In the second sentence, no such relationship can be established. Two separate ideas are presented:

The leader was absent. I was responsible for the group.

Here are some basic differences between the two constructions:

- The participial phrase in the first sentence relates specifically to the following noun or pronoun—in this case to *I*, which is not a part of the participial phrase itself.
- The participle in the second sentence is tied to a nominal, *leader*, within the confines of the phrase.
- The absolute phrase in sentence 2 does not appear to modify any single word within the following clause. In fact, if anything, it seems to modify the entire main clause.
- The subject of the main clause cannot be related to the object of the participle in sentence 2, as it can be in sentence 1.

Nominative absolute phrases are capable of mobility within a sentence, because they are not directly tied to any single sentence element. Participial phrases do not enjoy such mobility. Notice the placement of the absolute phrase in each of the sentences below:

> *The ship having sailed earlier than expected*, we were forced to take a plane to Europe.
>
> We were forced to take a plane to Europe, *the ship having sailed earlier than expected.*

Following are some sample sentences, some with participial phrases (in italics), others with nominative absolute phrases (in bold).

> We found the boys *shooting marbles behind the school building.*
>
> **The tree having fallen across the drive**, we were forced to walk to the store for groceries.
>
> The students were studying for the examination, **the finals having been scheduled for the next day**.
>
> *Choked by the weeds*, the flowers simply would not grow so tall as the climbing roses.
>
> **The dog having been found by its master**, the reward of $100 was canceled.
>
> The trucker spotted the hitchhiker *sitting under the overpass.*
>
> The scouts, *needing shelter from the storm*, entered the old house.
>
> **The jury having found the defendant guilty**, the judge, *having a luncheon engagement*, adjourned the court.
>
> We thought we had spotted a UFO *flying overhead.*
>
> *Seeing their English professor coming up the walk*, the class began studying, **the bell having already rung**.

Identifying Verbals

To better help you identify the various types of verbals, the following sentences contain infinitive phrases, gerund phrases, participial phrases, and/or nominative absolute phrases:

> The bell having rung, the students ceased their talking to friends.
> **the bell having rung:** nominative absolute phrase
> **having rung:** participial phrase
> **talking to friends:** gerund phrase
>
> We wanted to find our friends, so we began shouting to attract them.
> **to find our friends:** infinitive phrase
> **shouting to attract them:** gerund phrase
> **to attract them:** infinitive phrase
>
> By finding the north star, the scouts were able to find the trail leading out of the woods.
> **finding the north star:** gerund phrase
> **to find the trail leading out of the woods:** infinitive phrase
> **leading out of the woods:** participial phrase

Pray without ceasing, expect to receive nothing, find joy in loving.
ceasing: gerund phrase
to receive nothing: infinitive phrase
loving: gerund phrase

Realizing the professor was late, the class decided to leave early.
realizing the professor was late: participial phrase
to leave early: infinitive phrase

When we returned, the bus, having left early, was already departing.
having left early: participial phrase

The sun having set, we decided to make our camp early.
the sun having set: nominative absolute phrase
having set: participial phrase
to make our camp early: infinitive phrase

We refused to waste time by studying astrology.
to waste time by studying astrology: infinitive phrase
studying astrology: gerund phrase

Relying on Lynne's instructions, we tried eating wisely in an effort to lose weight.
relying on Lynne's instructions: participial phrase
eating wisely: gerund phrase
to lose weight: infinitive phrase

The thing to do in an emergency is to yell "Fire," hoping to attract attention.
to do in an emergency: infinitive phrase
to yell fire: infinitive phrase
hoping to attract attention: participial phrase (modifying an understood "you")
to attract attention: infinitive phrase

CLAUSES

A *clause* is a group of words having both subject and predicate and incorporated as a part of the sentence. The two main types of clauses are the following:

- Independent clauses
- Dependent (or *subordinate*) clauses

Independent Clauses

An *independent clause* conveys complete meaning and may stand alone. It could be a sentence in its own right; but because it patterns with other elements within the framework of a sentence, an independent clause is a part of a sentence. In the examples below, the independent clauses are in italics:

Because I was ill, *I was not able to attend class.*
We were all frustrated, since the sun wasn't shining.
Elmo and I were friends, but *we weren't roommates.*

Coordinate clauses

A clause connected to one or more other clauses of equal status is called a *coordinate clause*; such clauses are joined through the use of coordinating conjunctions such as *for, and, nor, but, or,* and *yet.* (Note that the coordinate conjunction is not considered part of the independent clauses it joins; however, subordinating conjunctions, such as *because* and *since*, are considered a part of *dependent clauses.*)

A coordinating conjunction joining coordinate clauses is preceded by a comma—unless a comma is already used in one of the coordinate clauses. If such is the case, a semicolon is used. The first sentence following shows the use of a comma; the second shows the use of a semicolon:

The puppy was playful, *but* the cat was not.
As expected, the bus was late; *but* we didn't mind waiting.

Coordinate clauses may pattern *without* the coordinating conjunction joining them. In such cases, a semicolon is employed to separate them:

We refused to cross the river; the current was too swift.

Very short coordinate clauses in a series may be written without coordinating conjunctions and separated by commas:

I ran, I fell, I broke my leg.

Dependent (Subordinate) Clauses

Subordinate clauses are called *dependent clauses* because they cannot stand alone—that is, they cannot function independently as sentences. Instead, they are employed as parts of speech (adjectives, adverbs, and nouns); as such, they may be used as the specific parts of speech are used. Dependent clauses usually begin with a relative pronoun (such as *who, which,* and *that*) or with a subordinating conjunction (*if, as, since, although, until, because, where, when,* and *although*).

Adjective Clauses

The *adjective clause*, as does the single-word adjective, modifies a noun or pronoun. It is introduced by a relative pronoun (*who, whose, whom, which, that*) or by a subordinating conjunction (*where, when,* or *why*):

> The boy **who** *is speaking* is my brother.
> Give the money to him **who** *needs it most.*
> The racket **that** *I bought* has nylon strings.
> This is the place **where** *we had a flat tire.*
> The boy **who** *caught the fish* <u>*that are displayed here*</u> is ten years old.

The underlined clause in the preceding sentence is also an adjective clause.

> Sue Nelson, **who** *is a fine tennis player* and **who** *arrived today,* will teach us how to improve our game.
> The reason **why** *he left* is a mystery to everyone.

The relative pronoun is an important part of the adjective clause. It may be a subject, a direct object, an object of a preposition, or a possessive modifier. *Where, when,* or *why* in an adjective clause modifies the verb within that clause.

Often the relative pronoun or subordinating conjunction that usually introduces an adjective clause is omitted or understood. In formal English, these *joining* words probably ought to be employed. In any case, you should be able to recognize adjective clauses without the relative pronouns and subordinating conjunctions and not confuse such clauses with independent clauses. Note these examples in which the missing relative pronoun or conjunction is shown in brackets and the empty brackets show where the relative pronoun or conjunction would normally occur. The adjective clauses are in italics:

> The puppy [ ] *you wanted* has been sold. [that]
> He knew the reason [ ] *my car wouldn't start.* [why]
> The man [ ] *you met* is my brother. [whom]

RESTRICTIVE VERSUS NONRESTRICTIVE CLAUSES

Adjective clauses that are not essential to sentence meaning should be set off by commas. Such clauses are called *nonrestrictive clauses* or *nonessential clauses.* They may be omitted from a sentence without a loss of the basic meaning of the sentence. Adjective clauses beginning with *that* are always restrictive clauses (that is, they are necessary to restrict the meaning of the sentence; in other words, they indicate the essential meaning of the sentence):

> The dog *that you saw* came back again. (restrictive)
> Mr. Smith, *whom you met at the lecture,* is from the state of Texas. (nonrestrictive)

In the preceding first sentence, the adjective clause, *that you saw*, is essential to the sentence to identify the exact dog that came back. In the second sentence, the nonrestrictive adjective clause, *whom you met at the lecture,* is merely an aside adding more information than is required to garner full meaning from the sentence.

That versus *which*

Although many people use *that* and *which* interchangeably, they should not be so used. *That* should be used only to introduce a restrictive clause; *which* should be used only to introduce a nonrestrictive clause:

Correct: The puppy that I trained tore up my Birkenstocks.

(This sentence implies that there is more than one puppy; the speaker is referring specifically to the one she trained. This is a restrictive clause.)

Correct: The puppy, which I trained, tore up my Birkenstocks.

(In this sentence, the clause "which I trained" simply provides more information about the puppy in question; if the clause were removed, the sentence's essential meaning would still be conveyed. This is a nonrestrictive clause.)

Adverb Clauses

The *adverb clause*, as does the single-word adverb, modifies a verb (including the verb form in a *verbal*—that is, a *gerund, infinitive*, or *participle*), an adjective, or an adverb. Adverb clauses are introduced by subordinating conjunctions such as the following:

even if
as though
when
although
because
as long as
as
until
before
than
wherever
while
whenever
though
after
whether
since
whereas
so that

provided that
where
as if
in order that
as soon as

Here are some examples of dependent (subordinate) clauses used as adverbs to modify the verb, adjective, adverb, infinitive, and a participle:

When the bell rang, everyone hurried into the building.
(Modifies the verb *hurried.*)

Today is much warmer *than yesterday was.*
(Modifies the adjective *warmer.*)

The boys come here more often *than they came before.*
(Modifies the adverb *often.*)

He wishes to leave before the rain begins.
(Modifies the infinitive *to leave.*)

Grumbling *because he was tired*, Don retraced his steps.
(Modifies the participle *grumbling.*)

Adverbial clauses may express nine relationships:

- Time
    The man fainted *when he saw the blood.*
    Since the sun came up, I have been watching the ducks.

- Place
    I found my wallet *where I had left it.*
    Wherever we go we find interesting people.

- Manner
    The colt runs *as if he were lame.*
    Copy the message *just as you received it.*

- Condition
    The boat will sink *if the hull isn't repaired.*
    Even if I lose the race, I'll feel good about it.

- Cause
    Jerry's car wouldn't start *because it was out of fuel.*
    Since the buses weren't running, we walked to the store.

- Purpose

  Our neighbors landscaped their lawn *so that they would win the prize.*

  In order that we would not forget to call, we wrote the number on the windshield.

- Result

  The trees fell *so that the road was completely blocked.*

  The wind blew so hard *that the fire went out.*

- Comparison

  A dog can run faster *than a cat (can run).*

  No one talks *as much as my roommate (talks).*

- Concession

  She delivered the lecture *although she felt unsteady.*

  Even though I have reservations, I can't find a seat.

In the following examples, the adverb clauses modify the verb *runs.* Each illustrates one of the typical adverbial functions of telling *how, when, where, why, to what extent,* and *under what conditions.*

He runs *as though he had been frightened.* (how he runs)
He runs *whenever he can.* (when he runs)
He runs *wherever he goes.* (where he runs)
He runs *because he likes to run.* (why he runs)
He runs *as far as he can.* (to what extent he runs)
He runs *if he feels like running.* (under what condition he runs)

DISCERNING BETWEEN ADVERB CLAUSES AND ADJECTIVE CLAUSES

The following sentences contain adjective and/or adverb clauses. Following each sentence is a listing of each clause, the type of clause, and the word(s) it modifies:

The coin that I found on the sidewalk had been there since the sun rose this morning.
  that I found on the sidewalk: adjective clause (coin)
  since the sun rose this morning: adverb clause (had been [there])

If you see the person who used this book, have him or her report to me.
  if you see the person who used this book: adverb clause (have)
  who used this book: adjective clause (person)

Until yesterday, we had never seen a cow that could dial a telephone.
  that could dial a telephone: adjective clause (cow)

This is the place where we were stuck in the mud yesterday.
  where we were stuck in the mud yesterday: adjective clause (place)

Try to be quiet when you come home late at night.
>   **when you come home late at night:** adverb clause (try)

If you are careful, you will be able to see the hawk that built its nest in the old oak tree.
>   **if you are careful:** adverb clause (will be able)
>   **that built its nest in the old oak tree:** adjective clause (hawk)

I like the report that you presented to our group when you were here.
>   **that you presented to our group:** adjective clause (report)
>   **when you were here:** adverb clause (presented)

I talked with a young man who wants to be a race car driver when he becomes old enough.
>   **who wants to be a race car driver:** adjective clause (man)
>   **when he becomes old enough:** adverb clause (wants)

We watched the volcano that erupted unexpectedly.
>   **that erupted unexpectedly:** adjective clause (volcano)

We became acquainted with the people who moved into the house that was rebuilt after the fire.
>   **who moved into the house:** adjective clause (people)
>   **that was rebuilt after the fire:** adjective clause (house)

When we returned home from school, I got a job for the summer.
>   **when we returned from school:** adverb clause (got)

Even though he is always very polite, he seems to annoy people.
>   **even though he is always polite:** adverb clause (seems)

We'll surely win the game if we play well.
>   **if we play well:** adverb clause (win)

I plan to travel to Europe, where I'll trace my family's roots.
>   **where I'll trace my family's roots:** adjective clause (Europe)

The boy who was lost ate ice cream at the police station.
>   **who was lost:** adjective clause (boy)

We sang songs until we were too tired to sing any longer.
>   **until we were too tired to sing any longer:** adverb clause (sang)

Whoever told you that story is not a person that I would trust.
>   **that I would trust:** adjective clause (person)

The witness identified the man who held up the bank.
> **who held up the bank:** adjective clause (man)

I hope the rain stops because we want to go camping.
> **because we want to go camping:** adverb clause (hope)

Oscar wrote one of the most interesting stories I have ever read.
> **(that) I have ever read:** adjective clause (stories)

The road crew worked hard in the morning so that they could take the afternoon off.
> **so that they could take the afternoon off:** adverb clause (worked)

I enjoy classical music, which is not popular with Sue.
> **which is not popular with Sue:** adjective clause (music)

The ballet, which was performed by professional dancers, lasted until the next act was ready.
> **which was performed by professional dancers:** adjective clause (ballet)
> **until the next act was ready:** adverb clause (lasted)

Whenever you are ready, we'll meet the people who are waiting for us.
> **whenever you are ready:** adverb clause (meet)
> **who are waiting for us:** adjective clause (people)

We knew where we were when we saw the sign that pointed the way to Nashville.
> **when we saw the sign that pointed the way to Nashville:** adverb clause (knew)
> **that pointed the way to Nashville:** adjective clause (sign)

When I was a college student, I made a decision that changed my entire life—I decided to become a singer.
> **when I was a college student:** adverb clause (made)
> **that changed my entire life:** adjective clause (decision)

Cover your head if you want to avoid sun damage to your skin.
> **if you want to avoid sun damage to your skin:** adverb clause (cover)

Noun Clauses

Noun clauses function in sentences just as nouns function. If you understand the use of nouns as subjects, direct objects, objects of prepositions, indirect objects, appositives, subject complements, and objects of verbals, you should have little trouble understanding the use of noun clauses in a sentence. Examples of noun clauses used as various parts of the sentence are given in the following examples:

What the professor said was very confusing to the students. (subject of the verb *was*)
I found *what I was looking for*. (direct object of *found*)
Give the tools to *whoever needs them*. (object of the preposition *to*)
Tell *whomever you see* the story of the missing pens. (indirect object of *tell*)
We all knew the reason *that Sarah won the award*. (object complement of the noun *reason*)
The loser is *whoever crosses the line last*. (subject complement)
You think *whoever smiles at you* to be your friend. (subject of the infinitive *to be*)

A noun clause is usually introduced by one of the following words: *that, who, what, where, when, why, how, which,* and *whether.* Remember that some of these words also introduce other kinds of clauses, so take care not to attempt to identify clauses solely by the words that introduce them. The particular use of a clause within the framework of a sentence determines what type of clause it is:

I knew him *when he was a baby*.
    (The clause is an adverb clause telling *when* the speaker knew him.)

I knew when he hurt himself.
    (The clause is a noun clause used as the direct object of *knew*. What was known? When he hurt himself. Therefore, the clause is the direct object.)

He ran off the road where it crosses the creek.
    (The clause tells *where;* therefore, it is an adverb clause.)

At the last moment, we realized *where we were*.
    (The clause tells *what* we realized; therefore, it is a direct object and a noun clause.)

As with adjective clauses, the noun clause may sometimes occur without the relative pronoun *that*. In fact, *that* is often unnecessary in a sentence and serves only to introduce a following clause. (Some texts, however, treat *that* as a major part of a sentence—the direct object—and the following clause as a complement of *that*.) In the following sentence, the parentheses indicate where *that* would sometimes occur:

The minister believed () his sermon was inspiring.

The following sentences contain noun clauses, and indicate how those clauses are being used (as subjects, direct objects, object complements, objects of prepositions, subject complements, appositives, or indirect objects.

We told whoever would listen to us our sad, sad story.
Noun Clause: whoever would listen to us
Usage: indirect object

He told us he would help us move our belongings.
Noun Clause: he would help us move our belongings
Usage: direct object

Our futures depend upon how we discipline ourselves.
Noun Clause: how we discipline ourselves
Usage: object of the preposition

Whatever you prepare for dinner will be fine with me.
Noun Clause: whatever you prepare for dinner
Usage: subject

The final decision will be whatever you choose.
Noun Clause: whatever you choose
Usage: subject complement

The doctor knew what it was to suffer extreme pain.
Noun Clause: what it was to suffer extreme pain
Usage: direct object

Who wins the race is secondary to how he or she wins it.
Noun Clause: who wins the race
Usage: subject
Noun Clause: how he or she wins it
Usage: object of the preposition

No one paid any attention to what the speaker told us about safety.
Noun Clause: what the speaker told us about safety
Usage: object of the preposition

We knew that our horse was becoming tired.
Noun Clause: (that) our horse was becoming tired
Usage: direct object

We were disappointed by what they told us.
Noun Clause: what they told us
Usage: object of the preposition

Most people are not impressed by how fast others drive.
Noun Clause: how fast others drive
Usage: object of the preposition

The message that the singer had canceled the engagement disappointed her fans.
Noun Clause: that the singer had canceled the engagement
Usage: appositive (actually, this is a complement to the noun "message")

Jack found his wallet just a short distance from where he thought he had lost it.
Noun Clause: where he thought he had lost it
Usage: object of the preposition

Everyone should know that the earth cannot support an indefinite number of people.
Noun Clause: (that) the earth cannot support an indefinite number of people
Usage: direct object

The family reached the decision that it would vacation at the seashore.
Noun Clause: that it would vacation at the seashore
Usage: object complement (this clause complements the direct object "decision")

Whoever told you that story is not a person that I would trust.
Noun Clause: whoever told you that story
Usage: subject

The president informed us that she was ready to have the meeting.
Noun Clause: that she was ready to have the meeting
Usage: direct object

I hope the rain stops because we want to go camping.
Noun Clause: the rain stops
Usage: direct object

The old mariner told whoever would listen his tale.
Noun Clause: whoever would listen
Usage: indirect object

We knew where we were when we saw the sign that pointed the way to Nashville.
Noun Clause: where we were
Usage: direct object

Whoever reads this book will find that things are different in California.
Noun Clause: whoever reads this book
Usage: subject
Noun Clause: that things are different in California
Usage: direct object

 # GENERAL OBSERVATIONS ABOUT SENTENCE PARTS

- A sentence may be comprised of many parts. Some of these parts, such as the following, are required:
  - Subjects and predicates
  - Punctuation
  - Direct objects
  - Indirect objects
  - Complements
  - Appositives
  - Sentence modifiers
  - Phrases
  - Clauses

- The English sentence comprises two parts, a subject and a predicate.
- With some sentences, answering a simple "who?" or "what?" question identifies the simple subject of the sentence.
- The *predicate* of a sentence is all the words that do not pattern with the subject, as long as the entire sentence (or clause) fits into one of the patterns discussed earlier in this part, in the section titled "Sentence Patterns."
- Punctuation is a mechanical aid to accurate written communication.
- Terminal punctuation is that punctuation that brings something, such as a sentence or an abbreviation, to an end. The various types of terminal punctuation include the following:
  - The period (.)
  - The question mark (?)
  - The exclamation mark (!)
  - The interrobang (‽)

- Internal punctuation separates, divides, and points out elements within an expression, thereby developing clarity and specific identity. Internal punctuation includes such marks as the following:

  - The comma (,)
  - The semicolon (;)
  - The colon (:)
  - The hyphen (-)
  - The em dash (—)
  - The en dash (–)
  - Parentheses (())
  - Brackets ([])
  - The ellipsis (. . . or . . . .)
  - Quotation marks ("")
  - The apostrophe (')
  - Italics

- A major sentence element contained in many predicates is the *direct object*, which occurs in sentences that have *transitive verbs*. A transitive verb is a verb that requires a direct object to give the sentence a sense of completeness. To identify direct objects, you may again ask the "what" question in conjunction with the verb.

- *Indirect objects* are those parts of the predicate that occur in sentences containing direct objects and that are closely related to the direct objects by identifying the person/thing to whom or for whom something is done or given, or of whom a question is asked. Indirect objects are usually nouns or pronouns.

- A *complement*, which may be a noun, adjective, pronoun, or phrase, is added to a verb to complete the predicate of a sentence. The complement provides information about a clause's subject or object. There are four main types of complements:

  - Object complement
  - Subject complement
  - Adverbial complement
  - Adjectival complement

- An *appositive* is a word, phrase, or clause usually located after a nominal (a noun, noun phrase, or noun substitute) to identify, explain, or describe the nominal. Although adjectives may be used in apposition, appositives are usually nouns and pronouns.
- Certain types of adverbials may be employed as *sentence modifiers*. Usually set off by commas, these modifiers relate to the entire sentence, not to any separate element within the sentence.
- The traditional definition of a *phrase* is somewhat as follows: "A phrase is a group of words not containing a subject and predicate and used as a single part of speech." The various types of phrases include the following:

  - Noun phrases
  - Prepositional phrases
  - Verbals

- A *clause* is a group of words having both subject and predicate and incorporated as a part of the sentence. The two main types of clauses are the following:

  - Independent clauses
  - Dependent (or *subordinate*) clauses

PART III

HANDLING CAPITALIZATION AND SPELLING

A couple elements of grammar are unusual in that they apply only to writers, not to speakers: capitalization and spelling. Although English does put forth some rules in regard to both these grammatical elements, the sad truth is that the language breaks those rules more often than not. In this part, you learn the rules—and exceptions—for capitalization and spelling.

Capitalization

The use of capital letters is a mechanical aid to clear written communication. When you write, you use capital letters to distinguish certain elements from other elements of the sentence. This section presents in a logical arrangement those elements that, according to custom, should be capitalized. It also emphasizes certain elements that should not be capitalized.

Although there are a few principles for the use of capital letters that do not readily submit to reason, you can easily learn the customs to follow by analyzing the general principles and the detailed illustrations presented in this section. If you follow these principles, you will be correct in all situations, with the possible exception of some journalistic writing, which tends to use less capitalization.

 Just as other conventions of language—and the language itself—are changing, so too is capitalization. Therefore, if you discover a practice that differs from this guide, you should pursue the matter to see how widespread the practice is. Bear in mind, also, that different publications use different style guides, and what may be acceptable style for one publication may need modifications for another.

The following should be capitalized:

- The first word of any sentence.
- The pronoun *I* and the vocative *0*.

> Are not these, O soul, the vision of Him? . . .

- The first word of a formal statement following a colon.

> Mrs. Smith released this statement to the press: "The fact that Smedley chose to resign is regrettable."

- The first word of a direct quotation for which the beginning has been included.

> Miss Grammarlove replied, "Today we shall study book reports."

 Do not capitalize the first word of a quoted fragment (unless the first word of the quotation is also the first word of the sentence):

> Was it Franklin who said that "fools will learn in no other"?
> I agree with Dr. Cole that Peter is his "own worst enemy."

- The first word of all outline topics and subtopics.
- The words *Resolved* and *Whereas,* and the first word that follows each of these expressions in a preamble and a resolution.

> Whereas, He has contributed unselfishly . . . .
> Resolved, That suffrage should be granted . . . .

- The first word of a statement or a question inserted into a sentence without quotation marks.

> Our problem is, How can we finish the work?

- The first word of a complete line of poetry.
- The first word after a strong interjection.

> Help! The shelves are falling!

- The first word and any noun in the salutation of a letter.

> Dear Friends and Neighbors,

- Only the first word of a complimentary close.

> Very truly yours,

You should capitalize initials; titles (or abbreviations of titles) preceding proper names; the abbreviations Jr., Sr., and Esq. following names; and the abbreviations of academic degrees.

Martin Luther King, Jr.
J.R. Ewing
Sir Anthony Hopkins
Mrs. Robinson
Superintendent Jones
Chief Maddox
Dr. James Herriott
Murgatroyd Peterson, Ph.D.

On the subject of academic degrees, the formal names of academic degrees should be capitalized.

Master of Arts degree
Doctor of Philosophy degree
Bachelor of Science

Do not, however, capitalize types of degrees unless the formal name is intended.

She received her master's degree last summer.
The university awarded more than a hundred bachelor's degrees in May.

Capitalize a title used alone or following a person's name only if the title refers to a high government official:

the Secretary of State
the secretary of our club
Dr. Jones, superintendent of schools
I was elected senator from my state.
   (*Senator* refers to an office, not a person; hence, no capitalization is
   needed.)
No, Senator, I don't agree.

In addition, you must capitalize proper nouns and proper adjectives. These include the following:

- The names of persons

   Before writing names beginning with *Mc* or *Mac,* find out
   whether or not the person spells his name with two capital
   letters. The custom is not constant: McDonald, MacKay,
   Macdonald, Macmillan, Macduff. Names beginning with *O'*
   usually contain two capital letters: O'Reilley, O'Toole,
   O'Callahan.

- Geographical names, including the names of the following:
  - Cities, townships, parishes, counties, states, provinces, countries, and continents
  - Recognized sections of the country or world
  - Islands, peninsulas, straits, beaches, and deserts
  - Bodies of water
  - Mountains
  - Forests, parks, canyons, and dams
  - Planets, stars, satellites, and constellations, except in the case of *sun, earth,* and *moon*

 It is considered correct to capitalize *earth* when it is used in a sentence with another capitalized astrological body.

 Do not capitalize east, west, north, and south when these words indicate direction (as opposed to when they are part of a geographic location's proper name, in which case they should be capitalized). Following are some examples:

> **Incorrect:** Jerry lives on the *East* side of town.
> **Correct:** Terre Haute is *west* of Indianapolis.
> **Incorrect:** I think the Pacific northwest is one of the most intriguing regions in America.
> **Correct:** There are many interesting books about the history of the South.

- The names of pets
- The names of firms
- The names of institutions

> Benton-Marshall County Hospital
> Notre Dame University

- The names of organizations

> Boy Scouts of America
> National Organization for Women
> Amvets

- The names of buildings and other man-made structures

> the Taj Mahal
> the Great Pyramids at Giza

- Brand names (note that the common noun that follows the name of the product should not be capitalized, except in advertising displays)

    Wrangler jeans
    Colt revolver

- The names of ships, planes, trains, railways, and airlines

    the Andrea Doria
    Air Force One
    Santa Fe Railroad
    Delta Airlines

- The names of historical events and periods

    the Civil War
    the Renaissance

- The names of historical documents

    the Bill of Rights
    the Declaration of Independence

- The names of holidays, including the words *day* and *eve*

    New Year's Day
    Christmas Eve

- The names of government bodies

    the U. S. Senate
    the House of Lords

- The names of races, religions, denominations, and nationalities

    Methodist
    Buddhism
    Asian
    Haitian

- The names of all languages
- The names of the months of the year and days of the week

Do not capitalize the name of a season unless the season is personified:

    I know that winter will soon arrive.
    I know you, Winter—an old, cold, grandfather.

- School subjects that are languages or that are followed by a numeral or a letter

  History 110
  history
  Chemistry B
  chemistry
  Biology 101
  biology
  French

- The names of political parties (but not the word *party*)

  Republican party
  States Rights party

- All things that are personified

  O Wind, if winter comes, can spring be far behind?

- An epithet or a nickname

  Jimmy Fritz Boomer

- Words referring to the Deity, to Christ, and to Mary, and the names applied to the Bible and its parts and to other sacred books

  O Lord
  the Virgin
  Genesis
  Koran
  Talmud
  Mishnah

- A noun, or an abbreviation of a noun, that is followed by a numeral or a letter, except the word *page*

  Stalag 14
  Laboratory C
  Deck A
  ER 6
  page 303

- The names of streets, boulevards, and other such road designations

  Maple Street
  Parklane Drive
  Glendale Road

Do not capitalize a generic term used in plurals:

> Chestnut and Walnut streets
> the Atlantic and Pacific oceans
> the Lutheran and Episcopal churches

- Words of family relationship when those words can be replaced by proper nouns or when they are used as part of the name

> Are you my friend's uncle?
> We hope Uncle Ed will sing for us.
> I know, Uncle, that you are very tired.

- Abbreviations of proper nouns

> WW II
> Ph.D.
> MBA
> AA
> AFL-CIO
> CIA
> GSA
> FFA
> 4–H
> FBI
> J.D. (Juris Doctor)

- Proper nouns used as parts of names

> Queen Anne's lace
> Alaskan husky
> Persian rug
> Lou Gehrig's disease
> Chinese checkers
> Russian roulette
> Donner's Pass (*Pass* is part of the name.)

- Copyrighted names of games, but not common names used to identify games

> Concentration
> Clue
> Stratego
> bingo
> checkers
> chess

- The abbreviations A.M., P.M., B.C., and A.D., as well as the abbreviations for any expressions that would be capitalized were it spelled out in full

Acceptable variations of *A.M.* and *P.M.* are *a.m.* and *p.m.*

In titles of publications, documents, musical compositions, radio and television programs, motion pictures, and works of art, you should capitalize the first word, the last word, and all other words except *a, and, the,* and prepositions and conjunctions that are one syllable or that contain fewer than five letters.

The following sentences demonstrate correct capitalization:

Jane said, "I suppose winter will be here before we know it."

Our family traveled to Eastern Kentucky to see Natural Bridge State Park.

Sarah presented this idea to the group: "We should all save our soft-drink cans until next spring."

The national anthem begins, "O say can you see . . . ."

The McGurtys have lived in the South for six generations.

The travelers drove north until they crossed the Mackinac Bridge into Michigan's Upper Peninsula.

Last Christmas Eve we watched the aurora borealis for over an hour.

Some members of the Presbyterian Church of America met in Louisville before the national convention.

I talked with Senator Wall Whistle about the national health situation.

He loved to quote Paul Goodman's "and may my buddy-seat carry friendly freight."

The resolution was, Resolved, That Jones performed honorable service.

The West is suffering from a number of years of drought.

She lived in Crittendon County until she became a U.S. senator.

The Panama Canal was built to aid intercontinental shipping.

I don't believe the "Spruce Goose" will ever fly again.

My uncle served in World War II until he was wounded.

Patricia is an engineer at nearby IBM Corporation.

Next semester, I will have to take French, History 111, Chemistry II, and linguistics.

We played with Skippy, my dog, for several hours.

Did the professor say, "Tomorrow this class will have a test"?

Have you met Aunt Sophie yet?

One of his favorite television shows is *Cheers.*

Pan Am Airlines has just completed a new financial arrangement with Delta Airlines.

The outlaw carried his Smith and Wesson revolver hidden in his Levi's jeans.

Have you ever watched the geese fly south for the winter?

GENERAL OBSERVATIONS ABOUT CAPITALIZATION

- The use of capital letters is a mechanical aid to clear written communication. When you write, you use capital letters to distinguish certain elements from other elements of the sentence.
- The rules regarding capitalization are rather complex and, seemingly, illogical. However, it is important to remember that you absolutely must capitalize the first word of any sentence, as well as proper nouns and proper adjectives.
- In titles of publications, documents, musical compositions, radio and television programs, motion pictures, and works of art, you should capitalize the first word, the last word, and all other words except *a, and,* and *the* and one-syllable prepositions and conjunctions.

Spelling

No matter how well you construct your sentences, a misspelled word in your text can result in the immediate loss of your credibility as a writer. Unfair though it may be, picky readers will, without doubt, hold misspellings against you, no matter how brilliant your prose may otherwise be.

Sadly, learning to spell correctly can be difficult due to the hodge-podge nature of the English language. Today's English has its roots in the language spoken by the Germanic tribes that colonized Britain in the middle of the fifth century; and in French, spoken by the Normans who conquered Britain in 1066. During the Renaissance, the English language borrowed numerous words from other languages, particularly from Greek, Latin, and French. Additionally, German, Yiddish, Italian, Spanish, and even Persian have contributed to the complexity of modern English.

That said, when it comes to learning how to spell correctly, you have a few strategies at your disposal:

- You can sound out those words you encounter of whose spelling you are unsure.
- You can use your dictionary to look up the correct spelling of the word.
- You can employ mnemonic devices to remember the correct spellings of words that baffle you.

SOUNDING OUT WORDS

One way to handle those situations in which you are unsure of a word's correct spelling is to "sound out" the word piece by piece. Although sounding out a word can be helpful in many instances, it is not the most reliable way of ensuring correct spelling. This is because a large number of words in the English language are not, in fact, spelled phonetically. (Ironically, an example of a word that is not spelled phonetically is *phonetically,* which, if it was spelled phonetically, would start with the letter *f.*)

In proving this point, many grammarians refer to a story in which a girl, when asked to spell the word "fish," writes "ghoti" on the chalkboard. Her reasoning? The letters *gh* generate an *f* sound, as in the words *laugh, trough,* and *cough; o* can be used to sound like *i,* as in the word *women;* and the letters *ti* can indicate an *sh* sound, as in the words *function, nation, intervention,* and so on.

Watching for Homophones

Further complicating the issue are homophones—that is, words that sound alike but that have different meanings and different spellings. Following are several examples of homophones; notice how many instances there are of multiple homophones for a single word.

 Definitions in the following entries derive from *Webster's New World College Dictionary, Fourth Edition.* (Only the first definition of each word is provided here.)

Air: The elastic, invisible mixture of gases (chiefly nitrogen and oxygen, as well as hydrogen, carbon dioxide, argon, neon, helium, etc.) that surrounds the earth; atmosphere

Err: To be wrong or mistaken; fall into error

Heir: A person who inherits or is legally entitled to inherit, through the natural action of the law, another's property or title upon the other's death

Aisle: A part of a church alongside the nave, choir, or transept, set off by a row of columns or piers
Isle: An island, esp., a small island: poetic except as part of a place name

Altar: A place, esp. a raised platform, where sacrifices or offerings are made to a god, an ancestor, etc.
Alter: To make different in details but not in substance; modify

Ate: Past participle of the verb *to eat*
Eight: The cardinal number between seven and nine; 8; VIII

Carat: A unit of weight for precious stones and pearls, equal to 3.0864 grains (200 milligrams): abbrev. *C*
Caret: A mark (^) used in writing or in correcting proof, to show where something is to be inserted
Carrot: A biennial plant (*Daucus carota*) of the umbel family, with fernlike leaves and compound umbels of white flowers, usually with one red flower in the center: only the cultivated variety is edible
Karat: One 24th part (of pure gold)

Cease: To bring or come to an end; stop; discontinue
Seize: To take forcible legal possession of; confiscate

Cede: To give up one's rights in; surrender formally
Seed: The part of a flowering plant that typically contains the embryo with its protective coat and stored food and that can develop into a new plant under the proper conditions; fertilized and mature ovule

Ceiling: The inside top part or covering of a room, opposite the floor
Sealing: Present participle of the verb *to seal*

Cel: Films: from use of celluloid, esp. formerly, for photographic films
Cell: A small convent or monastery attached to a larger one
Sell: To give up, deliver, or exchange (property, goods, services, etc.) for money or its equivalent

Cent: A monetary unit of the U.S., equal to 1/100 of a dollar; penny
Scent: To smell; perceive of the olfactory sense
Sent: Past participle of the verb *to send*

Cereal: Any grain used for food, as wheat, oats, or rice
Serial: Of, arranged in, or forming a series

Chute: A waterfall; rapids in a river
Shoot: To move swiftly over, by, across, etc.

Cite: To summon to appear before a court of law
Sight: Something seen; view
Site: A piece of land considered from the standpoint of its use for some specified purpose

Colonel: A military officer ranking above a lieutenant colonel and below a brigadier general, and corresponding to a captain in the navy
Kernel: A grain or seed, as of corn, wheat, etc.

Cue: A bit of dialogue, action, or music that is a signal for an actor's entrance or speech, or for the working of curtains, lights, sound effects, etc.
Queue: A line or file of persons, vehicles, etc., waiting as to be served

Ewe: A female sheep
You: The person or persons to whom one is speaking or writing

Flew: Past participle of the verb *to fly*
Flue: A tube, pipe, or shaft for the passage of smoke, hot air, exhaust fumes, etc., esp. in a chimney
Flu: Short for *influenza*

For: In place of; instead of
Fore: At, in, or toward the bow of a ship
Four: The cardinal number between three and five; 4; IV

Gibe: To jeer or taunt; scoff (at)
Jibe: To shift from one side of a ship to the other when the stern passes across a following or quartering wind

Holey: Having a hole or holes
Holy: Dedicated to religious use; belonging to or coming from God; consecrated; sacred
Wholly: To the whole amount or extent; totally; entirely

Key: An instrument, usually of metal, for moving the bolt of a lock and thus locking or unlocking something
Quay: A wharf, usually of concrete or stone, for use in loading and unloading ships

Knew: Past participle of the verb *to know*
New: Never existing before; appearing, thought of, developed, made, produced, etc., for the first time

Know: To have a clear perception or understanding of; be sure of or well informed about
No: Not

Meat: Food; esp., solid food, as distinguished from drink
Meet: To come upon or encounter; esp., to come face to face with or up to (a person or thing moving from a different direction)
Mete: To allot; distribute; apportion: usually with *out*

Medal: A small, flat piece of metal with a design or inscription stamped or inscribed on it, made to commemorate some event, or awarded for some distinguished action, merit, etc.
Meddle: To concern oneself with or take part in other people's affairs without being asked or needed; interfere (*in* or *with*)
Metal: Any of a class of chemical elements, as iron, gold, or aluminum, generally characterized by ductility, malleability, luster, and conductivity of heat and electricity
Mettle: Quality of character or temperament; esp., high quality of character; spirit; courage; ardor

One: Being a single thing or unit; not two or more
Won: Past participle of the verb *to win*

Pair: Two similar or corresponding things joined, associated, or used together
Pare: To cut or trim away (the rind, skin, covering, rough surface, etc.) of (anything); peel
Pear: A tree (*Pyrus communis*) of the rose family, with glossy leaves and greenish, brown, or reddish fruit

Peak: To become sickly; waste away; droop
Peek: To glance or look quickly and furtively, esp., through an opening or from behind something
Pique: Resentment at being slighted or disdained; ruffled pride

Poor: Lacking material possessions; having little or no means to support oneself; needy; impoverished
Pore: To read or study carefully
Pour: To cause to flow in a continuous stream

Rain: Water falling to earth in drops larger than 0.5 mm (0.02 in) that have been condensed from the moisture in the atmosphere
Reign: Royal power, authority, or rule; sovereignty
Rein: A narrow strap of leather attached to each end of the bit in the mouth of a horse, and held by the rider or driver to control the animal

Right: Formed by, or with reference to, a straight line or plane perpendicular to a base

Rite: A ceremonial or formal, solemn act, observance, or procedure in accordance with prescribed rule or custom, as in religious use

Wright: A person who makes, constructs, or repairs: used chiefly in compounds

Write: To form or inscribe (words, letters, symbols, etc.) on a surface, as by cutting, carving, embossing, or, esp., marking with a pen or pencil

Rote: A fixed, mechanical way of doing something; routine

Wrote: Past participial of the verb *to write*

Rye: A hardy cereal grass (*Secale cereale*) widely grown for its grain and straw

Wry: Turned or bent to one side; twisted

Sew: To join or fasten with stitches made with needle and thread

So: In the way or manner shown, expressed, indicated, understood, etc.; as stated or described; in such a manner

Sow: To scatter or plant (seed) for growing

Their: Of, belonging to, made by, or done by them

There: At or in that place

They're: A contraction from the words *they are*

To: In the direction of; toward

Too: In addition; as well; besides; also

Two: The cardinal number between one and three; 2; II

Vain: Having no real value or significance; worthless, empty, idle, hollow, etc.

Vane: A flat piece of metal, strip of cloth, etc., set up high to swing with the wind and show which way it is blowing; weather vane

Vein: Any blood vessel that carries blood from some part of the body back toward the heart

 If you are using a word-processing program on a computer to write, be wary of relying too heavily on your word processor's spell-checker. Although spell-checkers can help you locate and correct many misspelled words, most cannot determine whether you have misused a homophone—that is, if you correctly spelled the word *mettle*, it cannot detect whether you have used it incorrectly in place of the word *meddle, medal,* or *metal.*

Selecting the Correct Homophone

Following are numerous sample sentences that demonstrate the selection of the correct homophone:

The swimmer gasped for (*air, err, heir*) upon reaching the surface.
air

Luisa's father walked her down the (*aisle, isle*).
aisle

(*Ate, Eight*) of us went to the movie.
Eight

Jeff bought Lisa a two-(*carat, caret, carrot, karat*) diamond as an engagement ring.
carat

(*Cease, Seize*) this nonsense at once!
Cease

Billy agreed to (*cede, seed*) possession of his Buzz Lightyear figurine in exchange for Joey's Luke Skywalker toy.
cede

Ed painted the (*ceiling, sealing*) using a long-handled paintbrush.
ceiling

You can purchase an original *Scooby Doo* animation (*cel, cell, sell*) at this auction.
cel

Jillian refused to pay back one (*cent, scent, sent*) of the loan.
cent

Fruity Pebbles is my favorite type of (*cereal, serial*).
cereal

Phoebe's sweatshirt clogged the laundry (*chute, shoot*).
chute

When you write a research paper, you must (*cite, sight, site*) your sources.
cite

I think it was (*Colonel, Kernel*) Mustard in the hall with a candlestick.
Colonel

Erin hit Wanda over the head with a pool (*cue, queue*).
    cue

The (*ewe, you*) nuzzled her newborn kid.
    ewe

A bird just (*flew, flue, flu*) into the window!
    flew

I bought these flowers (*for, fore, four*) my mother.
    for

I typically (*gibe, jibe*) the ballplayers from the opposing team.
    gibe

Even though Renata's favorite jeans are (*holey, holy, wholly*), she wears them almost every day.
    holey

Brigitta lost her house (*key, quay*) and was stuck outside in the rain.
    key

Alas, poor Yorick, I (*knew, new*) him well . . .
    knew

I (*know, no*) the answer, but I've forgotten it.
    know

Vegetarians don't eat (*meat, meet, mete*).
    meat

Becky's father won a silver (*medal, meddle, metal, mettle*) in the 1976 Olympic Games.
    medal

(*One, Won*) of us will have to sleep on the sofa.
    One

It seems like every time I (*pare, pair, pear*) an apple, I cut my finger!
    pare

Solange climbed the (*peak, peek, pique*) while carrying a 40-pound backpack.
    peak

I urge you to (*pore, poor, pour*) these materials before the exam.
pore

After the heavy (*rain, reign, rein*), it seemed as though the garden sprouted weeds overnight.
rain

Returning the ring to its owner was the (*right, rite, wright, write*) thing to do.
right

Freddy learned his multiplication tables by (*rote, wrote*).
rote

I'll have a tuna sandwich on (*rye, wry*), please.
rye

Because I didn't have enough money to buy a dress, I decided to (*sew, so, sow*) one instead.
sew

My parents gave us (*their, there, they're*) old patio furniture.
their

Give the candle (*to, too, two*) me.
to

Some people think it's (*vain, vane, vein*) to have plastic surgery.
vain

To (*air, err, heir*) is human.
err

My grandmother was born on the (Aisle, Isle) of Wight.
Isle

After the show, we (*ate, eight*) pizza.
ate

To indicate where in the manuscript a comma should be placed, first draw a (*carat, caret, carrot, karat*).
caret

(*Cease, Seize*) the day.
Seize

Jessica put a (*cede, seed*) in the dirt to see if it would grow.
seed

Tiffany used a (*ceiling, sealing*) agent to caulk the window.
sealing

Time passes slowly in a prison (*cel, cell, sell*).
cell

What is that bewitching (*cent, scent, sent*) you're wearing?
scent

Ted Bundy was a (*cereal, serial*) killer.
serial

I don't think I could ever (*chute, shoot*) an animal.
shoot

(*Cite, Sight, Site*) is one of the five senses.
Sight

A popcorn (*colonel, kernel*) is stuck in my teeth!
kernel

If you are waiting to speak to the postmaster, please stand in this (*cue, queue*).
queue

I'll share the car with (*ewe, you*) if you'll help pay for the insurance.
you

Please open the (*flew, flue, flu*) before lighting the fire.
flue

Please bring your papers to the (*for, fore, four*).
fore

At this point in the course, the captain of the yacht must (*gibe, jibe*).
jibe

Christmas is a (*holey, holy, wholly*) day for Christians.
holy

The men who work on the (*key, quay*) reek of fish.
quay

The (*knew, new*) kid in school lives behind me.
new

Mom said that under (*know, no*) circumstances was I allowed to go to the party.
no

I plan to (*meat, meet, mete*) Sam after work.
meet

Leave it to Aunt Susan to (*medal, meddle, metal, mettle*) in our affairs!
meddle

I can't believe Randy's brother (*one, won*) the lottery!
won

Would you hand me that (*pare, pair, pear*) of socks?
pair

No, you cannot (*peak, peek, pique*) at your presents; your birthday isn't until tomorrow!
peek

Tax breaks could really benefit the working (*pore, poor, pour*).
poor

The (*rain, reign, rein*) of Queen Elizabeth I lasted from 1558 to 1602.
reign

Getting one's driver's license has become a (*right, rite, wright, write*) of passage in this country.
rite

Evelyn practically (*rote, wrote*) the book on horseback riding.
wrote

Kevin has a (*rye, wry*) sense of humor.
wry

Before you paint the wall, you cover it with primer like (*sew, so, sow*).
so

Could you please set those plates down (*their, there, they're*)?
there

I want to go (*to, too, two*)!
too

Edgar installed a new (*vain, vane, vein*) on the roof.
vane

Prince William is (*air, err, heir*) to the throne.
heir

Use shredded (*carat, caret, carrot, karat*) to add color to your salad.
carrot

Ian decided to (*cel, cell, sell*) his motorcycle.
sell

Jane says she (*cent, scent, sent*) the parcel yesterday.
sent

This plot of land is the building (*cite, sight, site*) for the new mall.
site

Jake caught a nasty strain of the (*flew, flue, flu*).
flu

I've made enough food for (*for, fore, four*) people.
four

Linda has proved herself to be (*holey, holy, wholly*) competent.
wholly

Because of the rationing, the baker was forced to (*meat, meet, mete*) out the bread.
mete

Many products that used to be made of (*medal, meddle, metal, mettle*) are now made of plastic.
metal

(*Pare, Pair, Pear*) is my favorite type of fruit.
Pear

Ned knew his decision would (*peak, peek, pique*) his father.
pique

Could you please (*pore, poor, pour*) me a glass of milk?
pour

Victor was so excited, we practically had to (*rain, reign, rein*) him in.
rein

William Shakespeare is probably the most famous play (*right, rite, wright, write*) of all time.
wright

You reap what you (*sew, so, sow*)!
sow

(*Their, There, They're*) the ones who wanted to visit Monticello in the first place!
They're

After Jake took a slice, only (*to, too, two*) were left.
two

Before the nurse could take a sample of my blood, she had to locate a (*vain, vane, vein*).
vein

This necklace is made of 24-(*carat, caret, carrot, karat*) gold.
karat

The hurricane really tested our (*medal, meddle, metal, mettle*).
mettle

Don't forget to (*right, rite, wright, write*) to your grandmother!
write

LOOKING UP WORDS IN A DICTIONARY

Looking up a word in your dictionary is the best way of ensuring you are spelling the word correctly. A simple pocket dictionary should suffice in most instances; that said, it would serve you well to invest in a more extensive dictionary for more obscure words. Additionally, spelling dictionaries are available; these dictionaries contain the correct spellings, but not definitions of, thousands of English words. Because these dictionaries lack the definitions of words, they are less cumbersome than full-sized regular dictionaries.

 If you're in the market for a new dictionary, consider *Webster's New World College Dictionary, Fourth Edition.*

There may be times when you can't even determine a word's first letter. For example, if you were trying to determine the correct spelling of the word *mnemonic,* it might not cross your mind to look under the *N*s in your dictionary. In times such as these, a *phonetic dictionary* may be helpful. Phonetic dictionaries enable you to look up words phonetically rather than alphabetically.

 If you have access to the World Wide Web, you'll find several online dictionaries at your disposal. To access several dictionaries, as well as other useful tools, visit `www.refdesk.com`.

 It's best to look up words during the revision phase of writing rather than as you compose your prose. Otherwise, you run the risk of losing your train of thought. As you write, simply highlight any words about whose spelling you are unsure.

USING MNEMONICS

A *mnemonic* is a memory device that you can use to remember something, such as how to spell a word. For example, a mnemonic device to help you remember whether the word for "a person who has controlling authority or is in a leading position" was *principle* or *principal* might be "*A* stands for *authority;* therefore, the correct ending is *al* and not *le.*"

SPELLING RULES

Aside from the strategies listed earlier in this section, there are several rules that you can learn to aid in the improvement of your spelling.

 You should be particularly careful to spell proper nouns—especially the names of people—correctly. Misspelling a person's name can be construed to indicate a general lack of interest on your part about the person whose name you've misspelled.

 The following are, of course, general rules. It should be noted that there are exceptions, even beyond those ones listed in the entries that follow.

I before E except after C

Nearly every person who attended grammar school in the United States knows this rhyme: "*i* before *e* except after *c.*"

I before E

shield	hygiene	sobriety
niece	wield	friend

E before I

deceit	perceive	ceiling

Exceptions to this rule include the following words:

weird
seize
either
neither
caffeine
foreign
forfeit
leisure

This rule is complicated by this exception: When the vowel combination is intended to sound like an *a,* the *i* should follow, not precede the *e.*

neighbor	weigh	eight
sleigh	vein	beige

Handling the Addition of Prefixes and Suffixes

The addition of a prefix to a word does not affect the spelling of the root word:

un + easy	uneasy
un + necessary	unnecessary
il + literate	illiterate
mis + spell	misspell
dis + content	discontent

Much spelling confusion arises, however, when a suffix is added to a root word. Should the silent *e* at the end of a root word be dropped before the suffix is added? If the root word ends in a consonant, should that consonant be doubled before the suffix is added? Following are some guidelines for answering these and other suffix-related questions.

Adding Suffixes to Words That End in a Silent *E*

When adding a suffix to a root word that ends in a silent *e,* drop the *e* if the suffix begins with a vowel.

ridicule + ous	ridiculous
hate + ing	hating
write + ing	writing

An exception to the preceding rule is this: If the root word ends in *ge* or *ce*, then the final *e* is not dropped (unless the suffix begins with the letter *i*, in which case, the *e* is dropped).

outrage + ous	outrageous
trace + able	traceable
age + ing	aging

Don't be surprised to discover exceptions to the exceptions. For example, some words ending in *ge* or *ce* do drop the final *e* when a suffix is added—for example, *mortgage + or* becomes *mortgagor,* and *pledge + or* becomes *pledgor.*

Additionally, if eliminating the silent *e* will create confusion or mispronunciation, it should remain.

acre + age	acreage
mile + age	mileage

When adding a suffix to a root word that ends in a silent *e*, keep the *e* if the suffix begins with a consonant.

love + ly	lovely
commence + ment	commencement

Likewise, if the suffix begins with the letter *y*, the silent *e* at the end of the root word is typically dropped.

ice + y	icy
ease + y	easy
rose + y	rosy

Exceptions to this rule include such words as *cagey, dicey,* and *pricey.*

If another vowel precedes the silent *e*, you should drop the *e*, regardless of whether the suffix begins with a consonant or with a vowel.

glue + ed	glued
true + ly	truly

If you are adding the suffix *ing* to a word that ends in *ie*, the *ie* is usually changed to *y* before the *ing* is added.

vie + ing	vying
die + ing	dying
lie + ing	lying

Adding Suffixes to Words That End in Y

When adding a suffix—whether it begins with a vowel or a consonant—to a word that ends in *y,* change the *y* to *i* when the *y* is preceded by a consonant.

happy + ness	happiness
hearty + ly	heartily

An exception to this rule is this: If you are adding the suffix *ing,* the *y* should remain as is.

ply + ing	plying
dry + ing	drying

Likewise, the *y* remains intact when a suffix is added if the *y* is preceded by a vowel.

play + ing	playing
stray + ed	strayed

Doubling the Final Consonant

When adding a suffix to a word that ends in a single consonant (except *w, x,* or *y*) preceded by a vowel (as in *hug, quip, strap, equip,* and so on), you should double the consonant at the end of the root word if the root word is monosyllabic or if the last syllable of the root word is accented:

hug	hugging
quip	quipped
strap	strapping
infer	inferred

If, in the case of a multisyllabic root word, the accent changes from the final syllable to the preceding one when a suffix is added, you should not double the final consonant.

defer + ence	deference
confer + ence	conference

Additionally, the final consonant of a multisyllabic root word should not be doubled if the root word ends in a single consonant preceded by a single vowel, and the accent is not on the last syllable.

prophet + ic	prophetic
diagram + ing	diagraming

Likewise, if the root word, whether it be monosyllabic or multi-syllabic, ends in a single consonant preceded by multiple vowels, the final consonant should not be doubled.

hear + ing	hearing
treat + ment	treatment
lean + ed	leaned
view + ing	viewing
cheat + er	cheater

If the root word, be it monosyllabic or multisyllabic, ends with more than one consonant, the final consonant is not doubled before the suffix is added.

sand + y	sandy
schuss + ing	schussing
health + y	healthy
mass + ive	massive
warm + ly	warmly

able versus *ible*

Many words in the English language end in either *able* or *ible*. Alas, there are no hard-and-fast rules about which suffix is correct in which situation. When in doubt, consult your dictionary.

Adding Suffixes to Words That End in *C*

If you are adding a suffix to a word that ends in the letter *c*, you must usually add the letter *k* to the end of the root word before adding the suffix to preserve the hard sound of the *c*.

picnic + ing	picnicking
traffic + ed	trafficked

Handling Plurals

Although most nouns are made plural through the addition of an *s*, as in *cats, dogs, sneezes,* and *files,* many nouns do not fit this pattern:

- Nouns ending in *s, ss, z, zz, x, ch, sh,* and *tch* are made plural by adding *es* to the singular form:

bus	buses
mass	masses
buzz	buzzes
fox	foxes
lunch	lunches
wish	wishes
watch	watches

- If a noun's singular form ends in a consonant plus *y,* you must change the *y* to *i* and then add *es:*

baby	babies
fly	flies
sky	skies

Proper nouns that end in *y* are exceptions to this rule:

Correct: the Kennedys
Incorrect: the Kennedies

- Some nouns that end in *o* are made plural by the addition of *es:*

hero	heroes
tomatos	tomatoes

You should be alert for variant spellings of the plural forms of some nouns. For example, *cargo* may take either the *s* or *es* to form the plural. *Bus* may be spelled with one *s* or two in its plural form (*buses* or *busses*).

- In the cases of some nouns ending in *f* or *fe,* the ending is changed to *ves* to form the plural:

wife	wives
shelf	shelves
elf	elves

Compound Words

Many writers have difficulty when it comes to spelling compound words. Should the words remain separate, should they be hyphenated, or should they be joined into a single word? For example, which is correct: horse play, horse-play, or horseplay?

Unfortunately, your only real way of determining which spelling is correct for any given compound word is to consult your dictionary. If the compound you seek does not appear, it's probably wise to assume the words should remain separate. Whether the words should be hyphenated depends on the role they play in the sentence. (For more information, refer to Part II, "Sentence Elements," under the heading "The Hyphen.")

COMMONLY MISSPELLED WORDS

Following is a list of commonly misspelled words:

absence	absorption	accessible	accidentally
accommodate	accumulate	achieve	achievement
acquaintance	acquire	acquitted	advantageous
advice	advise	affect	affiliated
aggression	aggressive	alignment	allege
all right	a lot	aluminum	amateur
ambience	among	analysis	analyze
annual	apartment	apparatus	apparent
appearance	appropriate	arctic	arguing
argument	arithmetic	ascend	asphalt
assistant	asterisk	athlete	athletic
attendance	auditor	balance	balloon
bankruptcy	battalion	beginning	belief
believable	believe	beneficial	benefit
benefited	besiege	boundaries	brilliant
Britain	bulletin	bureau	bureaucracy
burglar	business	calendar	camouflage
campaign	candidate	category	ceiling
cemetery	challenge	changeable	changing
choose	chose	clientele	collateral
coming	commission	committee	comparative
compelled	competitor	concede	conceivable
conferred	congratulations	connoisseur	conscience
conscientious	conscious	control	controversial
controversy	convenient	convertible	corroborate
counterfeit	criticism	criticize	deceive
defendant	deferred	definite	definitely
definition	dependent	describe	description
desirable	desperate	despise	develop
dictionary	dilemma	dining	disappear
disappearance	disappoint	disastrous	disbursement
discipline	discrepancy	dispensable	dissatisfied
dissipate	dormitory	duel	dyeing (to dye)
dying (to die)	ecstasy	effect	eighth
eligible	eliminate	emanate	embarrass
embarrassing	eminent	encouragement	encouraging
endorsement	environment	equipped	especially
exaggerate	exceed	excellence	exhaust
exhilarate	existence	existent	experience
exorbitant	explanation	extraordinary	fallacy
familiar	fascinate	February	fiery
flexible	fluctuation	foreign	foresee
forfeit	formerly	forty	fourth

frantically	fulfill	gauge	generally
gesture	government	grammar	grandeur
grievance	grievous	gruesome	guarantee
haphazard	harass	harassment	height
heroes	hindrance	holiday	hoping
humorous	hypocrisy	hypocrite	idiosyncrasy
illegible	immediately	immigrant	incidentally
incredible	indelible	independent	independence
indispensable	inevitable	infinitely	inoculate
insistent	intellectual	intelligence	interesting
intermediary	interrupt	irrelevant	irreplaceable
irresistible	jeopardy	jewelry	judgment
judicial	knowledge	laboratory	laid
latter	labeling	led	legitimate
leisure	license	lightning	litigation
loneliness	lose	losing	maintenance
maneuver	manufacture	marriage	mathematics
maybe	mediocre	mere	miniature
minimum	mischief	mischievous	missile
murmur	mysterious	naive	necessary
negligence	negotiable	newsstand	ninety
noticeable	occasion	occasionally	occurred
occurrence	omission	omitted	opinion
opportunity	optimist	optimistic	paid
parallel	paralysis	paralyze	particular
pastime	peaceable	perceive	performance
permanent	permissible	perseverance	persistent
personal	personnel	perspiration	persuade
phony	physical	picnicking	playwright
pleasurable	possess	possesses	possession
possibility	possible	practically	prairie
precede	preceding	precedence	predictable
preference	preferred	prejudice	preparation
prevalent	principal	principle	privilege
probably	procedure	proceed	profession
professor	prominent	pronunciation	psychology
pursue	quantity	questionnaire	quizzes
recede	receive	receiving	recommend
reference	referring	relevant	relieve
reminiscence	repetition	rescind	restaurant
rhyme	rhythm	rhythmical	ridiculous
roommate	sacrifice	sacrilegious	salable
salary	schedule	secretary	seize
sense	separate	separation	sergeant
severely	shepherd	sheriff	shining

(continued)

siege	similar	simile	sincerely
sophomore	sovereign	specifically	specimen
sponsor	statue	studying	subtlety
subtly	succeed	succumb	succession
suddenness	superintendent	supersede	suppress
surprise	tangible	tariff	technique
temperamental	tenant	tendency	than
therefore	too	tragedy	tranquility
transferred	transferring	tries	truly
tyranny	unanimous	unconscious	undoubtedly
unmistakable	unnecessary	until	unwieldy
usually	vacillate	vacuum	vengeance
vicious	village	villain	weather
weird	whether	wield	withhold
woeful	woman	women	

 Many words have alternate spellings. Sometimes, the alternate spelling is the less-common, and therefore, the less-acceptable, variant; other times, both variants of the same word are equally acceptable. Typically, if the two spellings are of equal acceptability, the dictionary will precede the second spelling with the word *or.* If one spelling is preferred, it will be listed first, with the second spelling preceded by the word *also.*

 Unless you are writing in the most informal of circumstances, avoid shortening or altering common words, as in the following:

    lite (light)
    nite (night)
    thru (through)

WORD DIVISION

If possible, you should avoid dividing a word at the end of a line using a hyphen; alas, there are occasions in which avoiding word division is impossible. If you find yourself in such a situation, attempt to divide the word according to pronunciation. That is, avoid dividing the word in the middle of a syllable; make the break at the end of a syllable:

    Correct: pronun-ciation
    Incorrect: pronunc-iation
    Correct: etymo-logical
    Incorrect: etymol-ogical

Beyond that, consider the following:

- Compounds should be divided in such a way that the words comprising the compound remain intact:

    Correct: dis-association
    Incorrect: disassoc-iation
    Correct: butter-fly
    Incorrect: but-terfly

- When two consonants separate a pair of vowels, it's best to divide the word between the two consonants:

    Correct: war-rant
    Incorrect: warr-ant
    Correct: mean-der
    Incorrect: mea-nder

- Avoid dividing words (or phrases) that already contain hyphens unless you divide them at the hyphen:

    Correct: complex-compound sentence
    Incorrect: comp-lex-compound sentence
    Correct: red-letter day
    Incorrect: red-let-ter day

- Avoid dividing proper nouns (especially names of people), and avoid separating a person's initials from the name itself:

    Correct: Marilyn Monroe
    Incorrect: Marilyn Mon-roe
    Correct: J.D. Salinger
    Incorrect: J.D. Salin-ger

- Avoid leaving a row of hyphens at the edge of your page; do not break the last word in more than two lines in a row.

BRITISH VERSUS AMERICAN SPELLING

If you enjoy reading, and have read books published in other English-speaking nations, you may have noticed inconsistencies in the spellings of certain words. Following are examples of words whose spellings differ depending on whether the writer is British or American:

American	British
canceled	cancelled
center	centre
check	cheque
color	colour
criticize	criticise

American	British
gray	grey
humor	humour
judgment	judgement
labor	labour
license	licence
realize	realise
theater	theatre
tire	tyre
valor	valour

FOREIGN WORDS

You may find yourself employing foreign words as you write. If so, you'll likely wonder whether you are presenting them correctly. For example, should the foreign word appear in italics? How can you ensure that they have been spelled correctly? What is the correct use of diacritical marks?

Italicizing Foreign Words

If the foreign word you are employing is familiar within the English language, as is the case with such words and phrases as the following, the word or phrase is not italicized.

barrio
soup du jour
haute couture
joie de vivre
protégé
bona fide
en route
non sequitur
Mardi gras
sangfroid
subpoena
gesundheit
al fresco

If, however, the foreign word is not a familiar one, then it should be italicized. The rub, then, is determining which foreign words are considered familiar. Here's a litmus test: If the word in question appears in an English-speaking dictionary, it can be considered familiar, and thus need not be italicized.

Ensuring That Foreign Words Have Been Correctly Spelled

To ensure that a foreign word has been correctly spelled, you should—you guessed it—consult your trusty dictionary. If the word does not appear in your English dictionary, you should then resort to using a dictionary for the language of the word in question.

If you have access to the Internet, visit the Language Automation Web site at `www.lai.com/lai/glossaries.html` for links to dictionaries for languages from Afrikaans to Yiddish, and everything in between. This site even provides links to dictionaries for artificial languages, such as Esperanto and Klingon.

Using Diacritical Marks

Unlike words in English, many foreign words employ diacritical marks—that is, accents, diacritics, or special alphabetic characters for native words. The diacritical marks most commonly used in European and Asian languages written in the Latin alphabet are listed in the following table.

Mark	Name	Purpose
´	Acute accent	Placed over a vowel to indicate length or high pitch, or to indicate primary stress of a syllable
`	Grave accent	Placed over a vowel to indicate length or low pitch, or to indicate secondary stress of a syllable
¨	Dieresis	Placed over a vowel to indicate that it is pronounced in a separate syllable
¨	Umlaut	Placed over the vowel to indicate a more central or front articulation
^	Circumflex	Originally used in Greek over long vowels to indicate a rising-falling tone; used in other languages to mark length, contraction, or a particular vowel quality
~	Tilde	Placed over the letter *n* to denote the sound *ny* or over vowels to indicate nasality
ç	Cedilla	Placed under a letter to indicate an alteration or modification of its usual phonetic value

Again, you should consult a dictionary for the language in question to determine whether a word in that language uses diacritical marks.

NUMERALS

The difficult part of using numerals in text is determining when those numerals should be spelled out and when they should be represented by numerical symbols. There are few consistent rules on this issue; in fact, different publications espouse the use of different styles. Some grammar texts urge writers to spell out whole numbers from one to ninety-nine, while representing all others with numerical symbols; others suggest that writers spell out whole numbers from one to twenty. Still others insist that only numerals one through ten be spelled out.

No matter which style you choose, however, a few rules do apply:

- Use the style you choose consistently within a single sentence or paragraph. For example, if a single sentence contains numbers that should typically be spelled out in addition to numbers that would normally be represented by numerical symbols, you should use numerical symbols for all the numbers in the sentence.

> **Correct:** Among the 482 graduates, 71 majored in German, 34 majored in French, and 111 majored in Spanish.
> **Incorrect:** Among the 482 graduates, seventy-one majored in German, thirty-four majored in French, and 111 majored in Spanish.

If the sentence or paragraph contains numbers in varying categories, it is acceptable to spell out some while representing others with numerals. Here's an example:

> In the last twenty years, I've read 43 books, watched 391 movies, and listened to 1,412 records.

Notice that twenty is spelled out, but the other numerals are not. This is because the other numerals are all members of the same category—that is, they are entertainment experiences, while the *twenty* refers to years.

- If your sentence or paragraph contains several numbers that would normally be spelled out, it's better to represent them with numerals to avoid creating cumbersome-looking text.

> **Correct:** I have several children; their ages are 1, 4, 7, 9, 10, and 14.
> **Incorrect:** I have several children; their ages are one, four, seven, nine, ten, and fourteen.

- Numbers that are approximations are typically spelled out.

- If the number is at the beginning of the sentence, it is always spelled out, even if it normally would not be.

  > **Correct:** Three hundred twenty members of Congress abstained from voting on the issue.
  > **Incorrect:** 320 members of Congress abstained from voting on the issue.

There may be times when spelling out a number that appears at the beginning of a sentence is cumbersome. In such cases, it's best to recast the sentence so that the number no longer appears at the beginning.

> **Incorrect:** Nineteen hundred forty six is the year my father was born.
> **Correct:** My father was born in 1946.

There are instances, however, where numbers that would normally be spelled out should not be (unless appearing at the beginning of a sentence), including the following:

- Percents and decimals
- Physical quantities (distances, masses, and so on)
- Sums of money
- Dates

Although dates are not spelled out, the numerical designation of centuries are (*twenty-first century, eighteenth century,* and so on).

> **Correct:** Colleen renovated a house that was built in the *eighteenth century.*
> **Incorrect:** Vermeer is a famous *17th-century* Dutch painter.

GENERAL OBSERVATIONS ABOUT SPELLING

- No matter how well you construct your sentences, a misspelled word in your text can result in the immediate loss of your credibility as a writer.
- Learning to spell correctly can be difficult due to the hodge-podge nature of the English language.
- You can sound out those words you encounter of whose spelling you are unsure.
- You can use your dictionary to look up the correct spelling of the word.

- You can employ mnemonic devices to remember the correct spellings of words that baffle you.
- Homophones are words that sound alike but that have different meanings and different spellings.
- Several rules can be learned to aid in the improvement of one's spelling. These are, of course, general rules. It should be noted that there are exceptions.
- Unless you are writing in the most informal of circumstances, avoid shortening or altering common words.
- The spellings of many words differ depending on whether the writer is British or American.
- If a foreign word or phrase you are employing in your text is familiar within the English language, the word or phrase is not italicized.
- The difficult part of using numerals in text is determining when those numerals should be spelled out and when they should be represented by numerical symbols. There are few consistent rules on this issue.

PART IV

ON WRITING

No doubt you'll use your newfound grammar expertise when you speak, but it's when you write that it really comes into play. After all, in order to speak correctly, you need not have a grasp on the correct use of the colon or the semicolon, or even on the accepted spelling of the words you're saying. In fact, grammar and writing are so intertwined that the word *grammar* stems from the Greek *gráphein*, meaning *to write*.

When writing, however, you must be concerned with more than the simple mechanics of grammar. It's not enough to ensure that every word has been spelled correctly, that every sentence has been correctly punctuated, that every verb agrees with every subject. Additional issues, such as structure and style, arise. And, as with speech, writers must consider their audience; it doesn't do to write as though your piece will be read by a girl-scout troop when, in fact, your cantankerous, male-chauvinist college professor is your audience.

Although there is no precise process for writing—whether it be a novel, a play, an article, a school paper, a screenplay, a case study, or a research grant—most writing involves four basic steps:

- Prewriting
- Writing
- Revising
- Proofreading

The amount of time you spend on each step will vary widely depending on the type of piece you are writing, and, subcategorically, on you yourself. For example, a person writing a research paper will likely spend more time in the prewriting phase than a person writing a novel, for the simple reason that the research paper probably involves more, well, research. That said, some novelists research copiously, and may remain in the prewriting stage for some time before moving on.

Prewriting

E. L. Doctorow once said, "Planning to write is not writing. Outlining . . . researching . . . talking to people about what you're doing, none of that is writing. Writing is writing." And of course, he's right. Only writing is writing. That said, however, the prewriting phase of a writing project can be an important one. In this phase, the writer might do any of the following:

- Generate ideas
- Research
- Organize the piece

GENERATING IDEAS

Generating ideas can occur in any number of ways. While reading the newspaper, for example, you may read a story that plants an idea in your brain. Or you may see a person on the street who captures your interest and begin imagining his life. You may even generate ideas through your own experiences—for example, if you're buying a house, you may be inspired to write an article about it. Then again, your writing may be the result of a school assignment, in which case you may be limited in your choice of topic. Even so, you'll need ideas about how you want to present your information, or what aspect of the topic you want to cover.

Regardless of what you are writing, the idea-generating phase is critical. Following are some ways in which you can get your creative juices flowing:

- **Live.** In *An American Childhood,* Annie Dillard writes, "Admire the world for never ending on you—as you would admire an opponent, without taking your eyes from him or walking away." The world is a fascinating place; participating in life, and observing the people and things around you, can inspire incredible stories, articles, plays, and more.

 Always carry a notebook with you. When you see or hear something that sparks an idea, write it down immediately so that you don't forget it.

- **Talk to people.** Every living person on this planet has at least one incredible story to tell. If you listen, you'll be amazed at the material you can gather.
- **Reflect.** Reflecting on your own experiences can lend incredible insight that can be very helpful in the realm of writing.
- **Write in a journal.** Recording the events in your own life, as well as your general observations about life itself and the world around you, can help you hone your writing in general, as well as help you decide what topics are worth pursuing.
- **Read.** Read anything you can get your hands on, be it the *Wall Street Journal, Hamlet,* or the back of a Cheerios box. Reading brings the world to you, and with it, ideas for your own stories. As an added bonus, by reading, you will develop a strong sense of language, and, as a result, almost surely improve your writing skills.
- **Brainstorm.** Give yourself time to think; open your mind, and let the ideas pour in. This process can be especially effective in a group setting.

When brainstorming, don't discard any ideas, no matter how farfetched they seem. Write down everything that crosses your mind, and evaluate your ideas later.

If you're still stumped, try visiting an idea generator on the Internet. There are several to choose from; a few are listed here.

- Old Dominion University Libraries Idea Generator (www.lib.odu.edu/research/idea/ideagenerator.shtml)
- Hatch's Plot Bank (www.angelfire.com/nc/tcrpress/plotbank.html)
- Story Idea Generator (www.carlsbadnm.com/ronjones/words.htm)

RESEARCHING

After you've generated your idea, you're probably eager to get started writing. Before you do, however, you'll likely need to engage in some research. Of course, this comes as no surprise if you are writing an academic paper; it goes without saying that that type of writing requires you to conduct at least some research before putting pen to paper. If, however, you're writing a novel or short story, you may be thinking that you're exempt from the research portion of the prewriting phase. If your story is rooted entirely in your own experiences, that may be the case—you conducted your "research" when you lived through the experiences you're writing about. If, however, your story is about people who are different from you—perhaps they live in a different town, or hold different jobs, or experience things you can only imagine—you'll need to do some research before moving on.

When it comes to research, more is better. Learn as much as you can about the topic at hand. As Ernest Hemingway once said, "If a writer . . . knows enough about what he is writing about, he may omit things that he knows . . . . The dignity of movement of an iceberg is due to only one ninth of it being above water."

Your research may involve any of the following:

- Reading books, magazines, newspapers, pamphlets, or other materials
- Watching films, videos, or other broadcasts
- Interviewing people
- Searching the Internet

 The Internet has revolutionized the way people research. No longer must you trek to the library to access information about a topic, no matter how obscure. That said, you must take care when using the Internet as a research tool; because the Internet is so wide open, information found on it can sometimes be of questionable value. For this reason, you should consider the following when conducting your research online:

- Make sure your source is valid. Pluck information only from those sites you trust.
- Make sure the Web site you're quoting is up to date.
- Avoid using the Internet to the exclusion of all other research methods.

 As you're researching, be sure to gather the information you find into a file so that you can refer to it as you write. Such a file may include photocopied passages from books you've used in your research, printouts of articles you've found online, newspaper clippings, brochures, and so on. Paper trails such as these are also useful in the event your finished piece is published; editors or other magazine staff can use them to fact-check your story.

ORGANIZING THE PIECE

There are some types of writing, such as journal entries and love letters, for which organization, or *structure*, is insignificant. Such pieces are, in essence, outpourings of the feelings or views of the writer, and the order in which those feelings and views are presented is unimportant. Other types of writing, such as academic papers, case studies, and certain types of poems, have strict rules on structure. Sonnets, for example, must contain fourteen iambic-pentameter lines. Most types of writing, however, fall somewhere in the middle, requiring you to pay at least some attention to organization and structure before putting pen to paper.

Suppose, for example, that you are writing a suspenseful novel. Most likely, you would want to withhold certain details until the end of the story rather than revealing them at the beginning; on the other hand, if your story ends with a twist, you must lay the foundation for that twist earlier in the book to make it believable. As another example, suppose your story jumps back and forth in time. You may begin with a relatively short section set in the present, flash back to a short section set in the past, and then slowly increase the lengths of subsequent sections as you go. All these issues relate to the organization of your piece.

USING AN OUTLINE

Although some people can park themselves in front of a computer and crank out the great American novel, organizing it in their head as they go, many writers need to construct outlines before progressing to the writing stage. Whether you're writing a *War and Peace*-type saga or a 500-word article for your school paper, an outline can help you focus your idea and organize your piece. Outlines can range from the very broad to the very detailed—some writers create outlines that are hundreds of pages long. Of course, the more detailed your outline, the easier it is to actually write your piece.

As you build your outline, pay particular attention to the way the parts of your outline relate to the whole. In other words, in addition to looking at the big picture, be sure to look at the individual pieces and find a logical way to connect them. For example, as I wrote this chapter, I first discussed writing as a whole, then broke down the various components of writing, and attempted to illustrate how those components relate to the whole as well as to each other.

If you are creating an outline for your own use—that is, no one but you will look at it—you can list out the key points in your piece any old way you want. If, however, your outline will be viewed by others, such as a professor or editor, it's best to use a more formal outline structure.

GENERAL OBSERVATIONS ABOUT PREWRITING

- In the prewriting phase, the writer might generate ideas, research, and organize the piece.
- When trying to generate ideas, try any or all of the following:
  - Live
  - Talk to people
  - Reflect
  - Write in a journal
  - Read
  - Brainstorm

- Your research might involve any of the following:
  - Reading books, magazines, newspapers, pamphlets, or other materials
  - Watching films, videos, or other broadcasts
  - Interviewing people
  - Searching the Internet

- Most types of writing require one to pay at least some attention to organization and structure before putting pen to paper.
- Many writers need to construct outlines before progressing to the writing stage.
- The more detailed your outline, the easier it is to actually write your piece.

Writing

You've come up with an idea. You've researched. You've organized your piece and (we hope) generated an outline. Finally, you're ready to begin writing. At this stage, your goal is to simply get your ideas on paper in a relatively cohesive form (you'll revise your work later), using your outline as a template. This first pass is called the *rough draft*.

When creating a rough draft, you should first examine your outline, making sure your research has addressed all the points contained in it. Then, formulate sentences that express the points in your outline, filling in the missing pieces as you go. When you finish, you should have a cohesive piece that conveys your idea.

Of course, these instructions for writing are rather simplified; unfortunately, the scope of this book does not permit an exhaustive examination of the writing process. There are, however, numerous titles on this topic available to the curious reader. A good one to try is *Webster's New World Student Writing Handbook* (published by Hungry Minds, Inc.).

 You don't necessarily have to start at the beginning of your outline. If you prefer, begin in the middle and catch up as you go.

As you write, don't fret if your sentences contain grammatical errors or misspellings, or if they don't seem to flow. You'll fix these problems when you revise your piece. Do, however, concern yourself with the following:

- Style
- Showing versus telling

STYLE

The word *style* typically means "a way of doing things." In terms of writing, *style* can refer to two things:

- The form of a piece of writing (for example, whether a letter has an inside address, salutation, and complimentary close)
- The use of words and sentence patterns

It is with the second sense with which this section is concerned. The two primary ways to describe a style are by its preference for words of a certain kind (for example, familiar or unfamiliar, monosyllabic or polysyllabic, ornate or spare, and so on) and by its preference for certain sentence patterns or structures. As you write, notice whether your style is spare or florid, simple or complex. Understand that there is no preferable style; find the one that suits you (and your piece), and go with it.

SHOWING VERSUS TELLING

Compare the following two paragraphs:

When he heard the news, Ethan was sad.
When Ethan learned that his mother was ill with cancer, his face crumpled and his shoulders slumped. He swayed momentarily before folding his unsteady frame into his threadbare recliner and covering his face with his hands.

Notice that the second paragraph conveys Ethan's sadness without explicitly stating that he was sad. This occurs through the use of specific details. You learn what "the news" is, and you "see" Ethan's reaction. This is, in the world of writing, known as "showing versus telling." By showing the reader what is happening and enabling him to draw his own conclusions about what Ethan is feeling, you engage him in a way that simply telling him how Ethan felt won't allow. In essence, by showing rather than telling, you are proving to the reader that what you say is true.

The use of details can also help readers understand what kind of person or event is being portrayed in your writing. For example, noting that your subject (fictional or real) drinks decaffeinated lattes with skim milk is more revealing than simply noting that she drinks coffee. Likewise, noting that your subject drives a mint-condition cherry-red 1968 Mustang convertible is more revealing than noting that she drives a car. Of course, the most effective details are the ones that are the least expected—a hard-nosed cop's hidden love of haiku, for example, or a kindergarten teacher's heavy-metal CD collection.

 ## GENERAL OBSERVATIONS ABOUT WRITING

- In the writing stage, your goal is to simply get your ideas on paper in a relatively cohesive form (you'll revise your work later), using your outline as a template. This first pass is called the *rough draft*.
- As you write, don't fret if your sentences contain grammatical errors or misspellings, or if they don't seem to flow. You'll fix these problems when you revise your piece.
- As you write, do concern yourself with the following:
  - **Style.** The word *style* typically means "a way of doing things." In terms of writing, *style* can refer to the form of a piece of writing (for example, whether a letter has an inside address, salutation, and complimentary close) or to the use of words and sentence patterns. It is with the second that you are concerned here.
  - **Showing versus telling.** By showing the reader what is happening and enabling him to draw his own conclusions about what he is reading, you engage him in a way that simply telling him won't allow. In essence, by showing rather than telling, you are proving to the reader that what you say is true.

Revising

After you finish your rough draft, it's time to hone your manuscript. This process is called *revision*—literally, "re-seeing." During this process, you "re-see" your piece, looking at it anew to determine what stays and what goes. During revision, you separate the wheat from the chaff of your piece, ensuring, as Rust Hills puts it in *Writing in General and the Short Story in Particular,* that "everything enhances everything, interrelates with everything else, is inseparable from everything else, and all this is done with a necessary and perfect economy."

During the revision phase of your writing, examine the following:

- Word choice
- Variety in sentence structure
- Flow

WORD CHOICE

To paraphrase the venerable William Strunk Jr., co-author of the classic grammar book, *The Elements of Style,* just as a machine has no extra parts and a drawing has no extra lines, your writing should have no extra words. You must make every word in your piece count. If you can strip words from paragraphs or sentences while still retaining your intended meaning, do so. If you can use a single word to convey the meaning of several words (while maintaining the intended tone), do so. If you can use expressive language rather than passive language, do so.

Stripping Words

Eliminating unnecessary words, also called *tightening,* can help you focus your prose. Here's an example of a paragraph that needs tightening:

> Since the beginning of time, technology has always been a business issue. From the growing copper-working industry looking for more efficient transportation methods, constructing two-wheeled carts in Mesopotamia about 3500 B.C., to today's struggle with information technology. Industry has struggled with taking the phone, fax, steam, electricity, etc., and implementing them within their business processes.

Here's the same paragraph, but after it's been tightened. Notice how much easier it is to read.

Technology has always been a business issue. Even in 3500 B.C., Mesopotamia's growing copper-working industry constructed two-wheeled carts for more efficient transportation; more recently, businesses struggled to implement steam and electricity into their processes.

One way to tighten your prose is to join several short sentences into one long one. Examine the sentences below:

I enjoy surfing. I also enjoy scuba diving. I would like to surf and scuba dive more often.

You could combine these sentences into a single sentence:

I enjoy surfing and scuba diving, and would like to do both more often.

Here are other examples of sentences that were combined:

Virgil was a Roman poet. Virgil is featured in Dante's *Inferno*.
Virgil, the Roman poet, is featured in Dante's *Inferno*.

Loveland Pass is a mountain pass. It is in the Colorado Rockies.
Loveland Pass, a mountain pass, is in the Colorado Rockies.

My neighbor is a painter. He painted our house.
My neighbor, who is a painter, painted our house.

Additionally, when tightening your prose, be on the lookout for wordy phrases that can easily be replaced by one or a few words, as in the following:

Wordy Phrase	Suggested Replacement
a majority of	most
a sufficient amount of	enough
along the lines of	like
at such time as	when
at the present time	now
at this point in time	now
be in a position to	can, be able
by means of	by

come to a conclusion	conclude
despite the fact that	although
due to the fact that	because
during the time that	while
for the purpose of	to, for
for the reason that	because
for this reason	thus, therefore
give consideration to	consider, examine
give indication of	show, indicate, suggest
in a number of	several, many
in all cases	always
in close proximity to	near
in many cases	often
in most cases	usually
in no case	never
in some cases	sometimes
in the event that	if
in the near future	soon
in the neighborhood of	near, about, nearly
in the vicinity of	near
in this case	here
in view of the fact that	because, since
is capable of	can
is found to be	is
is in a position to	can
it is our opinion that	we think
it is possible that	perhaps
manner in which	how
notwithstanding the fact that	although
on the basis of	from, because, by
prior to	before
provided that	if
put an end to	end
reach a conclusion	conclude
subsequent to	after
the question as to	whether
with reference to	about
with the exception that	except that

Similar to wordy phrases are phrases that contain redundancies, such as the following:

Redundant Phrase	Suggested Replacement
adequate enough	adequate (or enough)
advance planning	planning
basic essentials	basics (or essentials)
close proximity	proximity
definite decision	decision
first priority	priority
general rule	rule
green colored	green
increase in increments	increase
joint cooperation	cooperation
major breakthrough	breakthrough
most optimum	optimum
necessary requirement	requirement
outside periphery	periphery
rate of speed	speed
resemble in appearance	resemble
twelve in number	twelve
usual rule	rule
very unique	unique

Choosing the Right Word

If you take the time to select the exact word to express your intended meaning, you can increase the impact of your writing. When determining whether a word is the right one, you should consider the following:

- **Is the word specific?** That is, is there a word or phrase that would more completely convey your intended meaning? Mentioning that your character is watering a plant is less specific, and thus less descriptive, than mentioning that she is watering a Venus' flytrap.
- **Does the word have unwanted connotations?** Many car dealerships have begun advertising their vast selection of "pre-owned cars" because, in their view, the word "used" has a negative connotation. You can control the way readers respond to your writing by recognizing the emotional overtones of certain words.
- **Is the word ambiguous?** Some sentences contain words that can mean more than one thing. For example, "Eloise has a funny expression on her face" could indicate that her expression is funny as in "amusing" or funny as in "odd."

On clarity

Avoiding the use of ambiguous words is only one way to improve the clarity of your writing. Here are a few other tips:

- Be precise.
  Vague: You shouldn't watch too much television.
  Better: You shouldn't watch more than one hour of television per day.
- Eliminate misplaced modifiers.
  Incorrect: Jack gave Joe his toy.
  Correct: Jack gave his toy to Joe.
  Correct: Jack returned Joe's toy to him.
- Avoid squinting modifiers.
  Vague: Seeing the children eating quickly caused Mother to lose her temper.
  Better: Mother quickly lost her temper upon seeing the children eating.
  Better: Mother lost her temper upon seeing the children eating quickly.
- Avoid hedge words.
  Vague: Smith died of an apparent heart attack.
  Better: Apparently, Smith died of a heart attack.
  Better: Smith died apparently of a heart attack.

- **Is the word overused?** Has the word grown trite? Has its novelty gone? Such words are called *clichés* and should be avoided.

  If you must use a cliché, be certain you don't muddle it. For example, many people use the phrase "I could care less" instead of the correct version, "I couldn't care less," even though these two phrases convey opposite meanings.

- **Is it appropriate for the context in which it is being used?** If you are writing a novel about NASA scientists, it is unlikely that they would speak using street jargon, and vice-versa.

Employing Expressive Language

The use of expressive language can improve your writing by leaps and bounds. As an example, compare the following two paragraphs:

Bruges was pretty but the weather was lousy and I was in a bad mood. But I walked around and finally found a nice bench to rest on and read. Later, I walked back to the station but just missed a train to Brussels—I ran all the way from one end of the station to the other and took the steps to the platform two at a time, but an unsmiling worker wouldn't let me board.

Bruges, all cobblestones and spires, appealed to me, but the lousy weather wrecked my mood. After trudging around town all morning, I collapsed on a sheltered bench and read a few chapters of *A Year in Provence.* When the rain abated, I sauntered to the train station; as I straggled in, a voice on the intercom announced the imminent departure of the Brussels-bound train. I sprinted the length of the station and scrambled up the steps to the platform two at a time, but a domineering conductor blocked my way when I tried to squeeze through the closing doors of the train.

Notice how the text in the second paragraph seems more vibrant, more descriptive? The narrator doesn't just "walk around"; rather, she "trudges." She doesn't "rest on" a bench; she "collapses" on it. She doesn't "run from one end of the station to the other"; instead, she "sprints" and "scrambles." The use of powerful verbs and precise details makes the second paragraph come alive.

Following are some tips to help you employ expressive language in your writing:

- Use active voice rather than passive voice.

    Passive: The carpet was designed by Elias.
    Active: Elias designed the carpet.

- Substitute descriptive verbs for vague verbs.

    Vague: Katherine went to the mall.
    Better: Katherine walked to the mall.
    Even Better: Katherine ambled to the mall.

- Condense your sentences to avoid wordiness and redundancy.

    Wordy: An appointment will prevent me from attending the meeting. I am going to the dentist, so I won't be there.
    Better: A dentist appointment will prevent me from attending the meeting.

- Eliminate overkill.

    Overkill: A peninsula surrounded on three sides by ocean
    Better: A peninsula

- Delete pointless words.

    Wordy: There is a woman who lives nearby who works as a waitress.
    Better: A woman who lives nearby works as a waitress.

- Replace long words with short words when possible.

    Long Word: Rudy had a gigantic hematoma on his calf.
    Better: Rudy had a gigantic bruise on his calf.

- Eliminate adverbs that repeat an idea already expressed in the verb.

    Wordy: Jillian sped quickly to the scene.
    Better: Jillian sped to the scene.

- Eliminate adjectives that repeat an idea already expressed in the noun.

    Wordy: The ugly hag scolded us for trespassing.
    Better: The hag scolded us for trespassing.

VARIETY IN SENTENCE STRUCTURE

In addition to paring your sentences to their leanest, it's important that you use many different sentence patterns so that readers don't perceive your writing as monotonous. As discussed in Part II, in the section titled "Sentence Patterns," the English language supports nine basic sentence patterns, which are combined in various ways to construct longer sentences. Here, in simplified form, are the nine basic patterns of the English sentence:

- **Pattern 1:** Noun + Verb$_{\text{to be}}$ + Adjective

    The grass is green.

- **Pattern 2:** Noun + Verb$_{\text{to be}}$ + Adverb

    My bedroom was upstairs.

- **Pattern 3:** Noun$_1$ + Verb$_{\text{to be}}$ + Noun$_1$

    Some dogs are good hunters.

- **Pattern 4:** Noun + Intransitive Verb

    The shadows deepened.

- **Pattern 5:** Noun$_1$ + Transitive Verb + Noun$_2$

    The cat caught the mouse.

- **Pattern 6:** Noun$_1$ + Transitive Verb + Noun$_2$ + Noun$_3$

    My brother gave his wife some flowers.

or

Noun$_1$ + Transitive Verb + Noun$_2$ + *to* + Noun$_3$

My brother gave some flowers to his wife.

- **Pattern 7:** Noun$_1$ + Transitive Verb + Noun$_2$ + X, wherein X equals any one of several possibilities:
  - ◆ Another noun

    We elected Mabel president.

  - ◆ An adjective

    They considered Sam handsome.

  - ◆ A pronoun

    The FBI thought Jerry me.

  - ◆ An adverb of place

    We imagined him downstairs.

  - ◆ Verb, present participle

    We found the child crying.

  - ◆ Verb, past participle

    The boys found their clothes pressed.

  - ◆ Prepositional phrase

    They considered him in their way.

  - ◆ Infinitive phrase with *to be*

    Everyone considered Ella to be a friend.

- **Pattern 8:** Noun + Linking Verb + Adjective

  The milk smells bad.

- **Pattern 9:** Noun + Linking Verb + Noun$_2$

  Marie remained president until the election.

Even within a single sentence pattern, such as in patterns 1, 2, and 3, there are variations. For example, you have the traditional form:

The grass is green.

In addition, you can use this form:

Green is the grass.

Repetition

Although it's a good practice to avoid repetition—be it in sentence structure or in content—there are times when repetition can help you emphasize an important point, or can lend a lyrical quality to your prose. That said, repetition, even when it's intentional, should be used only sparingly.

In addition to using various sentence patterns, you should also use both loose sentences and periodic sentences. Before you learn about the difference between loose and periodic sentences, however, you must understand that every sentence, whether it's loose or periodic, contains a basic statement, which may stand alone, or may be buried in a longer sentence. Following are examples of basic statements:

Dogs slobber.
Snow is cold.
Christmas is on Tuesday.

A *loose sentence,* then, is one that contains a basic statement, along with a string of details. Loose structures typically expand the verb or object.

Basic statement: Snow is cold.
Loose sentence: Snow is cold, but is received each year with open arms by kids and grownups alike.

A *periodic sentence,* on the other hand, is one in which additional details are placed before or within the basic statement. Periodic structures typically expand the subject or verb.

Basic statement: Snow is cold.
Periodic sentence: Snow, although it is received each year with open arms by kids and grownups alike, is cold.

Some sentences are both loose and periodic:

Basic statement: Snow is cold.
Combination sentence: Snow, although it is received each year with open arms by kids and grownups alike, is cold, so cold that it freezes one's nose.

FLOW

You've pared down your sentences, taken care to choose the right words, revised your text to employ more expressive language, and made sure your sentences vary in structure—but something is still wrong. Chances are, your piece seems somewhat choppy. What's missing are *transitional devices,* which can help you ease your prose from one point to the next. These devices help you link each paragraph—or even each sentence—to the ones before and after it.

Following is an example of a paragraph lacking flow:

Jennifer was prepared for the test. Joseph was not. He hadn't even read the book on which he was being tested. He was nervous about the exam. He was sweating.

Here is the same paragraph, edited to improve the flow:

Jennifer was prepared for the test. Joseph, on the other hand, was not. Indeed, he hadn't even read the book on which he was being tested. For this reason, he was nervous about the exam. In fact, he was sweating.

The main type of transitional device is the transitional expression, of which there are several types:

- **Contrast and qualification.** Using this type of device, you heighten the contrast between the point you've just made, and the point you're about to make. This type of transitional device includes such words and phrases as the following:

  on the contrary
  however
  in contrast
  still
  yet
  nevertheless
  on the other hand

  The following sentences provide examples of the contrast and qualification transitional device:

  In light of the present circumstances, quitting your job seems the thing to do. *On the other hand,* the economy is slow, and may make finding new work difficult.
  I realize your husband drives you bonkers. *Nevertheless,* he is a decent man, and one worth hanging on to.

- **Continuity.** Using this type of device, you further the point you are attempting to make by providing a secondary argument. This type of transitional device includes such words and phrases as the following:

  besides
  furthermore
  in addition
  also
  secondly
  to continue
  next
  similarly
  likewise
  moreover
  indeed
  again
  in other words

These sentences make good use of continuity transition:

> Bill is an obnoxious man. *Furthermore,* his breath smells.
> You are much prettier than Tiffany is. *Besides,* she's an idiot.

- **Cause and effect.** Using this type of device, you illustrate how one point relates to the next. This type of transitional device includes such words and phrases as the following:

  > thus
  > therefore
  > as a result
  > consequently
  > hence
  > for this reason

The following sentences suggest cause and effect in their use of this type of transitional device:

> Patrick is very tall and athletic. *For this reason,* he is an excellent candidate for the varsity basketball team.
> You are a horrible cook. *Therefore,* I will cook dinner tonight.

- **Exemplification.** This type of device enables you to support a point you are attempting to make by providing specific details about that point. This type of transitional device includes such words and phrases as the following:

  > for instance
  > for example
  > in fact
  > more specifically
  > to illustrate

The following sentences provide examples of reinforcing a point with this type of transitional device:

> Felicia is attending one of the top colleges in the nation. *Specifically,* she is attending Yale.
> Dogs are very loyal. *In fact,* our dog follows me wherever I go and protects me from strangers.

- **Summation.** Using this type of device, you sum up points you've already made. This type of transitional device includes such words and phrases as the following:

  > finally
  > in conclusion
  > to sum up
  > in brief
  > lastly
  > as we have seen

  Lastly, these sentences demonstrate the summation transitional device:

  > *As we have seen*, dinosaurs were fascinating creatures.
  > *To sum up*, planning a wedding can be a daunting task.

GENERAL OBSERVATIONS ABOUT REVISING

- During the revision process, you "re-see" your piece, looking at it anew to determine what stays and what goes; in this process, you separate the wheat from the chaff.
- During the revision phase of your writing, examine the following:
  - Word choice
  - Variety in sentence structure
  - Flow

- Eliminating unnecessary words, also called *tightening,* can help you focus your prose. One way to tighten your prose is to join several short sentences into one long one; another is to replace wordy or redundant phrases with one or a few words.
- If you take the time to select the exact word to express your intended meaning, you can increase the impact of your writing. When determining whether a word is the right one, you should consider the following:
  - Is the word specific?
  - Does the word have unwanted connotations?
  - Is the word ambiguous?
  - Is the word overused?
  - Is it appropriate for the context in which it is being used?

- The use of expressive language can improve your writing by leaps and bounds. Following are some tips to help you employ expressive language in your writing:
  - Use active voice rather than passive voice.
  - Substitute descriptive verbs for vague verbs.
  - Avoid wordiness and redundancy.
  - Eliminate overkill.
  - Delete pointless words.
  - Replace long words with short words when possible.
  - Eliminate adverbs that repeat an idea already expressed in the verb.
  - Eliminate adjectives that repeat an idea already expressed in the noun.

- It's important to use many different sentence patterns so that readers don't perceive your writing as monotonous. The English language supports nine basic sentence patterns, which are combined in various ways to construct longer sentences.
- Try to employ both loose sentences and periodic sentences in your writing. A *loose sentence* is one that contains a basic statement, along with a string of details. A *periodic sentence*, on the other hand, is one in which additional details are placed before or within the basic statement.
- Transitional devices can help you ease your prose from one point to the next. These devices help you link each paragraph—or even each sentence—to the ones before and after it. The main type of transitional device is the transitional expression, of which there are several types:
  - Contrast and qualification.
  - Continuity.
  - Cause and effect.
  - Exemplification.
  - Summation.

Proofreading

A few summers ago, I drove past our neighborhood nursery and noticed posted signs that touted the myriad plants, trees, and other flora for sale. *TREES*, boasted one; *PLANTS*, promised another. And a third? *SHURBS*. I'm no gardener; I can't tell a hyacinth from a hydrangea. But I'm fairly certain that no member of the vegetable kingdom is called a *shurb*, not even in its Latin form. *Shrub*, on the other hand . . . .

It just goes to show you: No matter what type of writing you perform—be it an essay, a technical document, a novel, or a simple advertisement—proofreading is an important component of the writing process. It is the absolute last step of your journey, occurring after you have revised your piece—perhaps more than once—for clarity and accuracy (but, obviously, before you submit the final piece to your publisher, professor, or peers). Proofreading enables you to catch those small embarrassing mistakes that can make or break your writing.

 In its strictest sense, the word *proofreading* refers to the inspection and marking of proofs during the printing process. As such, proofreaders are concerned not only with grammatical errors, but also with such issues as spacing, leading, alignment, and the like. This section employs the word proofreading in a less strict sense—that is, as concerning the correction of grammatical errors.

WHAT TO LOOK FOR

Proofreading is, it would seem, a simple process: You read your piece and, drawing on what you've learned in earlier parts of this book, you locate and correct errors. You'll want to check in particular for errors in punctuation, grammar, and usage. Chances are, these errors will leap out at you as you carefully read your work; even so, here are some common problems for which you should be on the lookout:

- Misspelled words

  Incorrect: Our neighborhood nursery sells shurbs.
  Correct: Our neighborhood nursery sells shrubs.

- Improperly capitalized words

  Incorrect: Kevin and I visited Kevin's Mom.
  Correct: Kevin and I visited Kevin's mother.

- Subjects and verbs that disagree

  Incorrect: Gerry and I was exhausted after spending the day in the hot sun.
  Correct: Gerry and I were exhausted after spending the day in the hot sun.

- Pronouns and antecedents that disagree, either in number or in gender

  Incorrect: The smart painter cleans their brushes after finishing work.
  Correct: Smart painters clean their brushes after finishing work.

- Incorrect verb forms, particularly with irregular verbs

  Incorrect: We drug the garbage to the curb.
  Correct: We dragged the garbage to the curb.

- Inaccurate punctuation that dilutes the meaning of a sentence

  Incorrect: Franklin, and George, bought a puppy, at the pet store.
  Correct: Franklin and George bought a puppy at the pet store.

- Shifts in tense

  Incorrect: We walk into the bar, and the bartender served us a beer.
  Correct: We walked into the bar, and the bartender served us a beer.

- Shifts in person

  Incorrect: Janis is my favorite waitress. She'll never let a person down. She'll pour you a cup of coffee before you've even sat down.
  Correct: Janis is my favorite waitress. She never lets me down. She pours me my cup of coffee before I've even sat down.

- Misrelated modifiers

  Incorrect: Helen purchased a new jacket from the store that she liked.
  Correct: Helen purchased from the store a new jacket that she liked.
  Correct: Helen purchased a new jacket that she liked from the store.

- Run-ons and sentence fragments

  Incorrect: I saw Peter he was sleepy but he was going to work anyway.
  Correct: I saw Peter; he was sleepy, but he was going to work anyway.
  Incorrect: I was buzzing. Wired from the long flight.
  Correct: I was buzzing, wired from the long flight.

If you have written your piece using a word-processing program on your computer, you may be tempted to simply use that program's spell-checking feature instead of proofreading it with your own eyes. Relying on your word processor to find mistakes, however, is a risky endeavor.

For example, although your spell-checker will bring to your attention any words that do not appear in its dictionary, it will not alert you to words that are incorrectly used. Thus, common errors, such as the use of *there* instead of *their* or *it's* instead of *its* will be overlooked.

PROOFREADER'S SIGNS AND SYMBOLS

If you are proofreading your own work, and you will be the person to draft the final, corrected version, you can mark up your pages any way you want. You may have developed your own personal shorthand over the years; feel free to use it.

If, however, someone else will be applying your corrections to the final version (a secretary or typist, for example), or if you are proofreading the work of another person, you'll likely need to use the standardized proofreader's marks employed by journalists, editors, typesetters, printers, and the like.

The following table lists those proofreader marks you'll most likely encounter or need to use. (Note that there are more marks at your disposal than are discussed here; most omitted marks relate to typesetting rather than style or grammar per se. For a complete listing, refer to *The Chicago Manual of Style, 14th Edition*.)

 Be aware that proofreader's marks may vary somewhat; the ones shown in the following table are the currently in common, but not ubiquitous, usage.

Mark	Meaning
℘	Delete. Place this sign in the margin to indicate that something be removed from a line—be it a single letter, a word or words, or the entire line—without substitution. Do not use this sign when another letter, word, or line is to be inserted in place of the deleted matter. Draw a diagonal line through a letter to be deleted, or a straight line through a word or more to be deleted, to indicate where the deletion should be made. If you are deleting several lines, draw a circle around the lines to be deleted and add the delete symbol.
◡	Close up. You indicate too much space between letters by using this, the *close-up* sign, which is drawn in the text as well as in the margin.

Mark	Meaning
ℛ	Delete and close up. Use the delete-and-close-up sign when deleting a letter or letters within a word.
stet	Stet (let stand). You use this notation to indicate that a previous notation should be disregarded. To clarify what text should remain unchanged, place dots under the incorrectly marked word or words in the body of the text.
#	Insert space. Draw this symbol in the margin to indicate that a space should be added; place a vertical line or caret in the body of the text where the space should be inserted.
¶	Begin new paragraph. Place this symbol in the margin to indicate that a paragraph should be broken in two. To indicate the first word in the new paragraph, place an L-shaped mark to the left and partly under the word in the body of the text.
run in	Run in. Write run in in the margin and draw a line from the end of the one paragraph to the beginning of the next to indicate that the two paragraphs should be combined.
∿	Transpose. If you discover that words or letters are out of order, draw the transpose symbol over and under the affected text, and write *tr* in the margin. You can move a word or words to a different line by circling the text to be moved, and drawing a line from the circle to the spot where the text should be inserted (avoid drawing the line through words or punctuation).
(sp)	Spell out. Circle any abbreviations or numerals that should be spelled out, and place the spell-out sign in the margin.
ital	Set in italic type. Draw a single line under the word you want to italicize, and write *ital* in the margin.
rom	Set in roman type. If text has been incorrectly italicized, circle it and write *rom* in the margin.
bf	Set in boldface type. Draw a wavy line under the word you want boldfaced, and write *bf* in the margin.
lc	Set in lowercase. Draw a slash through any capital letters that should be changed to lowercase, and write *lc* in the margin.
cap	Set in capital letters. Circle or draw three short lines under any lowercase letter that should be capitalized, and write *cap* in the margin.

These marks should be made in the margin on the same line as the error. If a line requires more than one correction, the marks should appear in order, each separated by a slash.

MARKING CHANGES IN PUNCTUATION

As you proofread your work (or the work of others), you'll no doubt encounter instances of punctuation that you'd like to change either for accuracy or for effect.

The best way to change one punctuation mark to another is to circle or draw a line through the offending mark, and then place the correct mark in the margin. To supply a mark where none appears, draw a caret (∧) at the spot where the mark belongs, and again, draw the correct mark in the margin. Sounds simple, right? Well, it is— sort of.

The problem is that certain marks may seem indistinguishable from each other. For example, hand-written commas, apostrophes, and parentheses may appear identical. For this reason, you should draw these marks in the margin as follows:

- Place a caret over a comma.
- Place an inverted caret under an apostrophe or quotation marks.
- Draw your parentheses in such a way that they are large enough not to be confused with commas and apostrophes. Alternatively, you can draw two short, horizontal lines through each parenthesis to distinguish it from other marks.

Likewise, hyphens, en dashes, and em dashes are indistinguishable. Differentiate them by employing their appropriate symbols in the margin:

=	Insert hyphen
M	Insert em dash
N	Insert en dash

Here are a few more marks that can cause confusion:

- Periods can be so small as to seem invisible in the margin. For this reason, you should circle any periods you add.
- A question mark in the margin might be mistaken for a query. If you mean to add a question mark to a point in the text, you should follow the mark in the margin with the circled word *set*.
- A letter with a missing or incorrect accent or diacritical mark should be completely crossed out, and the letter and correct accent written in the margin.

Semicolons, colons, and exclamation points, if written clearly, need no further identifying marks.

The following sample paragraph has been proofread and marked using the symbols and techniques discussed in previous sections.

I'm on the train back to Nice after three incredible days in Provence. Today is ~~is~~ saturday. On Thursday, Marjorie and I drove back to Nice so we could reclaim Marjorie's luggage and make misc. arrangements. We took the autoroute and made it there in 2 hours by drivving more than 160km/hr (over 100mph. On the way back, we stopped in Aix en Provence, but were too tired to do much more than eat some poulet roti and fraises. Is there anything better than food from a market stall We went back to the château, sunned ourselves on the lawn, and were generlly lazy for the rest of the day. That evening, we went into St. Remy and ate well Chinese food. Robbie and his family got back from St. Tropez around 10 at night, so we didn't go out, but he gave me the SI with the Dennis Romdan article we had talked about, which I consumed that night in the Sitting room

Margin proofreading marks:

UC

UC x 2

(circumflex)

(circumflex)

s/l : l

tr

ital x 2

s/l ?

ital

lc/p

Try to find someone to look over your work for you. Sometimes, if you've been staring at the same piece of writing for several hours, it's impossible to catch the errors it contains. A fresh pair of eyes can be a lifesaver. Alternatively, if you have time, put the piece away for a few days, and then come back to it. You'll likely find many more errors than you would have otherwise.

GENERAL OBSERVATIONS ABOUT PROOFREADING

- Proofreading enables you to catch those small embarrassing mistakes that can make or break your writing. It is the absolute last step of your journey, occurring after you have revised your piece (but, obviously, before you submit the final piece to your publisher, professor, or peers).
- Here are some common problems for which you should be on the lookout when proofreading your work:
  - Misspelled words
  - Improperly capitalized words
  - Subjects and verbs that disagree
  - Pronouns and antecedents that disagree, either in number or in gender
  - Incorrect verb forms, particularly with irregular verbs
  - Inaccurate punctuation that dilutes the meaning of a sentence
  - Shifts in tense
  - Shifts in person
  - Misrelated modifiers
  - Run-ons and sentence fragments

- If someone else will be applying your corrections to the final version, or if you are proofreading the work of another person, you'll likely need to use the standardized proofreader's marks employed by journalists, editors, typesetters, printers, and the like.
- Proofreading marks should be made in the margin on the same line as the error. If a line requires more than one correction, the marks should appear in order, each separated by a slash.
- Try to find someone to look over your work for you; a fresh pair of eyes can be a lifesaver.

MISUSED WORDS AND EXPRESSIONS

Some problems of language command cannot be discussed according to principles of function. These problems consist of words and phrasal expressions that have been misused by many people over a long period of time. The ensuing list treats of such troublesome problems and gives a practical application in usage for many of the problem words or expressions.

Bear in mind that language is in a constant state of change and that what was once unacceptable may be acceptable today. The words *awful* and *sick* may be good examples. While *awful* once meant "inspiring awe" or "exalted," it now has taken on the meaning (in informal usage) of "very" or "unpleasant."

- My brother was awful tired after the race.
- We all felt just awful after eating the pie.

When the word is used with its original meaning of "inspiring awe," it is sometimes given a special (though generally unrecognized) spelling of *aweful*. The word is best avoided.

Likewise, many of us were informed as young children that *sick* and *ill* had special meanings: *sick* meant "mentally imbalanced," and *ill* meant "physically ailing." Of course, this distinction is no longer recognized. Now when *sick* is used, it may mean "affected with disease," "ill," "ailing in body or mind," or "suffering from an upset stomach." *Ill* means "not in good health" or "suffering from a physical disorder caused by poor health." In other words, the two terms are now generally used interchangeably. A distinction exists in formal usage, however, as the entry in this section suggests.

Nevertheless, various words have been used in specific ways and with specific meanings for a long enough period of time to be accorded certain stature in English usage. To be certain that your language employs words with precise meanings and reflects creditably upon you, you would indeed be wise to learn distinctions between similar words that are in common use. The guide presented in this Appendix is designed to help you learn such distinctions.

You will find a variety of definitions for most of the words presented in this section if you consult any standard dictionary. This guide cannot present all the many uses and definitions of any given word. Instead, the guide is intended to help you over *some* of the many trouble spots that exist and to serve as a quick reference. As always, when uncertainty about the use or definition of a word remains, you should rely on a good dictionary to help clarify the situation.

A, AN: Use *A* before a word beginning with a consonant sound, including the "long U" sound (as in *uniform*). Use *an* before a word beginning with a vowel sound, even if the first letter of the word is a consonant (as in *an honest person*).

> **Correct:** Most of us waited for *an* hour.
> **Correct:** He followed *a* usual procedure.
> **Correct:** John is truly *a* fine and honest fellow.
> **Correct:** Every band member has *a* uniform.
> **Correct:** No one should have *an* old uniform.

A LOT, A WHOLE LOT, LOTS, LOTS OF: Do not use these expressions to mean "much, many, a great deal." See *alot*.

> **Incorrect:** Almost everyone would enjoy having *lots of* money.
> **Incorrect:** We need *a whole lot* of help during the tournament.
> **Correct:** The visitor certainly had *many* friends.

A WHOLE LOT, LOTS, LOTS OF, A LOT: See *a lot, a whole lot, lots, lots of*.

A.D., B.C.: *A.D.* (*anno domini*) should always precede the date; *B.C.* should always follow the date (*A.D. 1936, 356 B.C.*).

B.C. is now frequently being replaced by *B.C.E.*, meaning "before common era."

A.M., P.M. (also a.m., p.m.): Use these expressions only with figures; do not use them to stand for the words *morning* and *afternoon*.

> **Incorrect:** We plan to be finished early in the *p.m.*

ABILITY, CAPACITY: *Ability* is one's power (mental or physical) to do a thing, or one's talent; *capacity* is the power to receive or to contain or acquire an ability.

> **Correct:** Carlita has the *ability* to do complicated problems in physics.
> **Correct:** Richard does not have the *capacity* to learn magic tricks.
> **Correct:** You have the *ability* to master calculus.

Correct: This much data are beyond his *capacity* to retain.
Correct: Mary has the *ability* to work advanced calculus problems.
Correct: Most landfills have the *capacity* to hold tons of garbage.

ABOVE: Avoid using *above* to refer to that which has already been written—except in legal documents, unless, perhaps, the reference is to something on the same page. Use *preceding* instead.

Incorrect: Be sure that you follow the *above* instructions.
Correct: The text in the *preceding* paragraph introduces the list that follows.

ACCEPT, EXCEPT: Do not confuse these two words as verbs. *Accept* means "to receive"; *except* means "to exclude."

Correct: John has been *accepted* into club membership.
Correct: The committee *excepted* his infraction of the rules and *accepted* his report.

AD: This is an unacceptable shortening of *advertisement*.

Incorrect: The fraternity ran a long *ad* in the campus newspaper.

ADMISSION, ADMITTANCE: *Admission* is the power to enter after paying a price; *admittance* is the physical act of entering.

Correct: Your *admission* to (your right to enter) the club depends upon your attitude and behavior.
Correct: The demonstrators' *admittance* to the president's home was blocked by the police.
Correct: Sally gained *admittance* to the theater after she paid the price of *admission*.
Correct: With this pass, I am guaranteed *admittance*.

ADVICE, ADVISE: *Advice* is a suggestion of how to act; *advise* means to suggest to another person a course of action or behavior.

Correct: May I offer you a piece of *advice* on handling your mother-in-law?
Correct: Please *advise* me on selecting a college.

AFFECT, EFFECT: *Affect* is a verb meaning "to influence" or "to have a bearing upon"; *effect* is both a verb and a noun. As a verb, it means "to bring to pass"; as a noun, "result."

Correct: How this weather will *affect* the crops is uncertain.
Correct: The *effect* (noun) of loud noise on hearing ability is well known.
Correct: We hope to *effect* (verb) a solution to the impasse.

> **Correct:** Will my absence from class *affect* my grade?
> **Correct:** What was the *effect* of the news upon your plans?
> **Correct:** Let's try to *effect* a solution to the problem.

AGGRAVATE, ANNOY, IRRITATE: *To aggravate* is to make worse an already bad condition; *to annoy* is to cause worry, trouble, or concern; *to irritate* is to cause to be inflamed or sore.

> **Correct:** The tight shoe *irritated* his foot until it bled.
> **Correct:** Yesterday's injury was *aggravated* by the tight boots she wore this morning.
> **Correct:** Children often *annoy* parents by their selection of music.
> **Correct:** The noise from the drill *annoys* me.
> **Correct:** The poison ivy *irritates* my skin.
> **Correct:** Do not *aggravate* the already sensitive mood of the teacher.
> **Correct:** By rubbing on the fence, the horse *aggravated* his injury.
> **Correct:** My father was really *annoyed* by my driving.

AIN'T: This is an illiterate contraction for *am not, are not, is not, has not,* and *have not.* Avoid using *ain't.*

ALIBI: Do not use this expression to mean "excuse." *Alibi* is proper only in its technical legal sense—proof that one could not have committed an act because one was not present at the time and place where the act was committed.

> **Correct:** What *excuse* do you have for arriving two hours late?
> **Correct:** The suspect had an *alibi* for the night of the crime.

ALL THE: *All the farther, all the faster, all the higher,* or similar expressions should not be used for *as far as, as fast as,* or *as high as.*

ALLOW, LEAVE, LET, PERMIT: *To allow* is to tolerate or to approve, to show forbearance. *To let* is to demonstrate indifference. *To permit* is to approve from a position of authority, to grant permission. *To leave* is to depart, to go away. Do not use these terms interchangeably.

> **Correct:** He *allowed* the children to play near the street.
> **Correct:** Our neighbor *let* his roof leak all spring.
> **Correct:** James *permitted* his brother to take the new boat.
> **Correct:** Will you *allow* me to go with you?
> **Correct:** *Let* me go, too.
> **Correct:** *Leave* me alone; I don't want any company right now!
> **Correct:** We cannot *allow* students to make noise all night long.

ALLUDE, REFER: *To allude* is to make indirect reference; *to refer* is to mention something specifically.

> **Correct:** The speaker *alluded* to the candidate's war record.
> **Correct:** The speaker *referred* to Act V, Scene ii, of *Macbeth*.
> **Correct:** The speaker *alluded* to his experiences as a sailor.
> **Correct:** Never *refer* specifically to your discomfort in this class.

ALLUSION, DELUSION, ILLUSION: An *allusion* is an indirect reference; an *illusion* is an unreal image or a false visual impression; a *delusion* is an error of the mind or a false belief.

> **Correct:** The lecturer made an *allusion* to Milton's blindness.
> **Correct:** The green oasis was only an *illusion.*
> **Correct:** Frank had *delusions* of being a great writer.
> **Correct:** Columbus disproved the *delusion* that the world is not round.
> **Correct:** I heard his *allusion* to the coming festival.
> **Correct:** The reflection of the sun upon the snow created beautiful *illusions.*
> **Correct:** The smoke on the horizon turned out to be an *illusion.*
> **Correct:** My aunt has *delusions* of extreme wealth.

ALL TOGETHER, ALTOGETHER: *Altogether* (one word) means "wholly, in all, thoroughly." *All together* (two words) means "in a group."

> **Correct:** We were *altogether* confused by the instructions.
> **Correct:** The family was *all together* for the first time in a decade.
> **Correct:** Ms. Brown said to the class, "Many of you have written thesis statements that are *altogether* too vague."
> **Correct:** Please bring your papers to me so that they will be *all together.*

ALL READY, ALREADY: *Already* (one word) means "prior to some specified time, either past, present, or future." *All ready* (two words) means "completely ready."

> **Correct:** I am *already* late for my own wedding.
> **Correct:** I am *all ready* to begin the ordeal.
> **Correct:** Are we *all ready* to go to the theater?

ALMOST, MOST: Do not use *most* in place of *almost*. *Almost* means "nearly"; *most* means "greatest in quantity or number."

> **Correct:** *Most* of the ponies were pintos.
> **Correct:** *Almost* all the money had been wasted on sweets.
> **Incorrect:** Yes, we have *most* finished the project.
> **Correct:** We are *almost* certain to go to the party tonight.

Correct: *Almost* all the students are late for class today.
Incorrect: *Most* all of my siblings are redheads.

ALOT: Avoid this misspelling and generally ineffective expression. See *a lot, a whole lot, lots, lots of*.

ALRIGHT: *Alright* is a corrupt spelling of *all right*. It is not generally accepted.

Correct: Betty is *all right* as our representative.
Incorrect: It will be *alright* for you to finish the test tomorrow.

ALSO: Do not use *also* as a connective; use *and*.

ALTAR, ALTER: An *altar* is a raised structure used in worship; *alter* means "to change or modify."

ALTERNATE, ALTERNATIVE: *Alternative* means "available as another choice," "unconventional," or "one of two possibilities." It should not be confused with *alternate*, as in "Our beading class meets on alternate Tuesdays."

ALTERNATIVE: Use *alternative* only to show an option between two things; for more than two, use *choice*.

Correct: He selected the most expensive of the many *choices*.
Incorrect: The stern father gave his son four *alternatives*.

ALTHOUGH, THOUGH: Both terms are acceptable and may be used interchangeably. However, you should be consistent in your use of the terms throughout a composition.

ALTOGETHER, ALL TOGETHER: See *all together, altogether*.

ALUMNA, ALUMNUS: *Alumnus* is a male graduate; *alumni,* two or more male graduates. *Alumna* is a female graduate; *alumnae,* two or more female graduates. *Alumni* is used when both male and female graduates are grouped together.

Correct: She and Bess are both *alumnae* of the same university.

AMATEUR, NOVICE: An *amateur* is one who does not accept payment for his efforts; a *novice* is an unskilled beginner in some endeavor.

Correct: The Olympics were originally designed for *amateur* athletes, although many professional athletes are now allowed to participate.
Correct: This knitting book is perfect for the *novice* knitter; it covers the basics of that craft.

AMONG, BETWEEN: *Among* always refers to more than two. *Between* literally refers to only two.

> **Correct:** The conquered territory was divided *between* the two victors.
> **Correct:** The candidate moved freely *among* the thousands who had gathered to meet him.
> **Correct:** Can we keep a secret *among* the four of us?

AMORAL, IMMORAL: *Amoral* means "without moral standards, without preconceived notions of right or wrong." *Immoral* means "contrary to moral codes or acceptable social standards, evil."

> **Correct:** Mrs. Sylvestor taught the history of the Aztecs from an *amoral* perspective.
> **Correct:** Many people think the government's treatment of the Indians was *immoral.*

AMOUNT, NUMBER: Use *amount* to refer to things in bulk or mass; use *number* to refer to objects that can be counted.

> **Correct:** The *amount* of dust in the air is disturbing.
> **Correct:** The *number* of termites in one nest is amazing.
> **Incorrect:** A great *amount* of the exiles sought to return to their homelands.
> **Correct:** The *number* of people at the concert was surprising.

AN, A: See *a, an.*

AND ETC.: Never place *and* before *etc.* The *and* is redundant, because *etc.* is an abbreviation for *et* (*and*) and *cetera* (*other things*).

> **Incorrect:** Write the alphabet in reverse order—that is, z, y, *and etc.*

AND WHICH, BUT WHICH: Do not corrupt subordination by inserting *and* or *but* before a subordinate clause. However, *and* or *but* may be used before *which* to join two *which* clauses.

> **Questionable:** He did not know *but what* I knew his secret. (Use *if.*)
> **Correct:** The car, *which* I bought yesterday and *which* was represented as being new was, in fact, well used.
> **Incorrect:** Katie read the trilogy by Crabb, and which she enjoyed very much.

ANGLE: Do not use *angle* to mean "point of view, phase, or facet."

> **Incorrect:** Let's look at another *angle* of this problem.
> **Correct:** If you want another *point of view* on the matter, ask Sue.

ANNOY, IRRITATE, AGGRAVATE: See *aggravate, annoy, irritate.*

ANTE-, ANTI-: *Ante-* means "before," as in *ante-bellum. Anti-* means "against," as in *anti-Castro.* The hyphen is used after *anti-* before words beginning with capital letters and before words beginning with the letter *I,* as in *anti-imperialist.*

ANYONE, EVERYONE, SOMEONE: Be sure to distinguish these words from *any one, every one,* and *some one. Anyone* (one word) means "any person." *Any one* (two words) means "any single person or thing." The same principle applies to *everyone* and *someone.*

> **Correct:** *Any one* of the three sisters will baby-sit for you.
> **Correct:** Can *anyone* help me lift this table?.

ANYPLACE: Do not use *anyplace* to mean "anywhere."

> **Incorrect:** Don't go *anyplace* until I have given you permission to move.

ANYWAYS: Do not use *anyways* for *anyway.*

ANYWHERES: This is a corrupt form of "anywhere."

ANXIOUS, EAGER: *Anxious* means "concerned, worried"; *eager* means "excited."

> **Correct:** The students were *anxious* about the final examination.
> **Correct:** The children were *eager* to begin coloring.
> **Correct:** Mother always becomes *anxious* when I am out late at night.
> **Correct:** All of us are *eager* to begin our new assignments.
> **Correct:** The students were *anxious* about the examination.
> **Correct:** I'm certainly not *eager* to see my test score.

APPARENTLY, EVIDENTLY: *Apparently* means "seems to be but may not be"; *evidently* means "both seems to be and is."

> **Correct:** *Apparently,* the mail carrier has not been here; we don't have any mail.
> (Perhaps we received no mail today.)
> **Correct:** *Evidently,* the mail carrier has been here; I see his tracks in the snow.
> (The evidence confirms the observation.)
> **Correct:** Leslie *evidently* is not here, since her seat is vacant.
> **Correct:** *Apparently,* students don't care for cold spaghetti.
> **Correct:** Since they won't eat it, they *evidently* don't like it.

APT, LIABLE, LIKELY: Use *likely* to express probability, *liable* to suggest the idea of responsibility, and *apt* to express predisposition or dexterity.

> **Correct:** Louise has shown that she is *apt* in music.
> **Correct:** You are not *likely* to win the lottery.
> **Correct:** The motorist is *liable* to pay for the damage.

AROUND: Do not use *around* to mean "about" or "near."

> **Incorrect:** We had *around* five dollars between us.
> **Incorrect:** We have read *around* 100 books in this class.
> **Correct:** The officer stopped *about* 20 cars.
> **Correct:** We had *about* 40 dollars in the bank.

AS: Do not use *as* in place of *if, that,* or *whether* to introduce a noun clause.

> **Incorrect:** I don't know *as* we'll have to decide immediately.
> **Incorrect:** I don't know *as* I shall be likely to go.

AS . . . AS . . . , SO . . . AS . . . : Use *as . . . as . . .* for a positive comparison; use *so . . . as . . .* for a negative comparison.

> **Correct:** My horse is *as fast as* your horse, but it is not *so fast as* LuAnn's.
> **Incorrect:** This new plane is not nearly *as* large *as* the older model.

AS, AS IF, LIKE: *Like* is a preposition and must have an object. *As* and *as if* are conjunctions; therefore, they connect but do not show an absolute relationship.

> **Correct:** Ellen acts *as if* she were ill.
> **Correct:** Tom looks *like* his father.

AS TO: Do not use *as to* as a substitute for *about* or *regarding*.

> **Incorrect:** He spoke *as to* the need for more effort.
> **Incorrect:** Mr. Fritzvold talked with me *as to* his conducting the tour.

ASSERT, MAINTAIN: To *assert* is "to declare, to state"; to *maintain* is "to affirm, to claim to be true, to defend."

ASSET: *Asset* is grossly overused to mean "resource, support, or source of strength." *Asset* means "a thing or quality of value."

> **Correct:** Rich soil is a great *asset* to a farmer.
> **Questionable:** Her friends were a great *asset* to her.
> **Incorrect:** Your being here is a real *asset* to our cause.

ASSURE, ENSURE, INSURE: *Assure* means "to guarantee, convince"; *ensure* means "to make certain"; *insure* means "to protect against financial loss by means of a legal contract."

Correct: I *assure* you, I have no intention of leaving.
Correct: To *ensure* our safety, the pilot demanded we wear seatbelts.
Correct: You should *insure* that necklace; it is very valuable.

AT: The *at* is redundant in such expressions as these: *Where is the book at? Where did you sleep at?* Avoid such uses.

AT ABOUT: The *at* is unnecessary. Use *about* without *at.*

AUGHT, NAUGHT: Aught means "anything"; naught means "nothing, zero."

Correct: He had *naught* (nothing) but good to say about his friends.
Correct: Go, my son, and see if *aught* (anything) be wanting. —Addison.
Correct: Do you have *aught* else to do?
Correct: Write out the digits beginning with *naught.*
Correct: *Naught* but trouble will come of that behavior.

AVAIL: *Of no avail* should be used only with some form of *be* or a linking verb.

Correct: Our efforts seemed *of no avail* against the flood.

AVOCATION, VOCATION: An *avocation* is a hobby; a *vocation* is one's regular work or profession.

Correct: Golf is his *avocation* above all other sports.
Correct: I'm a lawyer by *vocation*, but I sing for fun.

AWFUL: Do not use *awful* to mean "bad, fearsome." Do not use *awful* for such adverbs as "very," "really," and "extremely."

Incorrect: The accident had *awful* bad results.
Correct: We all felt *really* bad about the mishap.

A WHILE, AWHILE: Be sure to distinguish between the adverb *awhile* and the article and noun *a while.* As an object of a preposition, *a while* is always written as two words.

Correct: Wait *awhile* to see if we've been chosen to be delegates.
Correct: We played volleyball on the beach for *a while.*
Correct: We all watched television for *a while.*

B.C., A.D.: See *A.D., B.C.*

BACK OF: See *in back of*.

BAD: Do not use *bad* as an adverb; use *badly*. Use bad as an *adjective*.

> **Correct:** She feels *bad* about the loss of her pet.
> **Correct:** He needed the aspirin *badly*.
> **Correct:** He jumped *badly* because of the strong wind.
> > (*Badly* indicates how he jumped. It is an adverb.)
> **Correct:** We all felt *bad* about the accident.
> > (The verb *felt* in this sentence is a linking verb; *bad* is a predicate adjective.)

BADLY: Do not use *badly* to mean "very much" or with verbs to signify *want* or *need*. Use a word such as *truly, seriously, surely, really*.

> **Incorrect:** We *badly* need a new car.
> **Correct:** Because of his injury, he plays *badly*.
> **Incorrect:** The team *badly* needs your support.

BALANCE, REST: *Balance* is an accountant's term meaning "the excess shown on either side"; *rest* means "that which is left over."

> **Incorrect:** The *balance* of the students have left the campus already.

BANK ON, TAKE STOCK IN: Avoid these two expressions to mean "rely on" or "trust in."

> **Incorrect:** It is not a good practice to *bank* entirely *on* luck.

BE BACK: Do not use this expression to mean "return."

> **Correct:** I expect to *return* at noon.

BECAUSE: Do not use *because* to introduce a noun clause.

> **Incorrect:** The reason he did not attend is *because* he was in Chicago that evening.
> **Incorrect:** *Because* I'm angry is why I've resigned.

BEGIN, START: *Begin* means "to take the first step, to initiate action"; *start* means "to be startled" or "to cause something to begin."

> **Correct:** We *began* working on our project last night.
> **Correct:** The workers had to *start* the engine before they could move the tractor.

 Dictionary definitions now suggest that these terms are nearly synonymous with respect to using *start* to mean "begin."

BEING AS, BEING THAT: Do not use these two expressions to mean "since" or "because."

> **Incorrect:** *Being that* you are ready, why don't you go first?
> **Correct:** *Since* I was ill, I missed the last lecture.

BESIDE, BESIDES: Do not confuse these two words. *Beside* is a preposition meaning "by the side of." *Besides,* used chiefly as an adverb, means "in addition to."

> **Correct:** Martha usually sits *beside* me in class.
> **Correct:** Who *besides* Leslie knows the answer to that problem?

BETTER: See *had better, had rather, would rather.*

BETWEEN, AMONG: See *among, between.*

BLAME ON: Use *blame for.*

> **Correct:** They *blamed* us *for* the loss of power.
> **Incorrect:** The coach *blamed* the loss *on* the quarterback.
> (This sentence should be recast to read "The coach blamed the quarterback for the loss.")

BLOND, BLONDE: Following tradition, *blond* refers to males and to both males and females in groups; *blonde,* to females.

> **Correct:** They all have *blond* hair.
> **Correct:** That *blond* boy is my brother; the *blonde,* my sister.

BORN, BORNE: *Born* means "brought into being or existence"; *borne* means "carried" or "endured."

BOUND, DETERMINED: *Bound* means "obligated"; *determined* means "resolved." (The cliché "bound and determined" is acceptable.)

> **Correct:** The child seemed *determined* to have his way.
> **Correct:** This document makes you *bound* to remain for another year in your present position.
> **Correct:** The twins seemed *determined* to injure themselves.

BOYFRIEND, GIRLFRIEND (or BOY FRIEND, GIRL FRIEND): Avoid these informal expressions. Simply say, "friend" or "good friend." (Perhaps there is some logic in using these terms in referring to a person not present and whose sex may not otherwise be apparent. However, the terms are informal nonetheless.)

BRING, TAKE: Use *bring* to mean "to convey something to the person speaking"; use *take* to mean "to convey something away from the person speaking." *Bring* is related to *come; take,* to go.

> **Correct:** "Keep this book," said the professor, "and *take* it home with you."
> **Correct:** *Take* the papers to the principal's office when you go.
> **Correct:** I shall *bring* the books to class next time I come.

BUNCH: Do not use *bunch* to mean "group of people." *Bunch* properly refers to things that grow together in clumps—bananas, grapes, and so on.

> **Incorrect:** Did you see that *bunch* of people who boarded the plane?

BRUNET, BRUNETTE: *Brunet* is the masculine form; *brunette,* feminine. See *blond, blonde.*

BURSTED, BUST, BUSTED: These are corrupt forms of the verb *burst,* which has the same form for all its principal parts.

BUT, HARDLY, ONLY, SCARCELY: These words are negative in implication and should not be used with another negative.

> **Incorrect:** I'm *not hardly* about to breathe.
> **Incorrect:** We *couldn't scarcely* breathe.
> **Correct:** We *could scarcely* breathe.

BUT WHAT: Do not use this expression as a substitute for *that.*

BUT WHICH, AND WHICH: See *and which, but which.*

CALCULATE: Do not use this word to mean "think, guess, plan."

> **Incorrect:** What do you *calculate* that he will do about the error?

CAN, MAY: *Can* denotes ability; *may* denotes possibility or permission.

> **Correct:** Mother said we *may go* to the circus.
> **Correct:** Even with an injured leg, that horse *can* still run fast.
> **Correct:** *May* I help you with that package?

CANNOT HELP BUT: This is considered a double negative. Use *cannot help* with an *ing* word (a gerund).

> **Incorrect:** We *cannot help but feel* compassion for those unfortunate people.
> **Incorrect:** He *cannot help but feel* sorry for me.
> **Correct:** I *cannot help thinking* I made a favorable impression.
> **Correct:** She *could not help going* to the circus.

CAN'T HARDLY: This is a double negative. Use *can hardly*.

Incorrect: Susan *can't* hardly reach the instrument panel.

CAN'T SEEM: Use *doesn't seem* or *don't seem* (as appropriate, for correct number agreement).

CAPACITY, ABILITY: See *ability, capacity*.

CAPITAL, CAPITOL: *Capital* means "money invested" or "the location of the seat of government"; *capitol* means "state house" or "an edifice."

CENSURE, CRITICIZE: *Criticize* means "to examine" or "to judge as a critic"; *censure* means "to find fault with" or "to condemn as wrong."

Correct: Allow me to *criticize* your paper and point out its strengths and weaknesses.
Correct: My father *censured* us for our noisy behavior during the meeting.
Correct: Everyone seemed to *censure* Mable for her statement.

CENTER AROUND: Omit *around;* use *focus on* or *center on* or *upon*.

CHARACTER, REPUTATION: *Character* is what a person really is; *reputation* is what others think he is.

Correct: She is a person of outstanding *character.*
Correct: Her *reputation* is as unblemished as her character.
Correct: His philanthropic deeds have established for him an excellent *reputation.*
Correct: Your attitudes will surely reflect your true *character.*

CITE, SITE: *Cite* means "to quote from"; *site* is a geographical location.

CLAIM: Do not use *claim* to mean "assert, state, contend, maintain"; *claim* means "to demand on the basis of right."

Incorrect: He *claimed* that he was misquoted by the press.
Correct: I *claim* that car and the right to drive it.
Incorrect: Do you *claim* that you are innocent of all wrong?
Correct: The stranger *maintained* that he was a prospector.

CLOTH, CLOTHE: *Cloth* refers to fabric; *clothe* is a verb meaning "to cover" or "surround."

Correct: Rico was wearing a *cloth* shirt made of fine linen.
Correct: Mothers should *clothe* their young children in warm playsuits in the winter time.
Correct: The speaker seemed to *clothe* himself in an aura of self-righteousness.

COARSE, COURSE: *Coarse* means "base, crude, or rough"; *course* means "route, plan, academic pursuit."

Correct: The *coarse* material chafed my skin and caused a sore.
Correct: My cousin certainly has *coarse* manners at times.
Correct: Since we're out of money, we'll have to decide on a new *course* of action.
Correct: Patrice wanted to enroll in an advanced *course* in guitar.

COMMON, MUTUAL: *Common* means "belonging to more than one"; *mutual* means "being reciprocal" or "interchanged."

Correct: Jane and I have a friend in *common*, Sue.
Correct: Jane and I have a *mutual* respect for each other.
Correct: If we help each other, we can derive *mutual* benefits.
Correct: These two geometric figures share a *common* side.
Correct: Jane and Joan have a *common* friend—Jack.
Correct: They have made a *mutual* agreement about the use of the car.

COMPARE, CONTRAST: Use *compare* to indicate similarities or to examine two or more entities to ascertain similarities or differences; use *contrast* to point out differences only.

COMPLECTED: This is a corrupt form of *complexioned*.

Incorrect: Allison is an unusually *light-complected* girl.

COMPLEMENT, COMPLIMENT: *Complement* means "that which completes or accents, a full or total number"; *compliment* means "to flatter, a flattering remark."

Correct: My granddaughter has a full *complement* of Barbie dolls.
Correct: The new drapes certainly *complement* our furniture.
Correct: I wish to *compliment* you on your fine performance.

COMPLETE, FINISH: *Complete* is properly used to show that nothing is lacking; all parts are present. *Finish* is used to show that all that was required has been done.

> **Correct:** Both the model car and the puzzle were *complete*.
> **Correct:** We *finished* our drywalling by noon on Saturday.
> **Correct:** The student has already *finished* preparing his review.
> **Correct:** Have you *finished* all the assigned writing?
> **Correct:** The builders *finished* the house within two months.
> **Correct:** I hope to *finish* this test before I leave.
> **Correct:** *Complete* the structure before showing it to me.

COMPLIMENT, COMPLEMENT: See *complement, compliment*.

CONNECT TOGETHER: The *together* in *connect together* is redundant. Simply use *connect*.

CONSCIENCE, CONSCIOUS: *Conscious* means "being awake, alert"; *conscience* refers to one's feelings of right or wrong, one's morality.

> **Correct:** The player remained *conscious* while the doctor set his broken finger.
> **Correct:** My *conscience* would not allow me to peek at Carlita's answers.

CONSEQUENCE, IMPORTANCE: A *consequence* is a result; *importance* is significance.

> **Correct:** The accident was surely a *consequence* of carelessness.
> **Correct:** His objection is really of little *importance*.
> **Correct:** Everything of *importance* has been done.

CONSIDERABLE: This word is properly used as an adjective, not as a noun or an adverb. Use *considerably* as an adverb.

> **Correct:** Our endeavor involved *considerable* expense.
> **Incorrect:** The speaker was *considerable* upset by the noise.
> **Correct:** The farmer was *considerably* upset by the dry weather.

CONTACT: Do not use this verb form to mean "talk, consult, inform, query, talk with, telephone, or write to." *Contact* means "the coming together or joining of two things."

> **Correct:** The small boat made *contact* with the dock.
> **Correct:** I shall *consult with* [not *contact*] you by telephone tomorrow.
> **Incorrect:** All students should *contact* their advisors before registration day.

CONTEMPLATE: This verb should not be followed by a preposition.

> **Incorrect:** We'll *contemplate* on this matter later in the meeting.
> **Incorrect:** Oliver *contemplated on* the question for a long time.

CONTINUAL, CONTINUOUS: *Continual* means "occurring in steady, rapid, but not unbroken succession." *Continuous* means "without cessation or interruption."

> **Correct:** The *continuous* wind in the trees lulled us to sleep night after night.
> 　　　(The wind in the trees continued without cessation.)
> **Correct:** Today there seems to be a *continual* flow of interruptions.
> **Correct:** There is a *continuous* flow of the river from here to New Orleans.

CONTRAST, COMPARE: See *compare, contrast*.

COULD OF: This is a corrupt form of *could have*.

> **Incorrect:** Is it likely that anyone else *could of* won the election?
> **Correct:** No one *could have* lifted that huge stone by himself.

COUNCIL, COUNSEL: *Council* is a group of elected officials. *Counsel* means to advise someone or to receive advice.

> **Correct:** The student *council* approved the new dress code for the freshmen.
> **Correct:** The class advisor *counseled* the seniors about "skip day" regulations.
> **Correct:** My friend's *counsel* enabled me to understand my frustrations.

COUPLE: Do not use this word to mean "two."

> **Incorrect:** I have a *couple* dollars in my pocket.
> **Correct:** The *couple* is taking a delayed honeymoon.

 When referring to a man and a woman as a pair, *couple* may be either singular or plural. The plural form, the *"couple are,"* is becoming increasingly common today. Users of the term should be consistent: "The couple *are* planning *their* wedding," or "The couple *is* planning *its* wedding."

CREDIBLE, CREDITABLE, CREDULOUS: *Credible* means "capable of being believed"; *creditable*, "worthy of esteem or honor"; *credulous*, "inclined to believe or easily convinced."

> **Correct:** Tell this tale to your mother; she is more *credulous* than I.
> **Correct:** Your *creditable* performance deserves an award.

Correct: That account of the fiasco doesn't sound *credible* to me.
Correct: Carlos told us a very *credible* story
Correct: The skaters gave a very *creditable* performance last evening.
Correct: My mother—a very *credulous* person—believed the wild tale that we told her.

CRITICIZE, CENSURE: See *censure, criticize.*

CUNNING: Do not use this word to mean "attractive" or "pretty."

Incorrect: Don't you agree that she usually wears *cunning* clothes?

CUTE: Avoid this expression. Use *pretty* or *attractive.*

Incorrect: Joanna is thought of by many as being a *cute* girl.

DATA, MEDIA, PHENOMENA, STRATA: These words are the plurals of *datum, medium, phenomenon,* and *stratum.* As plurals, they require plural demonstrative modifiers and plural verbs.

Correct: *Those data are* quite reliable.

DATE: Avoid *date* to mean "an appointment for a set time" or "an engagement with one of the opposite sex."

Correct: I have an *appointment* to see the dean today.
Correct: I have an *appointment* with the hangman tomorrow.

DEAL: Avoid *deal* to mean "transaction" or "bargain."

Incorrect: I got a really good *deal* on a new motorcycle.
Incorrect: These people hope to settle the business *deal* before they adjourn.
Correct: Jim surely got a good *bargain* on his new bicycle.

DECIDED, DECISIVE: *Decided* means "definite, unquestionable, emphatic"; *decisive* means "final, conclusive, beyond any doubt."

Correct: The insurgents claimed a *decisive* victory against tyranny.
Correct: The chairman cast the *decisive* vote.
Correct: He made a *decided* effort to locate the missing dinosaur bones.

Do not confuse these words with the various forms of the verb *decide,* which means "to make a decision."

DEFINITELY: Avoid this word as a vague intensifier.

> **Incorrect:** The professor was *definitely* wrong in his answer. (Is there an *indefinite* wrong?)
> **Correct:** Sue was *surely* wrong in her assessment of Joe.

DELUSION, ILLUSION, ALLUSION: See *allusion, delusion, illusion.*

DEPENDING, DEPENDS: These words are always followed by *on* or *upon.*

DETERMINED, BOUND: See *bound, determined.*

DEVICE, DEVISE: A *device* is a gadget or tool; *devise* is a verb meaning "to formulate or invent."

> **Correct:** This handy *device* should enable us to open our broken lock.
> **Correct:** We should *devise* a plan to earn some money this summer.

DIDN'T, OUGHT: See *had ought, hadn't ought, didn't ought.*

DIFFER FROM, DIFFER WITH: Use *differ from* to indicate that two separate items are different. Use *differ with* to indicate disagreement.

> **Correct:** My report *differs from* yours.
> **Correct:** You may *differ with* me if you wish.

DIFFERENT FROM, DIFFERENT THAN: Use *from,* not *than,* after *different.*

DIFFICULT, HARD: *Difficult* means "not easy, demanding"; *hard* means "solid, firm."

Some dictionaries indicate that these terms are nearly synonymous and interchangeable for "not easy."

DISCOVERY, INVENTION: A *discovery* is the bringing to light of something that already exists. An *invention* is that which is created by ingenuity.

> **Correct:** The *discovery* of uranium did much to advance knowledge.
> **Correct:** The *invention* of the reaper was a boon to agriculture.
> **Correct:** The *discovery* of electricity has certainly helped us.

DISCREET, DISCRETE: *Discreet* means "careful, showing wise restraint"; *discrete* means "independent or separate."

> **Correct:** Sally was very *discreet* about the type of gossip she would tell her friends.
> **Correct:** The high school building was *discrete* from the technical school building.

DISINTERESTED, UNINTERESTED: *Disinterested* means "impartial"; *uninterested* means "having no concern or interest whatsoever."

> **Correct:** *Disinterested* persons make the most reliable witnesses.
> **Correct:** We were *uninterested* in the outcome of the trial, so we left early.
> **Correct:** The student appeared to be *uninterested* in the subject being discussed.
> **Correct:** All referees must be *disinterested* persons.
> **Correct:** A jury should remain *disinterested* in the outcome of the trial.
> **Correct:** How can anyone be *uninterested* in good novels?
> **Correct:** Negotiators for the government should be *disinterested* parties.

DISASSEMBLE, DISSEMBLE: *Dissemble* means to pretend or mislead one into a false belief. *Disassemble* means to take apart.

> **Correct:** He *dissembled* his intense shyness by singing a humorous song.
> **Correct:** My sister *disassembled* her watch and then could not assemble it again.

DONE: This is the past participle of *to do.* Do not use *done* as a past tense; use *did.*

> **Incorrect:** We knew that he *done* it on purpose.
> **Correct:** I knew immediately that he had *done* what he promised.

DON'T: This is a contraction for *do not,* but not for *does not* (*doesn't*).

> **Incorrect:** He *don't* hunt alligators anymore.

DRAGGED, DRUG: The past tense of *drag* is *dragged,* not *drug.*

DRUNK: *Drunk* is the correct past-participle form of *drink.* Do not use the past-tense form *drank* as the past participle.

> **Incorrect:** The baby has *drank* all her milk.

DUE TO: Do not use *due to* to give a reason; use *because of* (*as a result of*).

> **Incorrect:** *Due to* the bad roads, we were unable to proceed.
> **Incorrect:** Last night's performance was cancelled *due to* the blizzard.
> **Correct:** *Because of* his illness, he missed six class meetings.
> **Correct:** The flood was *due to* the recent heavy rains.
>> (In this sentence, the *due to* construction is adjectival in nature; in the preceding sentence, however, it is adverbial. Both constructions are widely accepted, the second without question.)

DUMB, MUTE, STUPID: *Dumb* means "not having the power of speech"; *mute,* "having the power of speech but choosing not to speak"; *stupid,* "dull witted, foolish." *Dumb,* even when used correctly, is falling out of favor.

> **Correct:** Because he chose not to incriminate himself, the witness remained *mute.*
> **Correct:** Removal of the vocal cords renders one *dumb.*
> **Correct:** The convict stood *mute* before the military tribunal.
> **Correct:** Because of his deafness, he has always been *dumb.*

EACH OTHER, ONE ANOTHER: Use *each other* to refer to only two; use *one another* to refer to more than two.

> **Correct:** Sarah, Sue, and Sally help *one another* regularly.
> **Correct:** The twins will surely hurt *each other.*

EAGER, ANXIOUS: See *anxious, eager.*

EFFECT, AFFECT: See *affect, effect.*

EITHER, NEITHER: Use these words to designate one of only two persons or things. For more than two, *not any* or *none* may be used.

ELEGANT: This word means "polished, fastidious, refined." Do not use *elegant* to mean "delicious, good."

> **Incorrect:** Don't you enjoy these *elegant* foods?
> **Correct:** The meal certainly tasted *delicious.*

EMIGRANT, IMMIGRANT: *Emigrant* means "one who has moved *out* of a country"; *immigrant* refers to one who has moved *into* a country."

> **Correct:** My new neighbor is an *immigrant* from South America.
> **Correct:** My ancestors *emigrated* from Europe to Canada in the eighteenth century.

EMIGRATE, IMMIGRATE: *Emigrate* means "to move out of a country"; *immigrate* means "to move into a country."

EMINENT, IMMINENT, PROMINENT: *Prominent* means "conspicuous"; *eminent* means "distinguished in character or rank"; *imminent* means "impending, about to occur."

> **Correct:** Place this picture of Uncle Oscar in a very *prominent* place.
> **Correct:** Dr. Rogers is an *eminent* nuclear physicist.
> **Correct:** The *imminent* flood resulted in a food shortage.
> **Correct:** Because of his business acumen, Mr. Carlson has become an *eminent* man in this city.
> **Correct:** Be sure to place this art treasure in a *prominent* place.

ENORMITY, ENORMOUSNESS: *Enormity* means "wickedness"; *enormousness* means "vastness."

> **Correct:** The *enormity* of his crimes is nearly beyond belief.
> **Correct:** The *enormousness* of Death Valley is quite intimidating.
> **Correct:** The *enormity* of his actions will surely not be forgiven.
> **Correct:** Were you in awe of the *enormousness* of the size of that building?
> **Correct:** The *enormousness* of the frontier startled some settlers.

ENSURE, INSURE, ASSURE: See *assure, ensure, insure.*

ENTHUSE: This is an illiterate attempt to develop a verb form to mean "make enthusiastic" or "become enthusiastic." While many words have been formed by this process of "back formation," this word has not yet gained the status of total acceptance. It is best avoided.

> **Incorrect:** Most everyone was *enthused* about the success of the team.
> **Correct:** I sincerely hope you become *enthusiastic* about the opera.

EQUABLE, EQUITABLE: *Equable* means "uniform, steady, consistently even, serene"; *equitable* means "just, impartial."

> **Correct:** Miss Wheat certainly has an *equable disposition*.
> **Correct:** An *equitable* solution is to cut the pie in half.
> **Correct:** A democratic form of government provides for *equitable* treatment of its citizens.
> **Correct:** The judge will surely remain *equable* in passing sentence upon the convicted man.

EQUALLY AS GOOD: The *as* is redundant. Use *equally good* or *as good as.*

> **Incorrect:** One of the poems is *equally as good* as the other.

EQUITABLE, EQUABLE: See *equable, equitable.*

ETC.: Use this abbreviation only when it is obvious what follows. Too often, the expression is used too vaguely to try to impress the listener or reader that the user knows more than he or she really does know.

EVERY BIT: Do not use this expression to mean "in every way" or "quite."

> **Incorrect:** He was *every bit* as happy as I thought he would be.
> **Incorrect:** My picture is *every bit* as good as yours.
> **Incorrect:** This man is *every bit as* guilty as you are.

EVERYONE, SOMEONE, ANYONE: See *anyone, everyone, someone.*

EVERYPLACE: This is a corrupt form of *everywhere*.

> **Incorrect:** We've looked *everyplace* for the lost kitten.

EVERYWHERES: This is a corrupt form of *everywhere*.

EVIDENTLY, APPARENTLY: See *apparently, evidently*.

EXAM: Do not use this substandard shortening of *examination*.

> **Incorrect:** Yesterday morning I wrote two *exams*.

EXCEPT, ACCEPT: See *accept, except*.

EXCEPTIONAL, EXCEPTIONABLE: *Exceptional* means rare or superior; *exceptionable* means objectionable.

EXCUSE, PARDON: *Excuse* is to grant leave; *pardon* is to forgive. However, in asking forgiveness, small indiscretions may be excused; greater faults are pardoned. In formal situations, adhere to the distinction listed first.

> **Correct:** *Pardon* me; I didn't mean to trip you.

EXPECT, SUSPECT: *Suspect* means "to have suspicions, to doubt or distrust"; *expect* means "to anticipate, to believe likely, or nearly certain."

> **Correct:** We all *suspected* Fritz of feigning illness.
> **Correct:** People in Alaska *expect* snow in winter.
> **Correct:** At what time do you *expect* him to return?

EXPLICIT, IMPLICIT: *Explicit* means "stated clearly or directly"; *implicit* means "suggested, implied."

EXTRA: Do not use this word to mean "unusually."

> **Incorrect:** The weather has been *extra* nice this spring.
> **Correct:** Maria is *unusually* perceptive.

FACTOR: Do not use this word to mean "element, circumstance, influence." A *factor* (noun) is an agent for another person. *Factor* also refers to at least two numbers or quantities that are multiplied to produce a result.

> **Incorrect:** There are several *factors* involved in this decision.
> **Correct:** Mr. Corry will serve as my *factor* in the negotiations for a new agreement.
> **Correct:** The *factors* of sixteen are two and eight (among others).

FAMOUS, INFAMOUS, NOTORIOUS: *Famous* means "well known, renowned, celebrated"; *notorious* means "well-known for unsavory reasons, disapproved of, deplored"—in other words, *infamous*.

> **Incorrect:** Rubinoff, the *notorious* violinist, gave a concert in the hall.

FARTHER, FURTHER: Use *farther* to express distance; use *further* to express the meaning of "more, in addition, to a greater degree."

> **Correct:** Aaron lives *farther* down the street.
> **Correct:** The dean promised to look *further* into the situation.
> **Correct:** We walked *farther* today than we did yesterday.
> **Correct:** Everyone should do some *further* reading on this topic.
> **Correct:** Cal lives *farther* down the street than I do.
> **Correct:** We need to discuss this problem *further*.
> **Correct:** The distance to the sea was *farther* than we had realized.
> **Correct:** This matter needs *further* discussion before we reach a decision.

FAVOR: Do not use this word to mean "resemble."

> **Incorrect:** Don't you think he *favors* his father in the face?
> **Correct:** Do you think Einer *resembles* his uncle Fritz?

FAZE: This word is not related to the noun *phase*. Use *faze* to mean "worry, disconcert."

FEATURE: Do not use this word to mean "imagine" or "believe." *Feature* means "form" or "appearance."

> **Correct:** One *feature* of high mountains is treeless peaks.
> **Incorrect:** Can you *feature* Ramon's doing that?

FELLOW: Avoid *fellow* in the general sense of "man, sweetheart, person." A *fellow* is a comrade or associate.

> **Incorrect:** Two *fellows* were riding in that red convertible.

FETCH: This word means both "go" and "bring." Do not use it with *go*.

> **Incorrect:** *Go fetch*, Charcoal.
> **Incorrect:** Will you *go and fetch* these items from the market?

FEWER, LESS: *Fewer* refers to numbers; *less*, to value, degree, amount. Use *fewer* with count nouns, *less* with mass nouns.

> **Correct:** I had *less* sleep last night than I usually have.
> **Correct:** My grandfather's trees have *fewer* apples this year than last.

Correct: This class has *fewer* students than has the other class.
Correct: I seem to have *less* money than you have.

FIGURATIVELY, LITERALLY: *Literally* means "strictly, truly, exactly"; *figuratively* means "in a similar way" or "in a manner of speaking, but not really true."

Correct: His clothes were *literally* smoking from the heat of the flames.
Incorrect: His car was *literally* flying when it made those marks on the pavement.
Correct: His father was *figuratively* boiling when he saw the dent in his new car.

FIGURE: Do not use this word as a verb to mean "plan, judge, deduce." Save *figure* for problems in mathematics.

Incorrect: I *figure* he's right about the cause of the fire.
Incorrect: No one *figured* that he would succeed.

FINE: This adjective is grossly overused as a vague word of approval. Choose a more nearly exact expression.

FINISH, COMPLETE: See *complete, finish*.

FIRST-RATE: Do not use this expression of quality as an adverb.

Correct: The orchestra gave a *first-rate* performance.
Incorrect: That dog hunts rabbits *first-rate*.
Incorrect: Luaci plays the piano *first-rate*.

FIX: Do not use *fix* as a noun to mean "predicament" nor as a verb to mean "repair" or "prepare." *Fix* means "to make secure."

Correct: I shall *fix* this lamp to the wall.
Incorrect: Now we are really in a *fix*!
Incorrect: Can you *fix* these leaky faucets?
Incorrect: Did you *fix* lunch for our visitors this noon?
Correct: I found myself in a really serious *situation* last night.

FLUNK: Use *fail*.

Incorrect: All too often students *flunk* classes that are quite easy.

FOLKS: Do not use this word to mean "family, relatives, parents."

Incorrect: Every holiday I go to visit my *folks*.
Correct: My *family* is worried about my going to Ohio this spring.

FORMALLY, FORMERLY: *Formally* means "high regard for correctness"; *formerly* means "in the past."

> **Correct:** The delegation was received very *formally* by the queen.
> **Correct:** She was *formerly* the senator from Kentucky.
> **Correct:** *Formerly* we played with another team.
> **Correct:** Everyone will dress *formally* for the dance.

FORMER: Use this expression to refer to the first of only two persons, things, or groups. See *later, latter.*

FORMERLY, FORMALLY: See *formally, formerly.*

FRIGHTEN, STARTLE: *Frighten* means "to induce fear, to cause to be afraid"; *startle* means "to surprise, to cause a reaction because of something unexpected."

> **Correct:** The howling of the wolves *frightened* the children at the camp.
> **Correct:** The noise of the door slamming shut behind me *startled* me.

FUN: Do not use *fun* as an adjective. Use *enjoyable, pleasant,* or a similar word.

> **Incorrect:** We had a *fun* time last evening.

FUNNY, STRANGE: Avoid *funny* to mean "queer, odd"; in this sense, use *strange. Funny* means "amusing."

> **Correct:** Isn't it *strange* that he doesn't care much for money?
> **Correct:** The children thought it *funny* when the clown swung from the rope.
> **Correct:** The squirrel was carrying a *strange* nut that it had found.

FURTHER, FARTHER: See *farther, further.*

GENDER, SEX: *Gender* refers to words in the study of grammar; *sex* is used in reference to creatures of the animal world.

GENTLEMAN, LADY: Use these two words when your purpose is to distinguish persons of refinement and culture from the ill-bred. Use the plural forms in addressing an audience: *Ladies and Gentlemen.* Otherwise, use *man* and *woman.*

> **Correct:** We counted four *men* who had lost their hats.
> **Correct:** In all matters, she shows herself to be a genteel *lady.*

GET, GOT: The verb *get* is one of the most useful words in the language. It is common in such idioms as *get along with* (*someone*), *get the better of* (*someone*), *get at* (*information*), *get up* (*a party*), *get on* (*a horse*), or *get over* (*an illness*). Always be certain that *get* or *got* is used in good idiom, not in slang. *Must* is often usable in its stead.

> **Incorrect:** I've *got* to leave soon.
> **Correct:** I *must* leave before the wind blows any harder.

GIRLFRIEND, BOYFRIEND (or GIRL FRIEND, BOY FRIEND): See *boyfriend, girlfriend (or boy friend, girl friend)*.

GOES: Do not use *goes* to mean "says, states, replies," and so on.

> **Incorrect:** He *goes*, "Where were you last night?"

GOOD, WELL: *Good* is properly a noun or an adjective; do not use *good* as an adverb. *Well* may function as either an adjective or an adverb, depending upon the meaning of the sentence.

> **Correct:** She looks *good* in her new dress.
>   (Good follows the linking verb looks and modifies she.)
> **Correct:** The choir sings *well*.
>   (*Well* is an adverb, modifying *sings*.)
> **Correct:** The senator looks *well*, even though she has been ill.
>   (*Well* (meaning "not ill") follows the linking verb looks and modifies *senator*.)
> **Incorrect:** He rides horses real *good*.
> **Correct:** He rides horses *really well*.

GOOD AND: Avoid *good and* in the meaning of "very" or "really."

> **Incorrect:** Father was *good and* angry with us last night.
> **Incorrect:** Be sure that the floor is *good and* clean tomorrow.

GOT, GET: See *get, got*.

GOTTEN: This is an acceptable past participle of *get*.

GRAND: Avoid the vague usage of *grand* to mean "excellent." Select the exact word to fit the desired meaning.

> **Questionable:** We had a *grand* time at the party last night.
> **Incorrect:** The class had a *grand* time at the reunion.

GREAT DEAL OF: Do not use this as a substitute for *many*.

> **Correct:** He knew *many* of the answers.

GUESS: Avoid *guess* to mean "think, suppose, believe." *Guess* means "to estimate, to conjecture"; *think* means "to reason, visualize, suppose."

> **Incorrect:** I *guess* I'll go to bed now.
> **Incorrect:** No one *guessed* that he would do what he had promised.
> **Correct:** I *think* I'll go to the theater tonight.

GUY: Do not use this word to mean "man, boy, person, fellow."

> **Incorrect:** Tell that *guy* to drive more slowly.

HAD BETTER, HAD RATHER, WOULD RATHER: These are good idioms used to express advisability (with *better*) or preference (with *rather*). Do not use *better* as a shortening of *had better*.

> **Incorrect:** We *better* do that work before dark.
> **Incorrect:** John *better* do his assignment.
> **Incorrect:** Do you think we *better* finish the work sooner than we planned?
> **Correct:** We *had better* do that work before dark.

HAD HE HAVE GONE: This is a corrupt expression of *had he gone*.

> **Incorrect:** *Had* he *have* gone, he'd be rich today.
> **Correct:** *Had* he *gone*, he'd be rich today.
> **Incorrect:** *Had* he *have* gone, we would have won.

HAD OF: This is a corrupt expression of *had*.

> **Incorrect:** *Had* we *of* done that, we'd be sleeping now.
> **Correct:** *Had* we done that, we'd be sleeping now.

HAD OUGHT, HADN'T OUGHT, DIDN'T OUGHT: Avoid these combinations. Use *ought* or *ought not*.

> **Correct:** You *ought* to be more careful.
> **Correct:** You *ought not* get involved in that situation.

HAD RATHER, WOULD RATHER, HAD BETTER: See *had better, had rather, would rather*.

HALF A, A HALF, A HALF A: Use *half a* or *a half*, but avoid the redundant *a half a*.

HANGED, HUNG: Use *hanged* rather than *hung* when speaking of an execution.

>   **Correct:** We *hung* the picture on the wall yesterday.
>   **Correct:** The outlaw was *hanged* at dawn yesterday.
>   **Correct:** The horse thief was *hanged* without benefit of trial.
>   **Correct:** Your picture was *hung* upside down.
>   **Correct:** The criminal was *hanged* at midnight.

HARD, DIFFICULT: See *difficult, hard.*

HARDLY, ONLY, SCARCELY, BUT: See *but, hardly, only, scarcely.*

HATE: Avoid this expression to mean "regret, dislike."

>   **Incorrect:** I *hate that I cannot* agree with you at all.
>   **Correct:** My sister *dislikes* having to get out of bed in the morning.

HAVE GOT: Do not use *have got* in the sense of "must" or to show mere possession. Use *have.*

>   **Incorrect:** *Have* you *got* an extra pencil in your pocket?

HEALTHFUL, HEALTHY: *Healthful* means "capable of giving health"; *healthy* means "having health."

>   **Correct:** Apples are certainly a *healthful* food.
>   **Correct:** My cat gave birth to seven *healthy* kittens.
>   **Correct:** Griffin appears to be a *healthy* person.
>   **Correct:** Many people consider carrots to be a *healthful* food.
>   **Correct:** Green beans are truly *healthful* foods.

HELP BUT: See *cannot help but.*

HIMSELF, MYSELF, YOURSELF: Use these forms as intensives or reflexives only. These forms are not substitutes for the nominatives and objectives. Also, never insert the word *own* between the syllables of these words.

>   **Correct:** You *yourself* are responsible for your problems.
>   **Incorrect:** You are responsible *your ownself* for your problems.
>   **Incorrect:** Alec and *myself* should prefer to deal with your brother and *yourself.*

HISSELF: This is a corrupt form of *himself.*

HOMEY: Avoid this term in the sense of *homelike, intimate.*

> **Incorrect:** We attended a *homey* little gathering at a friend's house.

HONORABLE, REVEREND: *Reverend* is not a title. It is an adjective that modifies a title such as *Mr., Dr., Ms. Honorable* is used as an official form of address for political figures.

> **Correct:** The *Reverend* Mr. Jones will speak to us on Sunday.
> **Incorrect:** I spoke with *Reverend* McDonald yesterday.

HOPEFULLY: *Hopefully* means "with hope." Avoid *hopefully* to mean "We hope that" or a similar phrase.

> **Incorrect:** *Hopefully* the engine will not fail us.
> **Correct:** We *hope* (or We are *hopeful*) that the engine will not fail us.
> **Correct:** The farmer listened *hopefully* for the sound of rain on the roof.

HOW COME?: Avoid this expression. Use *why* or *why not.* (*How come* is itself a corrupt form of "How did that come to be?" or "How came that to be?")

> **Incorrect:** *How come* you didn't answer as you should?

HUMAN, HUMANE: *Human* means "having the characteristics of homo sapiens"; *humane* means "merciful, having kindness or sympathy."

IDEA, IDEAL: Use *idea* to mean "thought, mental plan, or conception." Use *ideal* to mean "standard of excellence, perfection; a model."

> **Correct:** Chad had some great *ideas* about earning money.
> **Correct:** She selected John Cheever as her *ideal* writer.

IF, WHETHER: Use *if* to introduce clauses of condition; use *whether* (with *or* expressed or understood) to introduce noun clauses that contain alternatives.

 When *whether* fits, *if* is incorrect.

> **Correct:** *If* the sun shines, we'll go fishing.
> **Correct:** *Whether* you go *or* stay, you'll need some money.
> **Incorrect:** *If* you win or lose, you'll gain wide recognition.

ILL, SICK: Use *ill* to mean "not well" and *sick* to mean "*nauseated.*"

> **Correct:** We all became *sick* and had to vomit.
> **Correct:** Since Bob was *ill*, he didn't give his report.

ILLUSION, ALLUSION, DELUSION: See *allusion, delusion, illusion.*

IMMIGRANT, EMIGRANT: See *emigrant, immigrant.*

IMMIGRATE, EMIGRATE: See *emigrate, immigrate.*

IMMINENT, PROMINENT, EMINENT: See *eminent, imminent, prominent.*

IMMORAL, AMORAL: See *amoral, immoral.*

IMPLICIT, EXPLICIT: See *explicit, implicit.*

IMPLY, INFER: The writer or the speaker *implies* with his words; the reader or listener *infers* from what he or she hears.

>**Correct:** Are you *implying* that I failed the course?
>**Correct:** I *infer* from your comments that you are tired.
>**Correct:** What is he *implying* by that remark?
>**Correct:** I *inferred* from his actions that he did not choose to go.
>**Correct:** Did the speaker *imply* that we weren't well educated?

IMPORTANCE, CONSEQUENCE: See *consequence, importance.*

IN, INTO: *In* indicates *location within; into* indicates *motion or direction to a point within.*

>**Correct:** The children were jumping *into* the water (from the shore).
>**Correct:** The children were jumping *in* the water. (They were already in the water when they began jumping.)
>**Correct:** Brooke dived *into* the pool from the low board.
>**Correct:** Your book is *in* my desk.

IN-, UN-: Both prefixes have the meaning of "not." Check a dictionary if any doubt exists concerning the proper form to use.

>**Correct:** My friend is an *in*competent mechanic.
>**Correct:** That comment was *un*necessary.

IN BACK OF: Avoid this expression. Use *behind.*

>**Incorrect:** Park your car *in back of* the house.

IN REGARDS TO: Use either *in regard to* or *as regards.*

>**Incorrect:** The president wrote *in regards* to the motion before the house.

INCREDIBLE, INCREDULOUS: *Incredible* means "too extraordinary to admit of belief." *Incredulous* means "inclined not to believe on slight evidence."

> **Correct:** I truly believe your story about seeing a ghost to be *incredible* (unbelievable).
> **Correct:** Mother is too *incredulous* (unbelieving) to accept our story.
> **Correct:** His story was completely *incredible*.
> **Correct:** Frank cast me an *incredulous* glance as I discussed my experience.

INDIVIDUAL, PARTY, PERSON: *Individual* refers to a single person, animal, or thing. *Party* refers to a group, never to a single person (except in legal language). *Person* is the preferred word for general reference to a human being.

> **Correct:** Will the *person* who took my book please return it?

INFAMOUS, NOTORIOUS, FAMOUS: See *famous, infamous, notorious*.

INFER, IMPLY: See *imply, infer*.

INFERIOR THAN: Use *inferior to* or *worse than*.

> **Incorrect:** Your latest story is *inferior than* your earlier ones.

INGENIOUS, INGENUOUS: *Ingenious* means "clever, resourceful"; *ingenuous* means "open, frank, artless."

> **Correct:** Your invention is an *ingenious* device.
> **Correct:** He seemed to give *ingenuous* answers to my sincere questions.

INSIDE OF, OUTSIDE OF: The *of* is useless. Do not use *inside of* to mean "within." Do not use *outside of* to mean "besides."

> **Incorrect:** He said he'd be here *inside of* an hour.
> **Incorrect:** Look *inside of* the drawer to find more paper.
> **Incorrect:** He did nothing wrong *outside of* missing class ten times.
> **Correct:** The cat was *inside* the box.

INSURE, ASSURE, ENSURE: See *assure, ensure, insure*.

INTO, IN: See *in, into*.

INVENTION, DISCOVERY: See *discovery, invention*.

INVITE: Do not use *invite* as a noun. Use *invitation*.

> **Incorrect:** Have you received an *invite* to their party?

IRREGARDLESS: This incorrect form of *regardless* is often misused by speakers and writers because of its similarity to words such as *irresponsible, irrational,* and *irregular.* It is not acceptable.

> **Incorrect:** Larry seemed determined to go *irregardless* of my objections.

IRRITATE, AGGRAVATE, ANNOY: See *aggravate, annoy, irritate.*

IT'S: *It's* is the contracted form of *it is;* do not use *it's* as the possessive form of *it,* which is *its* without the apostrophe.

JUDGEMENT, JUDGMENT: *Judgment* is the more frequent spelling, the other (chiefly British) is sometimes considered an error.

JUST: Do not use *just* to mean "completely, simply, quite." *Just* means "fair, evenhanded, impartial, honest" or "only, precisely" and "barely."

> **Correct:** These potato chips have *just* enough salt.
> **Correct:** That meteorite *just* missed Jowana.
> **Incorrect:** I was *just* sick at the thought of quitting.
> **Correct:** That picture is *simply* beautiful.

KIND, SORT: These two words are singular forms and require singular demonstrative modifiers. *Kinds* and *sorts* are plural and require plural demonstrative modifiers.

> **Correct:** That *kind* of worker is very much appreciated.
> **Incorrect:** Not many people like these *kind of* programs.

KIND OF, SORT OF: Do not use these two expressions as adverbs to mean "somewhat, rather, after a fashion."

> **Incorrect:** The new senator was *kind of* naive about politics.
> **Incorrect:** After the game, I was *kind of* tired.

KIND OF A, SORT OF A: Omit the *a.* Usually, the article is placed *before* the first noun, not after the preposition.

> **Incorrect:** Do you enjoy this *kind of a* performance?
> **Correct:** All the girls thought he was *a kind of* jerk.
> **Correct:** She was *a sort of* mentor to the young people.

LADY, GENTLEMAN: See *gentleman, lady.*

LAST, LATEST: *Last* is final; *latest,* most recent.

> **Correct:** Yes, this is my *latest* book; I shall soon write another, however.

LATER, LATTER: *Later* is the comparative of *late* and means "more late"; alternatively, *later* means "at a time in the future." *Latter* refers to the second of two. If more than two are named, use *last* or *last-mentioned* instead of *latter*.

> **Correct:** I will try to mow the lawn *later* in the afternoon.
> **Correct:** We rejected the first plan but accepted the *latter*.

LATEST, LAST: See *last, latest*.

LATTER, LATER: See *later, latter*.

LAY, LIE: To *lay* means "to put" or "to place." To *lie* means "to rest" or "to recline." For more information, refer to the section titled "Troublesome Verbs" in Part I, "Parts of Speech."

> **Correct:** Let us *lie* here and rest.
> **Correct:** I *laid* the book on the shelf.

LEAD, LED: *Lead* (v) is the present-tense form; *led* is the past-tense and past-participle forms.

LEARN, TEACH: *Learn* means "to acquire knowledge"; *teach* means "to impart knowledge."

> **Correct:** I will *learn* from you if you will *teach* me.

LEAVE, LET, PERMIT, ALLOW: See *allow, leave, let, permit*.

LED, LEAD: See *lead, led*.

LEND, LOAN: *Lend* is a verb meaning "to make a loan." *Loan* is a noun meaning "the result of lending."

> **Correct:** Please *lend* me enough money for the plane fare.
> **Correct:** Can anyone here *lend* me a dollar until tomorrow?

LESS, FEWER: See *fewer, less*.

LET, PERMIT, ALLOW, LEAVE: See *allow, leave, let, permit*.

LET'S US: *Let's* is the contraction of *let us*. Therefore, *let's us* contains a redundancy (*us*).

> **Incorrect:** After the performance, *let's us* go out for coffee.

LIABLE, LIKELY, APT: See *apt, liable, likely*.

LIE, LAY: See *lay, lie*.

LIKE, AS, AS IF: See *as, as if, like*.

LIKE, LOVE: *Like* refers to taste or preference; *love* expresses affection.

> **Correct:** We all *like* to go swimming in the heated pool.

LIKE, SUCH AS: Do not use *like* to mean *such as*.

> **Incorrect:** I enjoy movies about female athletes, like *Love and Basketball*.
> **Correct:** Some books, such as *I Capture the Castle*, can be read very quickly.

LIKELY, APT, LIABLE: See *apt, liable, likely*.

LITERALLY, FIGURATIVELY: See *figuratively, literally*.

LOAN, LEND: See *lend, loan*.

LOCATE: Do not use this verb to mean *settle*. *Locate* means "to discover, to find"; *settle* means "to put into place or to establish in a permanent location."

> **Incorrect:** My ancestors wanted to *locate* in the valley near the river.
> **Incorrect:** Our former neighbors have *located* in Seattle.
> **Correct:** They *located* a fertile valley and *settled* there permanently.
> **Correct:** I hope those hillbillies don't *settle* in this neighborhood.

The definitions of these words tend to overlap with respect to location or establishing at a location.

LOOSE, LOSE: *Lose* means "to cease having." *Loose* as a verb means "to set free"; as an adjective, it means "free, not fastened."

> **Correct:** *Loose* the moorings so that we may set sail.
> **Correct:** Is that button *loose*?
> **Correct:** Did you *lose* your books?
> **Correct:** Try not to *lose* the money your father gave you.

LOSE OUT: The *out* is superfluous.

> **Incorrect:** I was afraid that he would *lose out* in the race.

LOTS, LOTS OF, A WHOLE LOT, A LOT: See *a lot, a whole lot, lots, lots of*.

LOTS OF, A WHOLE LOT, A LOT, LOTS: See *a lot, a whole lot, lots, lots of*.

LOVE, LIKE: See *like, love*.

LOVELY: Avoid the vague use of *lovely* to mean "very pleasing." Select the exact word to fit the meaning.

> **Incorrect:** We had a *lovely* time at your party last night.
> **Correct:** We had an *enjoyable* time at your party last night.
> **Correct:** Everyone had a *very pleasing* experience.

LUNCH, LUNCHEON: *Lunch* is a very light meal—food prepared for eating between regular meals at any time; *luncheon* is the midday meal.

> **Correct:** Let's have a light *lunch* before we retire for the night.
> **Correct:** The club entertained at a noon *luncheon*.
> **Correct:** The *lunch* was scheduled for four o'clock.

LUXURIANT, LUXURIOUS: *Luxuriant* means "profuse in growth"; *luxurious* pertains to luxury.

> **Correct:** My neighbors' lawn is certainly *luxuriant*.
> **Correct:** The new carpet in my sister's house is really *luxurious*.
> **Correct:** You certainly have *luxuriant* hair.
> **Correct:** The home is furnished *luxuriously*.
> **Correct:** The model had a *luxuriant* head of golden hair.

MAINTAIN, ASSERT: See *assert, maintain*.

MAJORITY, PLURALITY: *Majority* is more than half the total; *plurality* is the greatest of three or more numbers but less than half.

> **Correct:** Senator Smythe had the *majority* of the votes.
>   (The Senator had at least half plus one of the votes cast.)
> **Correct:** Perkins had a *plurality* of the votes for dog catcher.
>   (At least three candidates ran for office. Perkins had more votes than either of the other two (or more)—but not 50 percent of the total.)
> **Correct:** John received 103 votes; Sam, 27; Joe, 13; therefore, John received a *majority*.
> **Correct:** Because he has more votes than his opponent, Vernon has a *majority*.
> **Correct:** Thirty votes were cast; Bill had 14; Carl had 9; Sam had 7. Bill had a *plurality* of the votes.

MATH: Avoid this shortening of *mathematics* in formal writing.

MAY, CAN: See *can, may*.

MAY, MIGHT: The past tense form of *may* is *might*. That is, *may* expresses present or future intentions or possibility; *might* expresses past situations.

> **Correct:** I *may* go to the game; I'm not certain.
> **Correct:** I *might* have done it; I don't remember clearly.

Might is used in other special situations. For instance, *might* is used to state hypothetical situations.

> **Correct:** If the moon were nearer, we *might* be able to drive without lights.

Might is also used to express "weaker possibility or probability" than *may*.

> **Correct:** Martha *may* become an attorney some day.
> (A reasonable possibility exists.)
> **Correct:** Of course I can jump thirty feet. I *might* be able to pole vault to the moon, too.
> (The possibility is weak or nonexistent.)

MAY BE, MAYBE: Do not confuse the verb form *may be* with the adverb *maybe*, which means "perhaps."

MAY OF: Avoid this corruption of *may have*.

MEAN: Do not use *mean* for *ill-tempered*. This word means, among other things, *ignoble*, or *base*.

> **Correct:** The dictator had a *mean* motive for his decree.
> **Incorrect:** Don't be *mean* to the little children.

MEDIA, PHENOMENA, STRATA, DATA: See *data, media, phenomena, strata*.

MESSRS.: The plural of *Mr., Messrs.* should never be used without a name or names following it.

MIGHT, MAY: See *may, might*.

MIGHT COULD: This is a corruption of *may be able to*.

> **Incorrect:** We *might could* finish the project before Saturday.

MIGHT OF: Avoid this corruption of *might have*.

MIGHTY: *Mighty* means "strong"; do not use it to mean "very."

> **Incorrect:** There are times when I become *mighty* discouraged.

MORAL, MORALE: Distinguish the adjective *moral* from the noun *morale*.

> **Correct:** Since losing the game, the team has suffered a low *morale*.
> **Correct:** The *moral* standards of the community are above reproach.
> **Correct:** The team's *morale* was really high after the win.

MOST, ALMOST: See *almost, most*.

MOSTLY: *Mostly* means "almost entirely." Avoid using *mostly* to mean "in the greatest degree."

> **Correct:** The students were *mostly* freshmen.
> **Incorrect:** The people *mostly* affected by the new regulations are hunters.

MS.: This is an accepted title for a woman whose marital status is unknown or irrelevant to the situation.

MUCHLY: This is an unacceptable form of *much*.

> **Incorrect:** The mother was *muchly* disturbed because the train was late.

MUST OF: Avoid this corruption of *must have*.

MUTE, STUPID, DUMB: See *dumb, mute, stupid*.

MUTUAL, COMMON: See *common, mutual*.

MYSELF, YOURSELF, HIMSELF: See *himself, myself, yourself*.

NAUGHT, AUGHT: See *aught, naught*.

NEARLY, PRACTICALLY: *Practically* means "virtually" or "for all intents and purposes"; *nearly* means "almost" or "closely, as in space or time."

NECESSITY: Use *of* or *or* with this word, not *to*.

NEEDS, WANTS: *Wants* are things that one desires; *needs* are things required to continue as planned or hoped.

> **Correct:** His *wants* are few: a new car, a motorcycle, and a new fishing pole.
> **Correct:** The survivor's *needs* now are food and rest.
> **Correct:** The team is meeting its *needs* by wearing old jerseys.

NEITHER, EITHER: See *either, neither*.

NICE: *Nice* means "precise, exact." Do not overuse *nice* as a general word of approval.

> **Correct:** My mother has an *attractive* coat.

NO ACCOUNT, NO GOOD: Avoid these two expressions to mean "worthless" or "of no value."

> **Incorrect:** His check again proved to be *no account*.

NO PLACE: Avoid this corruption of *nowhere*.

> **Incorrect:** We could find the map *no place*.

NOT HARDLY: This is a double negative. Omit *not*. See *but, hardly, only, scarcely*.

NOTORIOUS, FAMOUS, INFAMOUS: See *famous, infamous, notorious*.

NOVICE, AMATEUR: See *amateur, novice*.

NOWHERE NEAR: Avoid this expression to mean "not nearly."

> **Incorrect:** Your essay is *nowhere near* as good as it should be.
> **Correct:** The paper is *not nearly* acceptable.

NOWHERES: Avoid this corruption of *nowhere*.

NUMBER, AMOUNT: See *amount, number*.

O, OH: Both are interjections. *O* is used in a very formal direct address, is always capitalized, and is never followed by a mark of punctuation. *Oh* expresses a wish, grief, pain, or surprise and is always followed by a comma or an exclamation mark. See the section titled "Interjections" in Part I, "Parts of Speech."

OBSERVANCE, OBSERVATION: *Observance* is the act of recognizing a holiday or honoring a special event. *Observation* refers to watching something or keeping a person or group under scrutiny.

> **Correct:** The banks will be closed in *observance* of the legal holiday.
> **Correct:** The reckless taxi drivers were kept under *observation* by the company manager.

OF: See *could of, had of, ought to of. Of* is never a substitute for *have*.

> **Incorrect:** You *should of* told him what you thought.

OFF OF: The *of* is unnecessary.

> **Incorrect:** The paper has blown *off of* my desk.

OH, O: See *O, oh*.

OK, O.K., OKAY: Avoid these expressions in formal contexts.

ONE ANOTHER, EACH OTHER: See *each other, one another.*

ONLY: Be certain that *only is* used only in conjunction with the word it is meant to modify. See *but, hardly, only, scarcely.*

> **Correct:** *Only* he wanted to play checkers.
> **Correct:** He wanted *only* to play checkers.
> **Correct:** He wanted to play *only* checkers.

ONLY, SCARCELY, BUT, HARDLY: See *but, hardly, only, scarcely.*

OR: Do not use *or* with *neither.*

OTHER, OTHERWISE: Use *other* as an adjective and *otherwise* as an adverb.

> **Correct:** The carpenter did some *other* work for my neighbors.
> **Correct:** He built the cabinets *otherwise* than we had planned.

OTHER TIMES: Use *at other times.*

> **Incorrect:** *Other times* I prefer to be alone.

OTHERWISE, OTHER: See *other, otherwise.*

OUGHT: See *had ought, hadn't ought, didn't ought.*

OUGHT TO OF: Avoid this corruption of *ought to have.*

OUT LOUD: Avoid this expression; use *aloud.*

> **Incorrect:** Will you read *out loud* to us?
> **Correct:** Emily cried *aloud* in her sleep.

OUTSIDE OF, INSIDE OF: See *inside of, outside of.*

OVER WITH: The *with* is superfluous.

> **Incorrect:** We were really pleased to see the game finally *over with.*

OWN UP: Do not use this expression to mean "admit, confess."

> **Incorrect:** The suspect practically *owned up* to the robbery.

P.M., A.M.: See *A.M., P.M.*

PARDON, EXCUSE: See *excuse, pardon.*

PARTY, PERSON, INDIVIDUAL: See *individual, party, person.*

PASSED, PAST: *Passed* means "exceeded, gained the lead" or "caused someone to receive something." *Past* means "(in) a bygone time."

> **Correct:** No one has every *passed* his test on the first try.
> **Correct:** Miranda *passed* me in the race to be valedictorian.
> **Correct:** The gambler *passed* his partner an ace under the table.
> **Correct:** Automobiles were much easier to work on in the *past*.

PEDAL, PEDDLE, PETAL: *Pedal* is either a verb meaning "to push with one's foot" or a noun meaning "that which is pushed with the foot." *Peddle* means "to sell or distribute something." *Petal* is the colored leaflet of a flower blossom.

> **Correct:** We must *pedal* faster if we wish to be home by lunchtime.
> **Correct:** He tried to *peddle* his ideas to a disbelieving audience.
> **Correct:** The flower had thirteen *petals* on its blossom, which means she loves me.

PER: Avoid using *per* except with a Latin word—*per annum, per diem*—or with statistics or units of measurement.

> **Correct:** This font prints at eight characters *per* inch.
> **Incorrect:** I prefer to work only four days *per* week.

PERCENT (or PER CENT): Use this expression only *after* a number. Do not use *percent* in the sense of *percentage*.

> **Incorrect:** A large *percent* of the students were unable to hear the speaker.

PERMIT, ALLOW, LEAVE, LET: See *allow, leave, let, permit*.

PERSON, PARTY, INDIVIDUAL: See *individual, party, person*.

PERSONAL, PERSONNEL: *Personal* means "belonging to someone," "private," or "confidential." *Personnel* refers to people associated with an organization such as a business.

> **Correct:** The President's *personal* plane was waiting to take us to Washington.
> **Correct:** We all respected his *personal* decision to resign as chairman of the club.
> **Correct:** The *personnel* of the First Armored Division were ready for the inspection.

PETAL, PEDAL, PEDDLE: See *pedal, peddle, petal*.

PHASE: See *faze*.

PHENOMENA, STRATA, DATA, MEDIA: See *data, media, phenomena, strata*.

PHONE: Avoid this shortening of *telephone* in formal contexts.

> **Incorrect:** No one is to use the *phone* without permission.

PHOTO: Avoid this shortening of *photograph*.

> **Incorrect:** Please send me one of your latest *photos*.

PIECE: Do not use *piece* to mean "distance, short distance."

> **Incorrect:** Several of us walked down the road a *piece*.

PLAN ON: Use *plan to*.

> **Incorrect:** Don't *plan on* leaving early from that test.
> **Correct:** I *plan to* visit Aunt Shelley in the fall.
> **Correct:** Our group *plans to* be in Paris next summer.

PLENTY: Do not use *plenty* as an adverb to mean "quite" nor as an adjective before a noun.

> **Incorrect:** That driver is *plenty* clever in finding a good route.
> **Incorrect:** There are *plenty* apples for all of you.

PLURALITY, MAJORITY: See *majority, plurality*.

POSTED: Do not use *posted* to mean "informed."

> **Incorrect:** I'll keep you *posted* on the situation.
> **Incorrect:** Let's keep well *posted* on this subject.

PRACTICABLE, PRACTICAL: *Practical* means "useful, not theoretical." *Practicable* means "capable of being put into practice."

> **Correct:** A screwdriver is a very *practical* tool to own.
> **Correct:** Sue presented a very *practicable* solution to the committee.
> **Correct:** John submitted a very *practicable* plan to his supervisor.

PRACTICALLY, NEARLY: See *nearly, practically*.

PRECEDE, PROCEED: *Precede* means "before"; *proceed* means "continue."

PRETTY: Avoid this word as an intensifier. Use *very, somewhat, greatly, rather.*

PRINCIPAL, PRINCIPLE: *Principal* means "first, leader, chief"; *principle* means "a general truth, a basic law, moral standard."

> **Correct:** The *principal* disagreement involved salary.

PROCEED, PRECEDE: See *precede, proceed.*

PRODUCE, PRODUCTS: *Produce* is raw material; *products* are manufactured items.

> **Correct:** Because of the flood, the farmer could not get his *produce* to market.
> **Correct:** What *products* does that factory make?

PROMINENT, EMINENT, IMMINENT: See *eminent, imminent, prominent.*

PROPOSE, PURPOSE: To *propose* is to offer; *to purpose* is to plan or to intend with determination.

> **Correct:** I *purpose* to change my name regardless of your objections.
> **Correct:** Will you *propose* a solution to this stalemate?
> **Correct:** Did you *purpose* to leave on the earlier plane?
> **Correct:** What new plan did he *propose*?

PROPOSITION: Do not use this word in the sense of *proposal, scheme, project,* or *undertaking.* A *proposition* is a statement of truth.

> **Incorrect:** All of us listened attentively to the unusual *proposition* contained in the motion.

PROVIDING: Do not use this word in the sense of *if;* use *provided.*

> **Incorrect:** We should like to hear more of this plan, *providing* you are not too tired to discuss it with us.

PURPOSE, PROPOSE: See *propose, purpose.*

PUT IN: Do not use this expression to mean *spend, occupy, applied.*

> **Incorrect:** I *put in* for promotion yesterday.
> **Incorrect:** I *put in* six hours at work this morning.
> **Incorrect:** Nora *put in* nine hours studying for her final examination.

QUITE: *Quite* means "entirely" or "all the way" and must not be used in the sense of *rather, somewhat, considerably,* or any other word of degree:

> **Correct:** You are *quite* correct in your analysis of the facts.
> *(Quite correct* means "entirely correct," not "almost correct.")

Further, *quite* must not be followed by a noun. Do not use the following or similar constructions:

> **Incorrect:** He caught *quite a few* fish before breakfast.
> **Incorrect:** We carried *quite a load* of wood to the kitchen door.

QUOTATION, QUOTE: *Quote* is a verb. Do not misuse it as the noun *quotation.*

> **Incorrect:** That statement is a *quote* from your last speech, Senator.

RAISE, RISE: *Raise* means "to lift something or force something upward"; *rise* means "to go higher, to gain elevation." See the section titled "Troublesome Verbs" in Part I for more information.

RAISE, REAR: Do not use *raise* to mean "bring up children." Use *rear.* Use *raise* in reference to animals or birds.

> **Incorrect:** Where were you *raised*?

RARELY EVER, SELDOM EVER, SELDOM OR EVER: Do not use any of these expressions for *seldom if ever, rarely if ever,* or *hardly ever.* In the cases of *seldom ever* and *rarely ever,* simply omit *ever* or change *seldom* and *rarely* to *hardly.*

> **Correct:** The stars *seldom* appear so bright as they do tonight.

REAL: Do not use *real* to mean "very" or as a substitute for *really* or *very. Real* means "genuine" or "authentic."

> **Incorrect:** I am *real* sorry for your misfortunes.
> **Incorrect:** It was *real* thoughtful of you to call me on the telephone yesterday.
> **Correct:** We all suffered a *real* setback in our plans.

REALLY: Avoid using the informal *really* when words such as *very* or *extremely* should be used.

REAR, RAISE: See *raise, rear.*

REASON IS BECAUSE: Use *reason is that.* See *because.*

> **Incorrect:** His *reason* for being late *was because* he could not find his hat.
> **Incorrect:** The *reason* he is late *is because* he had to change planes in Memphis.

REASON WHY: The *why* is redundant. See *reason is because.*

REFER, ALLUDE: See *allude, refer.*

REFER BACK: The *back* is superfluous. If more than one reference is made to an item, use *refer again.*

> **Incorrect:** If you need to do so, *refer back* to the original story.

REPUTATION, CHARACTER: See *character, reputation.*

RESPECTABLY, RESPECTIVELY: *Respectively* means "in a certain order"; *respectably* means "deserving of respect."

> **Correct:** Jane and Susan were elected president and vice president *respectively.*
> **Correct:** Their actions in behalf of the orphans were performed *respectably.*

REST, BALANCE: See *balance, rest.*

REVEREND, HONORABLE: See *honorable, reverend.*

RIGHT: Do not use *right* to mean "very" or "extremely."

> **Incorrect:** He was a *right* jolly old soul.

RIGHT ALONG: Do not use this expression to mean "continuously."

> **Incorrect:** It rained *right along* for the entire evening.

RIGHT AWAY: Do not use this expression to mean "immediately."

RISE, RAISE: See *raise, rise.*

SAID: Use *said* as an adjective meaning "before-mentioned" only in legal documents.

> **Correct:** Evidence shows that the *said* meeting did not take place.

SALARY, WAGES: *Salary* is a fixed amount of pay as remuneration for administrative, supervisory, or professional effort; *wages* refers to pay—usually at an hourly rate—for labor or physical effort.

SAME, SUCH: Use these two words as substitutes for *it, this,* or *that* only in legal documents.

SAYS: This is a corruption of *said* when reporting past conversations.

> **Incorrect:** Then I *says* to him, "Good-bye forever!"
> **Correct:** Einer sometimes *says* the strangest things.

SCARCELY, BUT, HARDLY, ONLY: See *but, hardly, only, scarcely.*

SELDOM EVER, SELDOM OR EVER, RARELY EVER: See *rarely ever, seldom ever, seldom or ever.*

SET, SIT: To *set* means "to put" or "to place." To *sit* means "to rest." See the section titled "Troublesome Verbs" in Part I for more information.

> **Correct:** She *sits* by the window to read.
> **Correct:** I *set* the book on the table.

SEWAGE, SEWERAGE: *Sewage* is waste material; *sewerage* is the system of pipes or channels for drainage.

> **Correct:** The city has proposed a bond issue to extend *sewerage* to the outlying residential areas.

SEX, GENDER: See *gender, sex.*

SHALL, WILL: *Shall* is used with the first-person pronoun; *will* is used with second- and third-person pronouns.

> **Correct:** I *shall* sing to you.
> **Correct:** You *will* be the first speaker tomorrow evening.
> **Correct:** He *will* lend you the money.
> **Correct:** The robin *will* build a nest in the tree.

SHAPE: Do not use *shape* to mean "condition, manner, state."

> **Incorrect:** Many homes in this area are in bad *shape.*

SHOULD, WOULD: The uses of *should* and *would* correspond to those of *shall* and *will.* For example, for expressing simple future, use *should* with the first person and *would* with second and third persons.

> **Correct:** I *should* like to tell you the story of my life.
> **Correct:** The workers *would* need more water in the noonday sun.

SHOULD OF: Avoid this corruption of *should have.*

SHOW UP: Do not use this expression to mean "expose" or "arrive."

Incorrect: At what time did he *show up*?

SICK, ILL: See *ill, sick*.

SIGHT: Do not use *sight* to mean "a great deal."

Incorrect: She did a *sight* better than expected.
Incorrect: The students have collected a *sight* of items for the yard sale.

SIT, SET: See *set, sit*.

SITE, CITE: See *cite, site*.

SIZE: Do not use *size* to mean "sized."

Correct: What *sized* hat does your uncle wear?
Incorrect: What *size* cap do you wear?

SIZE UP: Do not use this expression to mean "estimate, judge, evaluate."

Incorrect: After some serious observation, the officer *sized up* the situation.

SLOW, SLOWLY: Both are acceptable adverbs of long standing in formal English. Some unwarranted prejudice exists against *slow* in such constructions as "Drive slow."

SO . . . AS . . . , AS . . . AS . . . : See *as . . . as . . . , so . . . as . . . .*

SOME: Do not use *some* as an adjective to intensify (for instance, in place of *rather* or *somewhat*). Use *some* only to indicate amount or quantity.

Incorrect: Matilda is *some* better this morning.
Incorrect: That is *some* car that you have!
Correct: The travelers were somewhat surprised by the long delay.

SOMEONE, ANYONE, EVERYONE: See *anyone, everyone, someone*.

SOMEPLACE: This is a corruption of *somewhere*.

Incorrect: I hope to go *someplace* for a long vacation.

SOMEWHERES: This is a corruption of *somewhere*.

SORT, KIND: See *kind, sort*.

SORT OF, KIND OF: See *kind of, sort of.*

SORT OF A, KIND OF A: See *kind of a, sort of a.*

STANZA, VERSE: *A stanza* is a group of lines; a *verse* is one line.

> **Correct:** The second *stanza* contains six *verses.*

START, BEGIN: See *begin, start.*

STARTLE, FRIGHTEN: See *frighten, startle.*

STATIONARY, STATIONERY: *Stationary* means "fixed, unmoving, unmovable"; *stationery* is paper made especially for correspondence.

STATUE, STATURE, STATUTE: *A statue* is a figure, a graven image; *stature* is height or image; a *statute* is a written law.

> **Correct:** Our legislature placed this *statute* on the books two years ago.

STIMULANT, STIMULUS: *Stimulant* is that which increases physical or vital energy; *stimulus* is that which increases emotional or mental energy.

> **Correct:** The doctor gave the patient a prescription for a *stimulant.*
> **Correct:** Your remarks served as a *stimulus* for our new thinking on this matter.

STRANGE, FUNNY: See *funny, strange.*

STRATA, DATA, MEDIA, PHENOMENA: See *data, media, phenomena, strata.*

STUPID, DUMB, MUTE: See *dumb, mute, stupid.*

SUCH: *Such* is followed by *as* to introduce a relative clause and by *that* to introduce a result clause. Do not use *such* to mean "very." Refer to the section titled "Clauses" in Part II, "Sentence Elements," for more information about clauses.

> **Incorrect:** This is *such* a pleasant evening.
> **Correct:** The play was *such that* I had to walk out.

SUCH, SAME: See *same, such.*

SUCH AS, LIKE: See *like, such as.*

SUIT, SUITE: In its common usage, *suit* refers to items of apparel that serve as a unit and are meant to be worn together. *Suite* means "related things that are intended to be used as a single set" or "connecting rooms."

> **Correct:** My sister bought a new *suit* to wear to her friend's wedding.
> **Correct:** Our new bedroom *suite* consists of a bed, a dresser, and a nightstand.
> **Correct:** The conference was held in a *suite* of rooms at the new convention center.

SUPERIOR: This word should not be followed by *than*; use *to*.

> **Incorrect:** Does this material seem *superior than* the one we saw earlier?

SURE: Do not use *sure* as an adverb. Use *surely* or *certainly*.

> **Incorrect:** I *sure* hope we don't get any more rain tonight.
> **Correct:** I *surely* (or *certainly*) hope we don't get any more rain tonight.
> **Incorrect:** He *sure* does play a lot of tennis.

SURE AND, TRY AND: Use *try to, sure to*.

> **Incorrect:** Be sure *and* write to us while you are away.

SUSPECT, EXPECT: See *expect, suspect*.

SUSPICION: Do not use *suspicion* as a verb to mean "suspect."

> **Incorrect:** The officer *suspicioned* that we were not telling the whole truth.

SWELL: Do not use *swell* as an adjective to mean "excellent."

> **Incorrect:** We all had a *swell* time on the beach this morning.
> **Incorrect:** Margaret gave a *swell* book review to the club.

TAKE, BRING: See *bring, take*.

TAKE AND: Do not use this combination in sentences like this: "I'll *take and* hit the ball to the outfielders."

TAKE SICK: Do not use this expression for *become ill*. See *ill, sick*.

> **Incorrect:** Benny *took sick* of measles several days ago.

TAKE STOCK IN, BANK ON: See *bank on, take stock in*.

TEACH, LEARN: See *learn, teach*.

TEND TO: The *to* is superfluous.

> **Incorrect:** Everyone must *tend to* his own affairs.

TERRIBLE, TERRIBLY: Do not use these words to mean simply *bad*. Do not use *terribly* to mean "very."

> **Incorrect:** Helen was involved in a *terribly* bad accident.

THAN, THEN: *Than* is a conjunction used in comparisons; *then* is an adverb used to refer to a period or moment of time.

> **Correct:** Bill was able to catch fish much more quickly *than* I was.
> **Correct:** We all watched the sunset; *then* it was time to go home.
> **Correct:** Back *then*, bumpers were made of steel.
> **Correct:** Mary is taller *than* Roger.
> **Correct:** First we had rain, *then* we had snow, *then* we had more rain.
> **Correct:** The project involved more hard work *than* I had anticipated.
> **Correct:** *Then* came the rain.

THAT: Do not use *that* as an adverb.

> **Incorrect:** I know I didn't do *that* badly on the test.

THAT, WHICH: Although many people use *that* and *which* interchangeably, they should not be so used. *That* should be used only to introduce a restrictive clause; *which* should be used only to introduce a nonrestrictive clause:

> **Correct:** The puppy *that* I trained tore up my Birkenstocks.
> (This sentence implies that there is more than one puppy; the speaker is referring specifically to the one she trained. This is a restrictive clause.)
> **Correct:** The puppy, *which* I trained, tore up my Birkenstocks.
> (In this sentence, the clause "which I trained" simply provides more information about the puppy in question; if the clause were removed, the sentence's essential meaning would still be conveyed. This is a nonrestrictive clause.)

THAT, WHO: Use *who* instead of *that* to refer to persons.

> **Correct:** I caught the boy *who* broke the window.
> **Correct:** The man *who* repaired our car is a good mechanic.

THAT THERE, THEM THERE, THIS HERE, THESE HERE: These are all corrupt forms of *this, that, these, those.*

THEM: Do not use *them* as an adjective. Use *these* or *those.*

Incorrect: *Them* apples are all rotten.

THEN, THAN: See *than, then.*

THESE KIND, THESE SORT: See *kind, sort.*

THOUGH, ALTHOUGH: See *although, though.*

THUSLY: Use *thus,* except in pointing out method or direction (adverbial function).

Correct: According to the excavations, the ancient river flowed *thusly.*
Incorrect: Harold believed strongly in his convictions and wrote *thusly* to the dean.

TOWARD, TOWARDS: Either may be used; however, *toward* is more frequent today.

TRY AND, SURE AND: See *sure and, try and.*

UGLY: Do not use *ugly* to mean "ill-tempered."

Incorrect: The professor seemed to be in an *ugly* mood today.

UN-, IN-: See *in-, un-.*

UNINTERESTED, DISINTERESTED: See *disinterested, uninterested.*

UNIQUE: This word means "only one of its kind" and does not admit of comparison.

Incorrect: His rock collection is the *most unique* on campus.

UNITED STATES: When *United States* is used as a noun, it is always preceded by *The.*

UPDATE: This term refers to presenting information on or after the present day. It should not be used for a period that is not at least on the next calendar date.

Correct: The secretary will *update* her report on each workday of the week.
Incorrect: The news service *updated* its report every half-hour.

USE TO, USED TO: *Use to* is incorrect in reference to "an action once performed." The proper form is *used to*.

> **Incorrect:** He *use to* be a lifeguard at the city pool.
> **Correct:** He *used to* be a lifeguard at the city pool.
> **Correct:** A twenty-dollar bill was *used to* mark his place in the book.

USED TO COULD: This is a corrupt form of *used to be able*.

> **Incorrect:** Father recalled that he *used to could* throw a curve ball.

VERSE, STANZA: See *stanza, verse*.

VOCATION, AVOCATION: See *avocation, vocation*.

WAGES, SALARY: See *salary, wages*.

WAIT ON: Do not use this expression in place of *wait for*. *Wait on* means to serve, as in a restaurant.

> **Correct:** We will *wait for* you until dark.

WANT: *Want* should not be followed by a *that* clause.

> **Incorrect:** I *want that* you should be careful while swimming.
> **Incorrect:** Robert *wanted that* no one would interrupt him this morning.

WANT, WISH: *Want* means "to need, to require"; *wish* means "to desire."

> **Correct:** Do you *wish* to go with us?
> **Correct:** What do those poverty-stricken people *want*?

WANTS, NEEDS: See *needs, wants*.

WANT IN, OUT, UP, DOWN, OFF, THROUGH: These expressions are corruptions of *wish to come in* and the like.

WAYS: Do not use *ways* to mean "distance."

> **Incorrect:** Walk a *ways* with me while I tell you of my plan.

WELL, GOOD: See *good, well*.

WHERE: Do not use *where* for *that* to introduce a noun clause.

> **Incorrect:** We read *where* the school will be dismissed early.
> **Incorrect:** Did you read *where* the jury convicted the killer of the officer?

WHERE AT: The *at* is redundant.

Incorrect: No one knows *where* the books are *at*.
Incorrect: We think we know *where* the hidden treasure is *at*.

WHERE TO: The *to* is redundant.

WHETHER, IF: See *if, whether*.

WHICH, WHO, THAT: See *that, which* and *that, who*.

WHILE: Avoid using *while* as a substitute for *and* or *but* as a coordinating conjunction. *While* refers to time.

Incorrect: Felix enjoys opera *while* I enjoy blues.
Correct: Griffin enjoys country music, *but* I prefer pop.

WHO, THAT, WHICH: See *that, which* and *that, who*.

WIDOW WOMAN: The word *woman* is redundant.

Incorrect: The *widow woman* made an unusual request.

WILL, SHALL: See *shall, will*.

WIN OUT: The *out* is redundant.

Incorrect: Let's hope that our team *wins out* in the end.

WISH, WANT: See *want, wish*.

WORSE: Do not use *worse* to mean *more*.

Incorrect: The children wanted ice cream *worse* than they wanted spaghetti.

WORST WAY: Do not use this expression to mean *very much*.

Incorrect: I want to see you in the *worst way*.
Incorrect: The people need federal assistance the *worst way*.
Correct: He wanted to go to Hawaii *very much*.

WOULD, SHOULD: See *should, would*.

WOULD HAVE: Do not use *would have* to mean "had."

Incorrect: If we *would have* gone, we'd be rich by now.
Incorrect: If he *would have* asked me, I would have helped him move.
Correct: *Had* we gone, we'd be rich by now.
Correct: I *would have* done that *had* I been asked.

WOULD OF: This is a corrupt form of *would have.*

WOULD RATHER, HAD BETTER, HAD RATHER: See *had better, had rather, would rather.*

YOU ALL: Use this expression only in a plural sense for emphasis.

YOU WAS: This is corrupt form of *you were.*

YOURSELF, HIMSELF, MYSELF: See *himself, myself, yourself.*

GLOSSARY

A

absolute adjective an adjective that expresses within itself the highest degree of comparison, an absolute quantity, and thus will not submit to further comparison. Examples of such words are *unique*, *perfect*, *round*, *square*, *honest*, *vertical*, *horizontal*, *perpendicular*, *exact*, *endless*, *frozen*, *dead*, *full*, *empty*, and *straight*.

abstract noun a noun that names a quality, an attribute, an idea, or anything not having physical properties. Such words as *goodness*, *love*, *truth*, and *mercy* are included in this category. Many abstract nouns employ the suffixes *ness* (*goodness*), *ty* (*loyalty*), and *th* (*truth*) to name ideas and intangible qualities.

active voice describing a sentence in which the subject of the verb is the actor, or the doer of the action.

acute accent an accent (´) placed over a vowel to indicate length or high pitch, or to indicate primary stress of a syllable.

adjectival complement a complement that restricts or completes the meaning of an adjective in a sentence.

adjective a word that describes or "limits" a noun or pronoun. An adjective identifies by placing restrictions on any noun with which it is associated. For example, the adjective *small* in the phrase "the small boy" not only describes the boy, but it also limits the focus to a certain boy, not just any boy—specifically, to the *small* boy.

adjective clause a clause that, like a single-word adjective, modifies a noun or pronoun. It is introduced by a relative pronoun (*who, whose, whom, which,* or *that*) or by a subordinate conjunction (*where, when,* or *why*).

adjunct one of three forms of adverbials, adjuncts are integrated to some degree in the sentence or clause structure, and typically inform as to space, time, process, or focus (*in my neighborhood, next week, easily, primarily*).

adverb a word that modifies a verb, an adjective, or another adverb. In certain constructions, an adverb may also modify a preposition, a conjunction, a verbal, a noun, or a pronoun. As a general rule, adverbs tell how, when, where, why, under what conditions, and to what extent.

adverb clause a clause that, like a single-word adverb, modifies a verb (including the verb form in a verbal—that is, a gerund, infinitive, or participle), an adjective, or an adverb. Adverb clauses are introduced by subordinating conjunctions such as *even if, as though, when, although, because, as long as, as, until, before, than, wherever, while, whenever, though, after, whether, since, whereas, so that, provided that, where, as if, in order that, as soon as.*

adverbial an optional element in sentence or clause structure. Adverbials come in three main forms: adjuncts, conjuncts, and disjuncts.

adverbial complement functions as an adverb and is necessary to complete the meaning of the sentence that contains it. Adverbial complements are similar to subject complements, but usually convey the meaning of location, direction, progression, duration, condition, circumstance, or purpose.

adverbial conjunction an adverb that serves to connect independent clauses: *however, nevertheless, moreover, then, therefore, thus, consequently.*

antecedent the expression to which another expression refers. For example, in the sentence, "The person who gave you that book is my sister," "person" is the antecedent of "who gave you that book."

apostrophe a punctuation mark (') used to form possessives and various other semantic relationships, such as characterization, origin, measure, and so forth. Additionally, apostrophes are used in contractions, as well as to indicate missing letters.

appositive a word, phrase, or clause usually located after a nominal (a noun, noun phrase, or noun substitute) to identify, explain, or describe the nominal. Although adjectives may be used in apposition, appositives are usually nouns and pronouns. For example, in the sentence, "Pirmin Zurbriggen, the greatest ski-racer of his generation, retired last year," the appositive is "the greatest ski-racer of his generation."

appositive adjective an adjective (or set of adjectives) that follows the words that it modifies. These adjectives are usually used in pairs and employ the conjunction *and* or *but* between them.

article a member of a small group of words used with nouns to limit or define the noun.

aspect unlike tense, which indicates a verb's location in time in absolute terms (past or present), a verb's *aspect* refers to the way the time of the situation is regarded. Aspects are expressed by a combination of an auxiliary and a main verb.

attributive adjective adjectives found immediately before the word(s) that they modify.

auxiliary one of a small set of verbs that combine with a main verb to express various shades of meaning, usually of time or voice. The three primary auxiliaries are *be*, *have*, and *do*.

B

brackets punctuation marks ([]) used to enclose explanations within parentheses or in quoted material when the explanation is not part of the quotation, and to rectify a mistake such as may appear in a book or other manuscript.

C

case refers to the form of a pronoun, some of which, chiefly personal pronouns, change depending on their placement in a sentence. Pronouns being used as a subject of a sentence or clause are said to be in the *nominative case*; pronouns being used as an object are in the *objective case*; and pronouns being used to show ownership or similar relationships are in the *possessive case*.

cedilla a diacritical mark (ç), which is placed under a letter to indicate an alteration or modification of the letter's usual phonetic value.

clause a sentence or sentence-like construction within another sentence.

circumflex a diacritical mark (ˆ) originally used in Greek over long vowels to indicate a rising-falling tone; used in other languages to mark length, contraction, or a particular vowel quality.

cliché a word or phrase that is overused or has grown trite.

collective noun a singular noun that refers to more than one thing as members of a single unit. Some examples are *herd* (the single unit *herd* is made up of the individual members—cows, for example), *flock*, *jury*, *bunch*, *throng*, *committee*, *company*, *class*, *team*, *tribe*, *school* (*of fish*), *army*, *platoon*, *family*, *Congress*.

colon a punctuation mark (:) used after the salutation of a business letter; before a list of any kind that is introduced formally by such words as *the following* or *as follows*, by a number, or by any other "pointing out" expression; before a long and formal statement; between main clauses when the second clause explains or restates the first; and between numbers expressing the time by the clock, between the volume and page number of a magazine, between chapter and verse of a Bible passage, and between the title and subtitle of a book when the subtitle explains the title.

comma a punctuation mark (,) used to separate words, phrases, and clauses written in a series.

common noun a noun that is the name of a thing in general. Common nouns are divided into two groups: count nouns and mass nouns. See also *count noun, mass noun*.

comparative clause a clause containing a comparison.

complement a noun, adjective, pronoun, or phrase added to a verb to complete the predicate of a sentence. The complement provides information about a clause's subject or object.

complex sentence a sentence that contains one main clause; embedded in that main clause are one or more subordinate clauses.

compound sentence a sentence that contains multiple main clauses, which are often linked by a coordinating conjunction (*but, and*, and so on). Alternatively, a semicolon may be used to unite the two clauses. Clauses may also be linked with a conjunct, such as *however, therefore*, and the like.

concrete noun a noun that names a thing that has physical properties—that is, a thing that is a tangible item. Some examples of concrete nouns are *wood, rain, smoke, Mr. Peterson, ghost, car, moon, wind, pencil, Jennifer, sunshine, story, lie*, and *Saturday*.

conjunct one of three forms of adverbials, conjuncts, which are mainly adverbs or prepositional phrases, indicate logical relationships between sentences or clauses (*therefore, however, nonetheless, on the other hand*, and so on).

conjunctive adverbs adverbs used to connect subordinate clauses to the remainder of the sentence. The most widely used conjunctive adverbs are *where, when, whenever, while, as, why, before, after, until*, and *since*.

conjunction a "connective" word that joins single words, phrases, or clauses to the rest of the sentence.

coordinate clause a clause connected to one or more other clauses of equal status. Such clauses are joined through the use of coordinating conjunctions such as *for, and, nor, but, or,* and *yet.*

coordinating conjunctions a word that connects elements of equal rank in the sentence. The sentence elements may be single words, phrases, or clauses.

copular prepositional verb a prepositional verb (combination of verb plus preposition) that is complemented by a subject complement. Examples include *sound like, turn into, serve as.*

copular verb see *copulative verb.*

copulative verb also called a *copular verb.* A verb that usually patterns with a modifier or noun (or noun substitute) that is necessary to complete the meaning of the sentence. The most common copulative verb is *be*; others include *become, feel, get, seem.*

correlative conjunction a conjunction that functions normally, except that it patterns in a pair. The correlative conjunctions are *either . . . or, neither . . . nor, whether . . . or, both . . . and,* and *not only . . . but also.*

count noun a noun that identifies individual items, either singly or as members of groups.

D

declarative sentence a sentence whose primary role is to make a statement.

definite article a word, as in *the*, denoting a definite noun phrase, as in *the woman.* In this case, the speaker or writer refers to a specific woman (*the woman*), not just any woman (*a woman*).

demonstrative a word whose role is to locate a referent in relation to a speaker, an addressee, or some other person. Examples of demonstratives are *this* and *that.*

demonstrative pronoun a pronoun that serves to point out particular persons, places, or things, even though they may not be named directly.

dependent clause a clause that cannot stand alone. Also called a *subordinate clause.*

determiner a word that introduces and limits a noun phrase. Determiners specify number and quantity (*all, both, two, many, several*), or convey the denotation of a noun phrase (*a/an, the, my, this*).

diacritical mark accents, diacriticals, or special alphabetic characters for native words. The diacritical marks most commonly used in European and Asian languages written in the Latin alphabet are the acute accent (´), the grave accent (`), the diaeresis (¨), the umlaut (¨), the circumflex (^), the tilde (~), and the cedilla (ç).

diaeresis a diacritical mark (¨) placed over a vowel to indicate that it is pronounced in a separate syllable. See also *umlaut*.

direct object a major sentence element contained in many predicates. Direct objects occur in sentences that have transitive verbs. To identify direct objects, one may ask the "what question" or the "who question" in conjunction with the verb. For example, examine the sentence, "Joseph found a silver coin in the street." Then, ask the "what question": What did Joseph find? He found a silver coin. "Silver coin," then, is the direct object.

disjunct one of three forms of adverbials, disjuncts are of type style or content. Style disjuncts—which may be adverbs, prepositional phrases, finite clauses, and non-finite clauses—comment on the act of speaking or writing (*truthfully*, *in short*, *frankly speaking*, *since you mentioned it*). Content disjuncts, on the other hand, evaluate or comment on the truth value of what is said (*probably*, *unfortunately*).

E

ellipsis a punctuation mark (. . . or . . . .) used to indicate an omission from a quotation.

em dash a punctuation mark (—) used to indicate an important break in thought or in sentence structure; to set off an appositive that is a series; to mean *namely*, *in other words*, *that is*, and similar expressions that precede explanations; to indicate speech that is broken or faltering; and after an incomplete sentence (the em dash should be used without a period).

en dash a punctuation mark (–) used to connect continuing (that is, inclusive) numbers, as in dates, time, or reference numbers; to indicate a single period or season spanning parts of two successive calendar years; and in place of a hyphen in cases of compound adjectives when one element of the adjective is an open compound or when multiple elements are hyphenated compounds.

exclamation mark a punctuation mark (!) used after a strong interjection, or after phrases or sentences that show strong emotions.

exclamatory sentence a sentence that conveys a strong emotion. These types of sentences, which often contain no verb, sometimes consist of the word *what* or *how* followed by a noun phrase.

F

first person a manner of speaking or writing that refers to the speaker or writer through the use of certain linguistic sets, such as pronouns and verb forms. For example, the sentence "I ate fish for dinner" is in the first person, as indicated by the use of the pronoun "I."

function word a word that has a grammatical (syntactic) role in a sentence or clause as opposed to a lexical (semantic) meaning. Also called *structure words*, function words include determiners, prepositions, conjunctions, interjections, negativizers, and auxiliary verbs.

G

gerund a word that ends in *ing* that shares characteristics of nouns and verbs. For example, in the sentence "Sculpting hedges is Robyn's favorite activity," the gerund *sculpting* requires a direct object (*hedges*) in the same way many verbs require direct objects. At the same time, the phrase *sculpting hedges* acts as the subject of the sentence, much as nouns do.

gerund phrase a phrase recognized by two means, one of description and one of function. First, the gerund phrase is recognized by its characteristic verb form with an *ing* ending, although this is not always a sure-fire means of spotting a gerund. In addition to the *ing* ending, the gerund functions in a sentence in a manner similar to that of a noun. Of course, because this discussion concerns phrases, other words must be included with the gerund to form the phrase.

grave accent a diacritical mark (`) placed over a vowel to indicate length or low pitch, or to indicate secondary stress of a syllable.

guide word a key word that controls a preposition.

H

hedge word a word used to help the speaker or writer avoid making an absolute statement, such as *alleged* in "The alleged burglary occurred last night."

hyphen a punctuation mark (-) used between words that act as a single adjective modifier (including coined ones) preceding the word being modified; in two-word fractions only when the fraction is a single adjective that modifies directly; in numbers from *twenty-one* through *ninety-nine*; after a prefix that has been attached to a proper noun; after *self* and *all* when these words are prefixed to nouns; in compound titles containing *vice, ex,* and *elect*; in words when there may be doubt as to meaning; when the joining of a prefix with the root causes an awkward combination of letters; and to show the omission of a connecting word. Additionally, a hyphen should be used to divide a word at the end of a line.

I

idiom an expression that is peculiar to itself grammatically or that has a meaning that cannot be derived from the conjoined meaning of its elements.

imperative mood employed when a sentence states a request, command, or suggestion.

imperative sentence a sentence that gives an order or issues a command.

indefinite article a word, as in *a* or *an*, denoting an indefinite noun phrase, as in *a woman*. In this case, the speaker or writer is not discussing a particular woman.

indefinite pronoun a word that is substituted for a noun without referring to a definite person, place, or thing.

indefinite relative pronoun a pronoun introducing a noun clause. The indefinite relative pronouns are *who, whom, what, whoever, whomever, whatever,* and *whichever*.

independent clause a clause that, although it lacks the capitalization and punctuation of a sentence, could stand alone grammatically speaking.

indicative mood employed to state a fact or to ask a question. The indicative mood is the form common to most sentences, whether declarative or interrogative.

indirect object a major sentence element contained in many predicates. An indirect object is typically placed between the verb and the direct object, and typically has the role of recipient or beneficiary of the action. For example, *Maria* in "I told Maria the truth" is the sentence's indirect object.

infinitive the word *to* followed by the root form of a verb, such as *run, jump, play, work, buy, see*, and so on. Infinitives, then, look like this: *to run, to jump, to play, to buy, to see.*

infinitive phrase contains an infinitive and words that pattern with it—modifiers, objects, and subjects. Like verbs that are used as predicators in sentences, an infinitive may have objects—in this case called *objects of the infinitive* rather than direct objects.

inflection an affix that expresses a grammatical relationship, such as the plural *s* in *candidates* and the *ed* ending in *wanted*. In English, inflections are always suffixes.

intensifier an adverb that adds emphasis to or amplifies an adjective. The word intensifier is also used to describe an adjective that creates an emphasizing or amplifying effect.

intensive pronoun similar to the reflexive pronoun, except in their function within a sentence. Intensive pronouns are usually found immediately following a noun or pronoun for the purpose of lending emphasis to the noun or pronoun that they follow.

interjection a word or phrase "injected" into a sentence to express strong feeling or sudden emotion.

internal punctuation punctuation that separates, divides, and points out elements within an expression, thereby developing clarity and specific identity.

interrobang a punctuation mark (‽) used after an exclamatory question to which an answer is not expected.

interrogative adverb an adverb used in asking a question, as in "*Where* have you been?" "*When* were you in Texas?" and "*Why* did you burn that picture?"

interrogative pronoun a pronoun used when asking a question. The interrogative pronouns are *who, whom, whose, which*, and *what*.

interrogative sentence a sentence that asks a question.

intransitive verb a verb that shows action of some sort but does not require a direct object.

italics a style of font used for names of books, magazines, newspapers, long plays, long poems (book length), motion pictures, musical productions, works of art, ships, aircraft, and trains. Italics should also be used for words, letters, figures, and symbols referred to by name; for foreign words and phrases; and to lend emphasis.

L

linking verb a verb that requires a subject complement to complete the meaning of a sentence. Linking verbs are also copulative verbs. Any verb that can be substituted in the place of *looked* is probably a linking verb. Some common linking verbs include *appear, become, grow, remain, seem, get, look, sound, smell, feel, taste,* and *continue.*

M

mass noun a noun that identifies undifferentiated mass—that is, things not usually considered countable by individual items. Sometimes called *non-count noun.*

misplaced modifier a modifier located in a place other than near the word it modifies, therefore seeming to modify a word other than that it is intended to modify.

N

nominative case see *case.*

nominal relative clause a clause used as a noun substitute. The relative pronouns *who, whoever, whom, whomever, that, which, whichever, what,* and *whatever* may introduce nominal relative clauses.

non-count noun see *mass noun.*

nonfinite verb see *verbal.*

nonrestrictive clause a clause that may be omitted from a sentence without a loss of the basic meaning of the sentence. These types of clauses, which are also called *nonessential clauses,* should be set off by commas.

noun a word that names a person, place, or thing.

noun clause a clause that functions in a sentence just as a noun functions. A noun clause is usually introduced by one of the following words: *that, who, what, where, when, why, how, which,* and *whether.*

noun phrase a phrase (which may consist only of a single noun) that can be used in a sentence just as a noun is used: as the subject, direct object, indirect object, subject complement, object complement, object of a preposition, object of an infinitive, subject of an infinitive, and so on.

O

object complement a word or phrase that describes or "completes" the direct object, usually by adding a noun or adjective immediately after the direct object.

objective case see *case*.

P

parentheses punctuation marks [()] used to enclose parenthetical material that is only remotely connected with the content; to enclose references, directions, and incidental explanatory matter; to enclose figures repeated to ensure accuracy; and to enclose figures or letters used to mark divisions or enumerations that run into the text. Additionally, you should use a question mark within parentheses after a word or a statement of which the accuracy is questionable.

participial phrase a phrase that contains a participle. Such phrases can follow noun phrases; can function like subordinate clauses to indicate time, result, reason, and so on; or can follow an object and verb of the senses. Participial phrases are generally used as adjectives.

participial preposition a preposition that takes the *ing* form of certain verbs, such as *assuming, beginning, barring, considering, following, including, involving, regarding,* and a few others.

participle a non-finite form of a verb—that is, a verb that does not indicate tense. A participle combines characteristics of a verb with those of an adjective. Except for irregular verbs, the present participle of any verb ends in *ing*; the past participle of a regular verb is identified with the past tense, ending in *ed*. Participles are used to introduce participial phrases.

parts of speech word classes, that is, the different types of words contained in a language. In English, the parts of speech are nouns, pronouns, adjectives, verbs, adverbs, interjections, and function words (prepositions, conjunctions, and the like).

passive voice sentences that pattern with the actor-action-patient elements in a reverse order. In such sentences, the actor remains passive and often patterns as the object of a preposition at the end of the sentence. The element that is the direct object in a sentence in the active voice becomes the subject of the sentence in the passive voice.

past participle see *participle*.

period a punctuation mark (.) used after a declarative sentence; after an imperative sentence that is a polite request; after an indirect question; after a polite request that is put in the form of a question; after each initial in a proper name and after most abbreviations; as a decimal point; and after each numeral or letter division in an outline except those enclosed in parentheses.

personal pronoun used when a writer or speaker wishes to use a pronoun to substitute for a word that refers to a person, either himself or someone else (or, in the case of *it*, a thing).

phrasal preposition a unit of two or more words serving as a single preposition. Often the phrasal preposition is itself a prepositional phrase.

phrase a group of words not containing a subject and predicate that, together, function as a part of speech (noun, verb, adjective, adverb, preposition, and so on). The various types of phrases include noun phrases, prepositional phrases, and verbals.

plural more than one (as opposed to singular).

possessive case see *case*.

postponed preposition a preposition that patterns after its object.

predicate the part of the sentence that makes an assertion or a denial about the subject of that sentence; that is, it represents what is said about the sentence's subject. For example, in the sentence, "Cammy gave up skiing to become a champion snowboarder," *Cammy* is the subject, and "gave up skiing to become a champion snowboarder" is the predicate.

predicate adjective an adjective that occurs after linking verbs or after a form of the verb *to be* and that modifies the subjects of those verbs. As the name implies, these adjectives occur in the predicate of a sentence or clause, but they must modify the subject of the sentence or clause to be considered predicate adjectives.

prefix an affix attached to the beginning of a word, root, or phrase.

preposition a word or, in some instances, a short word group that functions as a connector between sentence elements. The element that it connects and patterns with is usually a noun and is identified as the *object of the preposition*.

prepositional phrase the combination of a preposition and the object of that preposition, and all words that pattern with it.

present participle see *participle*.

pronoun a word that can be substituted for a noun, two or more other pronouns, or a noun phrase without changing the meaning of the sentence or the basic construction pattern of the sentence.

proper adjective an adjective derived from a proper noun or a proper noun used as an adjective. These adjectives are generally written with capital letters.

proper noun a noun that names specific things that are identified with an individual name.

Q

quantifier indicates a relative or indefinite quantity, such as *all*, *many*, *several*, and *few*. These are distinguished from numerals, which provide an absolute indication of quantity (*nine* ladies dancing).

question mark a punctuation mark (?) used after a direct question; after each incomplete question in a series; and in parentheses to indicate historical doubt or uncertainty.

quotation mark a punctuation mark ("") used for quotations that employ the exact words from some source (either spoken or written).

R

reflexive pronoun a pronoun that reflects the person or thing already identified. Reflexive pronouns are used when the subject of a sentence performs an action on itself or refers to itself in some other way.

relative pronoun a pronoun that connects adjective or noun clauses to other elements of the sentence. That is, a relative pronoun substitutes for the noun being modified by an adjective clause and relates that clause to the noun.

restrictive clause an adjective clause that is necessary in order to restrict the meaning of the sentence; in other words, restrictive clauses indicate the essential meaning of the sentence. Adjective clauses beginning with *that* are always restrictive clauses.

S

second person a manner of speaking or writing that refers to the addressee through the use of certain linguistic sets, such as pronouns and verb forms. For example, the sentence "You ate fish for dinner" is in the second person, as indicated by the use of the pronoun "you."

semicolon a punctuation mark (;) used between main clauses that are not joined by *and, or, for, nor, but, so,* or *yet*; between main clauses that are joined by *and, or, for, but, nor, so,* and *yet* if there is a comma within any one of the main clauses; between the items in a series if any one of the items contains commas; and before such explanatory words and phrases as *namely, for example, in fact,* and *that is.*

sentence modifier an adverbial that relates to the entire sentence as opposed to relating to any separate element within the sentence. Sentence modifiers are usually set off by commas.

simple adverb a one-word adverb modifying the word or phrase appearing next to it.

simple preposition a preposition made up of either a simple or a compound word: *up, down, in, into, from, to, with, inside, around, before, upon, along, without,* and so on.

simple sentence a sentence that consists of one main clause, with no coordinate or subordinate clause.

singular describing one, as opposed to two or more (plural).

squinting modifier similar to a misplaced modifier, except that squinting modifiers are placed in a sentence in such a manner that they may modify either of two nouns in the sentence.

structure word see *function word.*

subject a sentence element that represents a person or thing of which something is said, usually the noun, pronoun, or noun phrase in a sentence or clause that comes before the verb or, in the case of interrogative sentences, after the verb. For example, in the sentence, "Alexia began taking ballet lessons at the age of five," *Alexia* is the subject of the sentence; it is being said of her that she "began taking ballet lessons at the age of five."

subject complement the complement of a copulative verb such as *be* or *seem.* The subject complement may be an adjective phrase, an adverb phrase, or a prepositional phrase, as well as a noun phrase or a nominal clause.

subjunctive mood employed to express a condition contrary to fact, a wish, a supposition, a prayer, or a doubt, as well as in "that clauses." The subjunctive mood is most commonly employed, however, in contrary-to-fact statements, as in "If I were rich, I'd quit my job."

subordinate clause see *dependent clause*.

subordinating conjunction a conjunction that connects two clauses of unequal rank. Subordinating conjunctions begin dependent clauses (usually adverb clauses) and show the relationship of those dependent clauses to the independent clauses of which they are a part. Some of the subordinating conjunctions are *if*, *because*, *after*, *since*, *when*, *while*, *until*, *unless*, *although*, *for* (meaning *because*), *wherever*, *than*, *till*, and *as*. The relative pronouns *who*, *whom*, *whose*, *which*, *what*, and *that* also function as subordinating conjunctions.

suffix an affix attached to the end of a word, root, or phrase.

T

tense refers to the time of a situation. English makes use of two tense categories, present and past, which are indicated by the form of the verb.

terminal punctuation punctuation that brings something, such as a sentence or an abbreviation, to an end.

third person a manner of speaking or writing that refers to neither the speaker/writer nor the addressee. For example, the sentence "He ate fish for dinner" is in the third person, as indicated by the use of the pronoun "he."

tightening in writing, the act of eliminating unnecessary words in prose.

tilde a diacritical mark (˜) placed over the letter *n* to denote the sound *ny* or over vowels to indicate nasality.

transitional device in writing, a device that helps you ease your prose from one point to the next.

transitional expression the main type of transitional device. There are several types of transitional expressions: contrast and qualification, continuity, cause and effect, exemplification, and summation.

transitive verb those verbs that pattern with direct objects—that is, they express an action that directly affects a grammatical unit (usually a noun or pronoun) elsewhere in a clause or sentence. Stated another way, a transitive verb shows an action that is "passed on" to the direct object.

U

umlaut a diacritical mark (¨) placed over a vowel to indicate a more central or front articulation.

V

VAC see *verb-adverbial composite*.

verb a word that expresses an act, occurrence, or a state of being.

verb-adverbial composite (VAC) a word used as a preposition or as a single-word adverb is sometimes linked to a verb to form a *verb-adverbial composite* (VAC).

verbal a type of phrase. Verbals, which include infinitives, gerunds, and participles, incorporate verb forms in their basic constructions. Verbals are employed as grammatical units within sentences, usually as nouns or modifiers. They are often classified as *nonfinite verbs*, because they are not inflected (do not change form) to indicate person, number, or tense.

W

word class see *parts of speech*.

INDEX